Weaving the Word

Weaving the Word

The Metaphorics of Weaving and Female Textual Production

Kathryn Sullivan Kruger

SUP

Selinsgrove: Susquehanna University Press
London: Associated University Presses

Associated University Presses
440 Forsgate Drive
Cranbury, NJ 08512

Associated University Presses
16 Barter Street
London WC1A 2AH, England

Associated University Presses
P.O. Box 338, Port Credit
Mississauga, Ontario
Canada L5G 4L8

The paper used in this publication meets the requirements of the American National Standard for Permanence of Paper for Printed Library Materials Z39.48-1984.

Library of Congress Cataloging-in-Publication Data

Kruger, Kathryn Sullivan, 1960–
Weaving the word : the metaphorics of weaving and female textual production / Kathryn Sullivan Kruger.
p. cm.
Includes bibliographical references and index.
ISBN 1-57591-052-7 (alk. paper)
1. English poetry—History and criticism. 2. Women in literature. 3. Tennyson, Alfred Tennyson, Baron, 1809–1892. Lady of Shalott. 4. Tennyson, Alfred Tennyson, Baron, 1809–1892. Lady of Shalott—Illustrations. 5. Blake, William, 1757–1827. Four Zoas. 6. Homer—Characters—Women weavers. 7. Mythology, Greek, in literature. 8. Weaving in literature. 9. Women authors. 10. Women weavers. I. Title.

PR508.W6 K78 2001
821.009'355—dc21

00-066078

PRINTED IN THE UNITED STATES OF AMERICA

To my life teachers
Sant Darshan Singh Ji Maharaj
and Sant Rajinder Singh Ji Maharaj
"The warp and woof of life is love."

Contents

Acknowledgments

THIS WAS WRITTEN WITH THE ASSISTANCE OF MANY COLLEAGUES AND friends. I especially think Dr. Lindsey Tucker, whose guidance and support made writing this book possible. She was the first to see my vision and helped to keep it alive. Thanks, also, to my talented mentors—Drs. Mihoko Suzuki, Shari Benstock, Kathryn Freeman, and Paula Harper—for their thoughtful and astute observations.

To Julia Kerr of ArtMagick (www.artMagick.com) I extend my appreciation for working so assiduously to locate the owners of some hard-to-find Pre-Raphaelite portraits.

I am grateful to many who have shared their ideas with me, read various drafts, as well as provided articles and other leads for my reasearch. My appreciation goes to Cheri Carooll-Levinson, Dr. Thomas Goodman, Natalie Gilbert, Carolyn Howd, Suzanne and Maryline Kruger, B. J. Lang, Judith Mesa-Pelly, Anita Miller, Mike Petroski, Dr. Diane Richard-Allerdyce, Peter Schmidt, Kathleen Sullivan, Ruth Seader, Pearl Sunrise, Diane Thiel, and Ken Uyemura, as well as the weavers at Penelope's Breads and Threads. With special thanks I salute my brother, Douglas Kruger, for his careful and thought-provoking reading of this manuscript.

I am indebted to my two families—my fathers, Tom Sullivan and Edward Kruger, and my mothers, Kathleen Sullivan and Suzanne Kruger—for their kindness and affection that can never be repaid. Most of all, I thank my dear husband, Jonathan, our delightful daughter, Sasha Nicole, and our sweet son, Ion Jacob, for their love and for their faith in my work.

* * *

I am grateful to the National Gallery of Victoria, Melbourne, Australia for permission to reprint William Holman Hunt's *The Lady of Shalott* (1850), to the Tate Gallery for permission to reprint John William Waterhouse's *The Lady of Shalott* (c. 1888), to the Pre-Raphaelite Trust and their representative, Julian Hartnoll, for permission to reprint *'I am half-sick of shadows,' said the Lady of Shalott* by Sidney Harold Meteyard (1913), to Wadsworth Atheneum, Hartford, the Ella Gallup Sumner and Mary Catlin Sumner Collection Fund, for permission to reprint William Holman Hunt's *The Lady of Shalott* (1886–1905), and to the Victoria & Albert Museum for permission to reprint Dante Gabriel Rossetti's wood engraving, *"The Lady of Shalott."*

Introduction

> The contemporary practice in many fields of cultural studies of considering only the most recent historical periods threatens to trap us in an extraordinarily narrow definition of culture. . . . The study of ancient history allows us to see the particularity of our own culture, to be critical of its categories, to imagine otherwise.
>
> —Page duBois, *Sowing the Body*

TODAY, WE ARE FAR REMOVED FROM THE WORLD OF TEXTILE PRODUCtion. Because most of us purchase clothing from catalogs or stores, we disregard the enormous labor involved in making cloth, forgetting this singular fact: producing textiles occupied a major part of our ancestors' lives. Unlike the stories wherein a fairytale character like Penelope or the Lady of Shalott weave (literally) to wile away the time, weaving was a harsh reality. Producing cloth often supplemented other incomes and was intensely laborious.[1]

Because cloth took so long to produce, it became very valuable in the ancient worlds. Whether decorating floors, walls or bodies, cloth was woven with attention to *intention,* communicating not only cultural meaning, but also bestowing (or preserving) power. Whether the heavily brocaded robe of a bishop, the colorfully woven jacket of a Peruvian merchant, or a translucent veil hung before a face—these textiles, like a sheet of paper, convey meaning, their language consisting of a grammar of fiber, design and dye.

The relationship between texts and textiles is, historically, a significant one. Anthropologists have long been intrigued at the various ways in which cloth embodies the unique ideas of a culture. They can trace the history of a culture through the record of its textiles, "reading" cloth like a written text. Indeed, this cloth transmits information about the society which created it in a manner not dissimilar from a written language, except in this case the semiotics of the cloth depend on choice of fiber, pattern, dye, as well as its method of production.

As artifacts, textiles are vulnerable, and unlike pottery disintegrate rapidly over time; but like pottery, those pieces that survive furnish important cultural and historical information. Records of trade and invasion, for instance, can be traced through changes made in the textile's design or in its method of production.[2] Reading textiles at this level is the job of anthropologists, yet there exist many other ways to read textiles, even today.

Not only does cloth provide information about a society's natural, economic, and social changes, but in early cultures the making of textiles became an important signifying practice. By carrying the words and symbols integral to a culture's social and religious beliefs, cloth conveys meaning. Cloth, according to anthropologist Elizabeth Wayland Barber, "from our first direct evidence twenty thousand years ago, has been the handiest solution to conveying social messages visually, silently, continuously."[3] From this standpoint, we begin to observe that if one of the main functions of a textile is to bear meaning, then the traditional distinctions we make between text and textile begin to fade.[4]

I propose that when we talk about literature and its history, we should also include in our discussion the ancient production of texts in the form of textiles (even if these texts via textiles survive only in the form of stories). In other words, how the texts of textiles function in any specific story tells us about a very important form of communication heretofore ignored. From such an examination we might come to see a connection between the history of woven cloth and our attitudes toward literature; we might further speculate that the older tradition of weaving—one which dates back between nine thousand and twenty-five thousand years—-has influenced the newer one of writing. Writing was invented around fifty-five hundred years ago, and has only become a widespread practice in the last four hundred years or so. Before written texts could record and preserve the stories of a culture, cloth was one of the primary modes for transmitting these social messages.[5]

Moreover, when re-establishing the connection between the written text and the textile, we must also concede that there exists a significant relationship between women, who wove textiles, and textual production. By recuperating a textile history and including it in our awareness of literary history, we will recover a large community of female authorship. I do not mean to imply that the history of textile production is peculiar only to women, nor do I suggest that female authorship is privileged with a special kind of literary structure, closer to the origin of civilization.[6] I agree with Rita Felski, in her resistance to interpreting literature or history solely through the categories of gender.[7] Nor do I intend to replace the reading of literary history from a dominant male perspective with a reading that emphasizes only a female one.

Instead, I am arguing for an expanded definition of literary history, one that includes this larger group of women who, from the beginning of ancient civilization, participated in the traditions of mythmaking and storytelling, preserving as well as perpetuating these stories in designs of woven fabric. I also maintain that during the time when weaving and storytelling were analogous, female participation was not always marked as a subculture, but that women's endeavors were equal to culture and were not considered beneath culture or marginal to it.[8]

In writing *Weaving the Word* my purpose was twofold: first, to argue that we can not consider the heritage of the written text without including in this history its ancestor, the textile, and that the ancient production of texts first occurred in the form of textiles; and second, to analyze specific weaving stories in which the difference between a text and a textile becomes blurred. These stories portray women weavers transforming their domestic activity of making textiles into one of making texts by inscribing their cloth with both personal and political messages.

For a more complete understanding of how texts as textiles are produced and then released into the world of language and symbols, I am indebted to Julia Kristeva's early theories on the literal relationship of the body to signification. By extending Jacques Lacan's theories of language and the body, Kristeva's work in semiotics and psychoanalysis provides a metaphoric lens for understanding the relationship between the textile-body and its text. Their models for the development of language and how identity is established through entry into the Symbolic finds a striking analogue in the metaphor of weaving and the language of textiles. Because of the complexity of Kristeva's theory of signification, and because the way I engage with this theory informs so much of the book, the second chapter deals exclusively with this subject and provides the metaphoric net for the remaining chapters.

As an industry, weaving centers wielded tremendous economic power in different parts of the world at different times in history. Along with economic strength came subjugation. Since textiles could be exchanged easily, if not easier than money, the market demanded a steady supply. Women as well as men were turned into loom slaves, working under harrowing conditions for twenty hours at a time. Quickly summarized, the tasks in making cloth are fourfold: producing fibers, preparing fibers, spinning fibers, and weaving. Our ancestors either grew fibers from plants like flax (linen), hemp, or cotton, or they raised animals, the most common being sheep (wool), goats (mohair and angora), and silkworms (silk). Plant fibers needed to be beaten and soaked to make them supple enough so they could be spun into thread, whereas animals fibers had to be washed and carded (combed) to take out the twigs and leaves in order to make the wool soft enough for spinning. Because weaving requires a great deal of spun thread, spinning always needed to be done. In those societies where servants or slaves were kept, a large portion of women were often employed solely as spinners. Occasionally, dying the fibers added another step in cloth production wherein the fiber was colored with natural dyes, generally from parts of plants such as bark, flowers, or roots, and occasionally from animal sources such as shellfish, where murex, or a deep blue dye, could be extracted.

Weaving these fibers together performed the final stage. We define weaving as the interlacing of two sets of threads at right angles. The first set of threads (called a *warp*) is attached to a frame to give it enough tension to hold the shape of the cloth. The second set of threads, called the *weft* (archaic: *woof*) is woven into the steady warp threads. *Plain weave* constitutes the simplest design where one thread goes over and then under the warp threads, alternating this pattern for each line.

While weavers clothed members of their society, they wove and embroidered into these fabrics the symbols and designs significant to their culture. One of the most effective ways human beings have created identity is by marking themselves with a symbol or sign that visually conveys an important idea. Today, a particular logo like *Ralph Loren* or *Armani* designates prestige and authority, whereas ten thousand years ago a simple geometric shape would convey the same message. The different plaids in Scotland, for example, indicate affiliation to specific clans. Sacred emblems embroidered on the robe of a Catholic priest, a Muslim fakir, or a Hopi medicine man bespeak spiritual authority, whereas the ensignia on an admiral's sleeve or a general's lapel conveys worldly power. In these ways, cloth homogenizes groups of people by expressing membership in a specific community.

Cloth need not be embellished with a specific symbol to impart a message, however. Plain cloth that has been produced, cut, or worn in a specific way may also convey meaning. The weaving of homespun cloth or *khadi* that Ghandi encouraged in his attempt to free India from British rule, when worn, signified resistance to England. Because England outlawed the spinning and weaving of cloth in the American colonies during the American revolution, even preventing loom parts from being shipped outside of England, wearing homespun clothing also signified opposition to the English Monarchy.[9]

Today, in American society, the blue twill cotton of blue jeans fully expresses a spirit of social equality. I would not be exaggerating to say that almost everyone in the United States owns a pair of blue jeans. A powerful symbol, jeans bridge the gap between all segments of society. No matter one's age, race, religion, or economic status, everyone wears jeans. Certain logos may seem to differentiate between one pair of blue jeans and another, but since no one is prevented from purchasing an expensive pair of jeans, a specific logo like *Guess* or *Tommy Hilfiger* is not an accurate indicator of social difference based on affluence. Indeed, says Barber, "human cultures have over time built a sort of language through clothing, allowing us to communicate even with our mouths shut."[10]

Although this book focuses on the metaphor of weaving as writing, and although it depends almost exclusively on Kristeva's theories for an analysis of how and why textiles work as texts, an understanding of some textile history will render the analysis more clear. Hence, the first chapter, "Myth, History, and the Material World," deals with the contribution women have made to the creation of culture— its history and its stories—through weaving. Here, I take a closer look at the relationship between semiotics and textiles by giving examples from different cultures of how cloth conveys meaning, and how in some societies cloth itself becomes a metaphor for language. John Lechte remarks in his study, *Julia Kristeva,* that "it would be quite incorrect to see literature . . . as isolated from history and society; rather, textual practices have to be seen to be—at least in part—the basis of history and society."[11] This study depends on a historical perspective concerning the relationship between textile practices and signification.

In the second chapter, "The Semiotics of Cloth and Thetic (Re)Production," I employ Julia Kristeva's early theory of signification as a model for this text/textile relationship. By exploring particular scenes in literature in terms of this model, I demonstrate ways in which the material nature of the text (the textile of the text) interacts with its semiotics, as well as how together they convey meaning.

In the third chapter, "The Greek Web: Arachne and Philomela, Penelope and Helen of Troy," I explore the stories of these four weavers. I consider how their different modes of signification, through weaving, reflect their relationship toward the patriarchal culture that either sustains or silences them. Whereas Arachne's tapestry is woven with forbidden signs that style her as an outlaw, Penelope's textile is "blank," indicating her identification with society and her place within it. Yet because she resists being caught within her obedient text by refusing to complete it, the message in her text becomes just as radical as Arachne's.

The fourth chapter, "The Loom of Language and the Garment of Words in William Blake's 'The Four Zoas,'" examines the relationship between weaving and linguistic performance, in which a body is created simultaneously with the word. Weaving scenes function for Blake as a place in which he can explore the creative process. As a metaphor that literally embodies the imagination and its processes, the textile inhabits a position that, like a mirror, informs Blake's readers about the difference between "true" and "false" creativity. Of particular interest is the relationship of gender to weaving; Blake assigns this important role and symbol for the creative process, almost solely, to his female characters.

In chapter five, "'A Magic Web with Colors Gay': Representations of the Lady of Shalott in Pre-Raphaelite Art," I consider the relationships between Tennyson's poem and six different Pre-Raphaelite paintings depicting the Lady of Shalott. The Pre-Raphaelite credo emphasized verisimilitude, and so the interrelationship between the poem and its multiple representations performs an interdisciplinary dialogue unique, I believe, in the history of art. Whereas in the first two sections of the poem, Tennyson offers his reader a portrait of a female artist fully engrossed in her weaving, the artists of the pictures I have collected here choose to illustrate the Lady as either dead, about to die, or within her tower in a failed relationship to her work. Weaving, therefore, becomes secondary or incidental (mere decoration) to these illustrations.

Chapter six, "Uniquely Feminine Productions," distills and synthesizes the ideas developed in the previous chapters, and introduces the concepts of fate, sacredness and time in textile production.

Much has been written on the history and influence of textiles in the ancient and modern worlds. Although I refer often to the history and weaving practices of cloth, my research focuses specifically on the connection between texts and textiles, language and cloth. This theme finds expression and continuity in the following chapters.

In drawing from the various disciplines of history, anthropology, Kristevan psychology, myth, and literature, I have attempted to show how texts as textiles constitute another form of literature. I believe that we must challenge ourselves to look outside a specific field when seeking answers to our questions and instead examine those areas where connections are made, where energy exists. The forces that go into creating any work of art, be it a story, a painting, a dance, or a piece of woven cloth, are too rich and varied to be understood merely by one discipline. Hence, I have attempted to weave the unique strands and hues of these disciplines into one theme, one work, but I have inevitably fallen short in my task. To do justice to my subject, to keep focused and maintain balance, I have left many things unsaid. There is much yet to be accomplished in this field. It is my hope that the following study will begin a dialogue between the disciplines, one that will continue for a long time to come.

Weaving the Word

1

Myth, History, and the Material Word

I dreamed marvelously. I dreamed there was an enormous web of beautiful fabric stretched out. It was incredibly beautiful, covered all over with embroidered pictures. The pictures were illustrations of the myths of mankind but they were not just pictures, they were the myths themselves, so that the soft glittering web was alive. In my dreams I handled and felt this material and wept with joy.
—Doris Lessing, *The Golden Notebook*

I

CONTEMPORARY WESTERN CULTURE DOES NOT REPRESENT WOMEN'S work as contributing to the making of culture or of history, but as an activity marginal to both. In his well-known essay "Femininity," Sigmund Freud proposed that though "women have made few contributions to the discoveries and inventions in the history of civilization," the "one technique which they may have invented [is]—that of plaiting and weaving."[1] I am inclined to believe that Freud's comment on the origins of weaving was based on his own anthropological research, which most likely supplied him with enough evidence to represent weaving as a female practice. Freud refused to give this invention its due, however, and heralded it not as an important achievement and organizer of culture but rather (since it is a female invention) as a metaphor for lack.[2]

Anthropological evidence, on the contrary, suggests otherwise, that weaving and cloth were not incidental to culture but were vital forces in establishing, homogenizing, and perpetuating many societies. Although weaving represents only one kind of cloth-making activity, it did evolve out of the earliest civilizations and to a great extent served as a catalyst for their progress. Women wove textiles, not metaphors for lack. This cloth, whether it was embroidered, woven, or dyed with the stories or symbols peculiar to their tribe, indicates the important presence of the contribution of women to the creation of culture, its texts, and its history.

Recent evidence has pushed back the dates of weaving from the Neolithic period of settled tribes to the dim prehistory of the Paleolithic period. Until a few years ago, the earliest known woven fragment was excavated in Catal Huyuk in southcentral Turkey and carbon dated to over eight thousand years ago.[3] However, in 1995, four clay fragments impressed with the pattern of a textile or basket were dated from 24,870 to 26,980 years ago. The fiber was plant, and the weave suggested a warp. No one was able to determine whether the impressions were made from a piece of cloth or a basket, but the discovery has changed how anthropologists think about weaving, even in its rudimentary stage of twining. Dr. James Adovasio stated that "prehistorians underestimated the importance of woven materials in early peoples' lives." He further commented that "stone tools have been overemphasized in archeologists' interpretations of prehistoric economies."[4] The new dates establish that an early form of weaving was in practice for over fifteen thousand years longer than previously thought. Hence, the remarkable quality of fine weaving found in the textile at Catal Huyuk had been developing much earlier. Such discoveries emphasize the significance of textile production in human history.

Traditionally, the history of weaving is a history of women's work. Anthropological research has concluded that invariably women produced most of the textiles in the ancient world. By participating in the production of textiles—as well as in the community that existed *because of* that production—women took part in the first textual practices, recording their society's stories, myths, and sacred beliefs in symbols woven or embroidered on their textiles. The scene they conveyed constituted society's first texts.

There are archaeologists who have esteemed the importance of textiles and the weaver who produced them. Junius Bird, an expert in ancient South American textiles, exemplifies this kind of researcher. His work significantly advanced the study of South American textiles, but did so in a way that "personalized" this field of research. As one colleague has written of Bird: "A newly detected knot in an old textile would be something that 'she did,' and 'she,' the person who made the fabric thousands of years ago, deserved commendation."[5] Indeed, our understanding of history needs to expand to include women as significant contributors to culture. As Page duBois proposes, we need "to imagine otherwise."[6]

To many of my readers, such a remark may seem redundant if not passe, particularly in the wake of many recent books in feminist and cultural studies that are gradually changing the way we read and think about the past. Such works are recouping and rewriting history by showing women participating in its making. I suspect, however, that no matter how determined scholars may be to engraft feminist studies onto the root of historical and cultural studies, no real change in the view of women in history will occur until modern society changes its perception of those tasks that make up this female experience, tasks like weaving and sewing, cooking and childbearing—and begins to esteem them. Without respect for this work, the history of female experience will always be considered less valuable than its historical male counterpart in male experience. Thus, I can not over-emphasize the importance of the role weaving and female weavers had in the creation of culture. Because we habitually link female involvement to textile history, the recuperation of this history recovers a record of women's participation in the creation of culture and its texts, thereby reclaiming a female authorship.

Of particular interest to me are those scenes in literature wherein weaving becomes, in the hands of women, a tool for signifying, and their textiles represent a text inscribed with a personal and/or political message. If the weaver is in league with the dominant patriarchal society, this text will reproduce its signs of prerogative, but if she is not a confederate of the dominant culture her textile will unmask these signs and represent them as marks of tyranny.[7]

The "Arachne and Athena" story as told by Ovid (which I examine more closely in chapter 3) provides a good example of how textiles bear meaning, and how the messages they bear (like their counterparts in writing) are often political in nature. In this story, the Olympian goddess, Athena challenges a young girl, Arachne, to a weaving contest. Arachne's response to Athena's command is to weave a rug with scenes wherein the gods betray humanity. Such a representation smacks of an affront to Athena and the patriarchal cosmogony she represents. On the other hand, Athena's rug boasts of the gods' supremacy. The two rugs function not merely as different points of view but as dual opposites, the obverse of each other. They are potent and dangerous objects, powerful words that unleash a force or energy that threatens the existence of both weavers and the world in which they live.

Weaving has long been a metaphor for the creation of something other than cloth, whether a story, a plot, or a world. Hence, it follows that the weaver is a natural metaphor for the Creator, and just as a cloth can be woven and thus a world created, so can it be unraveled. Hence, this creator has the power to destroy.

A tale from the Sioux tribe describes this phenomenon. It tells the story of an Indian woman who weaves a blanket strip for her buffalo robe. Next to her blazes a fire on which she cooks her dinner, a delicious soup made of berries. Her dog arouses her every time the soup spills into the fire. When she goes to stir her dinner, turning her back on the loom, the dog jumps up and begins to unravel her blanket. The story explains that this process of creating and effacing, weaving and unraveling, day followed by night, has been going on for centuries. The tale also prophesizes that the moment this weaver finishes her blanket the world will come to an end.[8]

As stated, whereas in some tribes men wove, for most ancient cultures textile production was a female activity. It is no coincidence that this work was supported and sanctioned by a female goddess. Among the most famous are Isis of Egypt (who invented weaving with the help of her sister, Nephthys), Ixchel of the Mayans, Tlazolteotle of Mexico, Spider Woman of the Navajo (Dine), Mokusa of Russia, Uttu from ancient Sumer, Toci of pre-Columbian Mexico, Athena of Greece, Ukemochi of Japan, and Brahma/Maya of India.

Throughout the *Upanishads* of the Hindus, Brahma (along with his consort Maya) represents the supreme god of all creation "on whom the worlds are woven as warp and woof." Whereas Brahma weaves the universe on a web of eternity, Maya weaves the products or illusions of time, things of this world "woven of clay." From her loom stream veils of illusion through which eternity (Brahma) flows unseen.[9]

Significant to my argument toward an expanded definition of literary history is the fact that many deities identified with textile production are also associated with linguistic development. This phenomenon is discussed at length in each of the following chapters. For now it is sufficient to mention a few of these deities. Athena of ancient Greece not only functions as the patron goddess of weavers, but as *Athene Parthenos* is patron of the literary arts as well.[10] Spider Woman taught weaving to the Navajo people (Dine), and was also their first Storyteller. Paula Gunn Allen writes, "All tales are born in the mind of Spider Woman, and all creation exists as a result of her naming."[11] For the Dogon of Africa, Nummo (a male deity in this case) spoke the first creative "Word" by passing his tongue over a loom strung between his teeth.

For many African tribes and for almost all of the North American Plains Indian tribes, the Spider as weaver is considered a beneficent creature and is thought to be either the Creator or a trickster figure.[12] Anansi the Spider constitutes one such creature. An Ashanti trickster figure whose antics occupy many folk tales, Anansi's primary function is to weave stories (generally about his own escapades). His talent for telling stories manifests alongside his other traits, primarily those of cunning and "art-ifice." By using these innate qualities, Anansi tells us, he once captured leopard, python, hornet, and Mmoatia the fairy and sold them to the Sky God in exchange for the Sky God's stories.

Just as Anansi occupies the central position of storyteller in African lore, so, too, Spider Woman occupies this position for the Diné (Navajo) of the Southwestern United States. The story of Spider Woman constitutes another origin myth wherein weaving like that of Maya creates the revealed world. During the late seventeenth century, the Pueblo Indians taught the Dine how to weave. The figure Spider Woman began to appear in Dine oral tradition, assuming greater importance as weaving became a major vocation. Called by the names of Grandmother Spider, Spider Old Woman, and Thought Woman, she conceives all beings, stories, and every aspect of the natural world in her mind and on her web. By singing and naming them, she manifests them into existence and simultaneously into language. Prairies, mountains, fresh springs, coyotes, yucca, and human beings all exist because she has woven them on her web and given them her life's breath in song. She weaves all human activity and relationships into a living tapestry. Hers is the first and last song.[13]

Today, Spider Woman as a Creator and Storyteller is still worshipped by the Dine. The tradition of weaving is so integral to the female community that a ceremony is performed within the first twenty-four hours of the birth of a female child. Late in the evening a medicine man will scout out a spider's web and gather enough wood for a fire. Then, around four in the morning, the mother and baby will be taken to the spider's web, and the medicine man will begin his prayers and chanting to Spider Woman, while the fire burns to keep the mother and child warm. As the first rays of the sun rise over the horizon and touch the child's eyes, her hand is inserted into the spider's web. From that moment on she is considered to be a weaver, blessed by the goddess of weaving and storytelling to excel in that art.[14]

A striking anecdote that associates language with spiders and webs occurs in speculations that the alphabet was discovered by tracing the mysterious angles of a spider's web.[15] Conjectural as this statement might sound, it intrigues nevertheless. Given the fact that our early ancestors studied the natural world so closely, finding it full of mysteries that still elude us today, it is conceivable (albeit unknowable) that the spider's web suggested an early form of an alphabet.

Since fabric clothes the body as well as marks that body with the social text, the weaver participates in the creation of culture. In the spider figure we confront a being who represents thought and whose web constitutes the material produced from thought. Thought, like a web, is spun from the body of a thinking, creating being. This metaphor implies that whether we spin fibers or thoughts, human beings participate in a system that clothes society with the fabric of belief as well as the fabric of cloth.

Such abundant mythological evidence attests to the natural association between the weaving of fabric and the weaving of stories that bring together a community. From these ancient myths we can see that the manipulation of language and symbol was not solely a male prerogative; through the process of weaving, many forms of signification were also available to women. David Jongeward remarks, "Every weaver, when engaged in the act of interlacing one thread with another, participates in a process that for countless generations has been a primal metaphor for creation, including creation of the world itself."[16]

The importance of the semiotic power of textiles largely escapes a modern Western audience. In an anecdote from the Columbian invasion of the New World, Gemeentemuseum Helmond writes:

> After Columbus discovered the New World, its inhabitants were surprised by the thirst for gold of the Spaniards and other Europeans. The Spaniards in turn uncomprehendingly watched the fleeing Inca warriors who did not bother to protect their stocks of gold and silver. However, the Incas did their utmost to destroy their warehouses of textiles to keep them from falling into the hands of the invaders. . . . Textiles were the pre-eminent medium to record and convey mystical and religious conceptions.[17]

Jane Schneider and Annette B. Weiner note in *Cloth and Human Experience,* "once cloth attains a degree of permanence, absorbing value from the passage of time, political elites attempt to hoard and store it."[18] Destruction of this cloth, through erasing the historical record of its privilege, consequently guarantees that those who might obtain the cloth are not endowed with its mystical power nor its political endorsement. By destroying their textiles, the Incas insured that the authority contained in the cloth's semiotic material was not transferred to the Spaniards. "Precisely because it wears thin and disintegrates, cloth becomes an apt medium for communicating a central problem of power: Social and political relationships are necessarily fragile in an impermanent, ever-changing world."[19] Even when cloth cannot be preserved, due to damp conditions or age, the traditions for making that cloth can be passed on from generation to generation, and sometimes are considered so sacred that they become guild secrets.

Fabrics printed with words and symbols reflect not only a culture's religious and social beliefs, but also demarcate gender, age, occupation, and status in various ways. The semiotics of cloth depend on the kind of material used to produce a piece of cloth, the way in which the cloth was made, the way cloth was worn, as well as the designs printed or woven into the material itself.

In the Western world, from ancient times until the late eighteenth and early nineteenth centuries, textile production represented one of the principal activities around which a culture organized its economic and social structure. One of the most interesting kinds of records that cloth retains is its culture's religious or spiritual beliefs. In most cultures the priest and the worshipper wore "sanctified, prescribed garments, which were usually woven—often with decorative symbols or designs."[20]

The concept of such garments was to ensure through cloth the continuity of power through the centuries. A good example of how these garments resist change over time is in the Buddha robe. When Buddhism spread from India to China (circa A.D. 100) and Japan (circa A.D. 600), the Buddha robe traveled with it. The robe's basic construction has altered little from its origin in India. The only addition has been sleeves and garments under the robe for wear in colder climates. The fabric used and embroidered symbols have altered with time, indicating the wealth or poverty of Buddhism, depending on where it is practiced. The lack of change in the formation of the robe signifies its connection to the past, whereas its embroidered symbols indicate how Buddhism has changed through history. The story of cloth is not only a figurative one, but how cloth is made and what fibers are used are as important to the narrative as the symbolic language or text.[21]

Distinctive garments or vestments are an integral part of most religious traditions. To this day the Roman Catholic and Greek Orthodox religious services are distinguished by the richly embroidered and elaborate robes and headgear worn by all of the participants in the service, from the altar boys to the priests, bishops, cardinals, and the Pope himself. These vestments confer a kind of privilege and power, and are embroidered with elaborate figures that reify this power.

Likewise, in the Islamic Middle East, around A.D. 640, passages from the Koran were incorporated into patterns of design, decorating formal robes as well as casual attire. These inscriptions, called *tiraz,* were woven in two styles of calligraphy: *kufic* (angular letters) and *naskhi* (cursive style). The calligraphy was designed to look like interlocking, repeated patterns rather than language. Only the religious devotee, privileged to read the Koran, would know what these designs of blessing and protection actually said. Not incidentally, the word *tiraz* (sometimes *taraz*) "forms a verb in Persian that means to weave, to adorn, or to compose poetry. As a verb stem it also appears in compounds such as *sukhan taraz* (word weaving, eloquent) that is used to describe poets."[22] From such examples we can see how literary history and textile history were, at one time, interdependent.

The inter-relatedness of text and textile, word and cloth, is superbly illustrated in the mythology of an ancient African tribe. For the Dogon of Africa, weaving is not only akin to speaking, but, according to their mythology, both activities occurred at the same time and were derived from the same primal cause.

The Dogon attribute language and weaving to one called Nummo—a male deity who buried himself inside the womb of a female Nummo who had become part of the earth. When his mouth emerged from an anthill, it took the form of a loom warped with cotton threads between his upper and lower teeth. "As the threads crossed and uncrossed, the two tips of the Spirit's forked tongue pushed the thread of the weft to and fro, and the web took shape from his mouth in the breath of the second revealed Word."[23] The Dogon are thus literally clothed in language: "The weaver . . . sings as he throws the shuttle, and the sound of his voice enters into the warp, adding to and taking along with it the voice of the ancestors."[24] As the beater (part of the loom that combs the fiber into the warp) strikes the threads into place, the song enters the space between the threads and the spoken becomes written, so that the song itself escapes through the narrative of warp and weft, pattern and dye.

For the Dogon, cloth is language: "To be naked is to be speechless."[25] The oral word is captured in the textile, and each word itself is given a body of fiber; many words linked together become the body and voice of the textile. Whereas the textile gives form to the word, the word as textile endows the human body with language. Whoever wears this cloth is transformed from an animal without language into a speaking, rational being—a member of the tribe.

Although cloth can sanction power through its symbolic language, how the semiotics of cloth works and what it guarantees varies according to every culture. In China, for example, because of the high cost of silk, only the royal or the wealthy could afford to purchase it. Yet even a peasant woman on the day of her marriage "was permitted to wear a red silk bridal jacket embellished with the symbols of the Imperial family; she was said to be 'Empress for a day.' "[26] By wearing the Imperial insignia, the bride participated in a symbolic contract not only between two individual families but within a larger social lineage. As "empress for a day," the bride is momentarily raised in status but not in freedom. By participating in the representation of royalty, the bride is a symbolic and silent guarantor of the authority of that system, a commodity of the state and an object for its maintenance and exchange. Her offspring from this marriage also exist as signs of the politically sanctioned union. These signs guarantee perpetuation of privilege by the Imperial family and its government.

The textile's primary meaning exceeds its purpose to clothe and protect by providing information about its wearer. Not only can clothing become symbolic of the person it is made for, but clothing can also have the opposite effect and turn its wearer into an abstraction or sign. Marked with the symbolic text of its society, the textile in turn marks its wearer, so that a body becomes identical to the "text." Thus, uniforms of any kind homogenize large groups of people, transforming the individual into an abstract ideal, marking them with ideas of prejudice or privilege, wherein their individuality is subsumed by the needs or claims of a larger community. When we wear uniforms of any kind, whether the orange robe of a renunciate, army fatigues and cap, a judge's cloak, or a college basketball uniform, we feel different about ourselves because we have now stepped outside of our world as an individual and entered a larger world of representation.

From the evidence of myth and history, we now have an idea of the significance weaving has had in the creation of culture. In the following section I look at how terms for cloth production have permeated the English language. When any activity penetrates our experience as human beings, the rhetoric of that activity finds expression in any given language through metaphor. Like terms for farming, terms for cloth production are used to describe many things other than the making of cloth.

II

The connection between weaving (textiles) and language (texts) becomes so entangled as to be almost impossible to separate. In many languages, including English, the verb *to weave* defines not just the making of textiles, but any creative act. Likewise, the noun *text* comes from the Latin verb *texere,* also meaning "to construct or to weave."[27] In Greek this verb, *tekhne,* refers to art, craft, and skill. Therefore, a weaver not only fashions textiles but can, with the same verb, contrive texts. Roland Barthes states that "etymologically the text is a cloth; *textus,* meaning 'woven.' "[28] Likewise, in Hinduism, and later Buddhism, sacred esoteric texts were called *Tantras.* The etymology of *Tantra* "derives from the weaving craft and denotes interpenetration . . . inter relatedness."[29] A Tantra is not only a woven text, then, but is thought to have innate power to weave the reader into a more integrated understanding of the sacred and secular worlds.

A network of terms exists in English contending that a written text is like a fabric—spun, woven, knitted, quilted, sewn, or pieced together. So many of our phrases in English are colored by our ancestors' experience of making cloth. We talk about the "fabric" of our society when characterizing our collective ideas. When someone makes up a story, we say that they are "spinning a yarn." Our thoughts can "unravel," "tangle," or "fray." Sometimes our ideas have too many "loose ends," which is a term for something woven but not yet tied off the loom, and hence in danger of falling apart.

When we refer to work as being "shoddy," we are refering to poorly woven material that was sold at greatly reduced prices. Someone who is dreamy or inattentive is said to be "woolgathering," which alludes to the actual profession of a woolgatherer who appeared to wander aimlessly through the fields gathering tufts of wool from the branches and bushes that the flocks rubbed against while grazing. When we are under a great deal of tension we may say that we are "on tenter hooks," which is a term for stretching wool to prevent shrinkage after it has been washed.

Finally, the word *clue* derives from the Anglo-Saxon *cliwen,* originally meaning "ball of yarn." There are many stories in which a ball of yarn has been used to help one find one's way out of a forest or maze, thus any help given to solving riddles became known as "clues."[30]

We call unmarried women "spinsters," originally meaning women employed at spinning, one of the only legitimate professions for women from the European Renaissance through the nineteenth centuries in both England and America. Consequently, the matriarchal family line is often called the "distaff" side of the family.

Many terms of this kind pervade our language. What intrigues me is not their number but the odd fact that we no longer consider these terms as being used metaphorically. Although attesting to the importance of cloth making in human history, the terms no longer have any explicit reference to cloth making but now seem almost exclusively used to describe the realm of human emotions and mental activity.

Just as our language is "shot through" with references to cloth making, so too exist a network of terminologies that perpetuates the idea that a text is like a fabric—spun, woven, knitted, sewn, or pieced together.

In literature the presence of a textile as well as a weaving scene always refers to two things: the production of literature (i.e., the text in which this smaller scene occurs) and the history of that production (i.e., the text's relationship to the textile). Regarding this four-way relationship (literature/text/text/textile), the production of fabric as a metaphor for the making of a text occurs across cultures and across time. It functions in various ways, but always contains within it the notion that the text constitutes a "material" object, a woven fabric that may be unraveled at any time.

This idea forms the basis of J. Hillis Miller's important book *Ariadne's Thread: Story Lines.* Miller proposes that a text's architecture is really a labyrinth created from the thread of thought on which words are strung. Accordingly, literary criticism may take up the narrative "thread" of any given text and follow it "deep into the labyrinth of the text" in order to discover the way a text "deconstructs itself in the process of constructing its web of storytelling."[31]

Conversely, Virginia Woolf emphasizes the materiality of the text as a whole. She equates literary texts with textiles by proposing that "fiction is like a spider's web, attached ever so lightly . . . to life at all four corners."[32] Woolf refers not so much to the similarities in the production of texts and textiles as to the fragile nature of literary texts, which, like textiles of any kind (including spider webs), are impermanent and ancillary manifestations of the society (or nature) that produces them. Her metaphor also makes cursory mention of the spider, a common image in mythology for the creator. Often, this spider represents a female deity, an author of creation, who, in this analogy, constitutes an author of fiction or any kind of literary text. Such an idea finds exquisite expression in John Keats's letter to J. H. Reynolds, dated 19 February 1818:

> Now it appears to me that almost any Man may, like the Spider spins from his own inward his own airy Citadel—the points of leaves and twigs on which the Spider begins her work are few and she fills the Air with a beautiful circuiting: man should be content with as few points to tip with the fine Webb of his Soul and weave a tapestry empyrean—full of Symbols for his spiritual eye, of softness for his spiritual touch, of space for his wandering.[33]

I find this passage remarkable not only for its metaphorical quality but for its tactile image. Because reference to texts as textiles charge the language with sensorial images, writers often turn to this analogy. This physical quality of a text/textile, the idea that it constitutes a kind of body or garment that can be worn or shorn, informs the language and our literature in surprising ways. I will give further discussion to this idea in a later chapter.

Woolf and Keats hint at a premise more fully elaborated by Sir Walter Scott: any analogy between text and textile can expand to include the weaver (or writer); the author's or narrator's task is to weave, knit, or quilt together a story. In Sir Walter Scott's novel, *The Heart of Midlothian,* the narrator's responsibility—to connect the different threads of his story—is compared to "what a knitter (if stocking looms have left such a person in the land) might call our dropped stitches, a labour in which the author generally toils much, without getting credit for his pains."[34] Here, Scott refers not to the material out of which a text is made (Miller), not to the possible deterioration of this material (Woolf), nor to the creator's self-sustaining power of imagination (Keats), but to the work involved in creating literary texts, likening his task to the painstaking manual labor of the textile trade. These dropped stitches refer to divergent points in a complex plot that must be retrieved and linked together at some point as the author develops the story.

Finally, Roland Barthes penetrates the heart of this metaphor, positing that textiles and texts are analogous because "etymologically the text is a cloth."[35] These analogies of text/cloth and textile laborer/author support the idea of a material text and the text-like nature of cloth. Indeed, our distinctions between the two begin to blur.

A further correlation exists between the textile-body and the text in recent feminist criticism, which states that the text represents a body, more particularly a female body, colonized by an author's need to make the text signify his own desire. Taken from an historical perspective, however, the textual body cannot be regarded merely as a "blank page," as a silenced female voice or body waiting to be written upon.[36] Instead, the textual body is itself a textile that speaks through the written text, emerging through the words, and controlling the narrative in surprising ways. This textile "speaks" in a manner akin to what Geoffrey Hartman calls the "volcanic silence," of poetry. I suggest, however, that this "volcanic silence," this "historical ground" in any text, derives as much from "the buried life" or history of the textile as it does from "the buried life of words."[37] Susan Gubar claims in her essay, "'The Blank Page' and the Issues of Female Creativity," that "no woman is a blank page: every woman is author of the page and author of the page's author."[38] A text's "blank page," in this sense, represents an "active" agent that signifies neither silence nor absence; instead, it constitutes the body of a textual/textile history, implying that this history includes a female experience and authorship.

Because weaving constitutes one of the first signifying practices that recorded the world's ancient myths and symbols, I propose that reference made within a written text to either a textile or to the weaving process recalls this history. Toward this view, the written text is a recent form of textile, ancillary to those primary texts "told" or "tooled" in cloth.

In the next chapter, I move away from weaving in the contexts of mythology and history and into an explication of Kristeva's theories. Here I posit that the literal relationship of the body to signification reproduces, metaphorically, a relationship between text and textile. This chapter establishes the theoretical context for the literary analysis that forms the rest of the book.

2

The Semiotics of Cloth and Thetic (Re)Production

> [T]he jackal, the deluded and deceitful son of God, desired to possess speech, and laid hands on the fibres in which language was embodied, that is to say, on his mother's skirt.
>
> —Marcel Griaule, *Conversations with Ogotemmeli*

> Among the Arabs of Moab a childless woman often borrows the robe of a woman who has had many children, hoping with the robe to acquire the fruitfulness of its owner.
>
> —Sir James George Frazer, *The Golden Bough*

> Whatever man makes and makes it live lives because of the life put into it. A yard of India muslin is alive with Hindu life. And a Navajo woman, weaving her rug in the pattern of her dream must run the pattern out in a little break at the end so that her soul can come out, back to her.
>
> —D.H. Lawrence, "Whatever Man Makes"

WE HAVE ESTABLISHED THAT WEAVING AND TEXTILES HAVE BEEN significant to creating cultures in a variety of ways. As an industry, weaving centers wielded tremendous economic power in various parts of the world at different times in history. As a signifying practice, the weaving of textiles allowed human beings to shape cultural identity. Finally, as a metaphor for creation, the concept of weaving is embedded in different languages and mythologies all over the world. In these ways weaving links us to a past that even now shapes our future.

Besides the fact that textiles can be marked with signs and symbols that in turn mark their wearer, how else can textiles be considered texts, and conversely, in what way can we regard texts as textiles? I examine this question by turning to an explication of Julia Kristeva's theories about the literal relationship of the body to signification toward a theory that posits the affinity between text and textile as one which reproduces, metaphorically, this relationship.

For those of my readers who are not yet familiar with the use of Lacanian or Kristevan theories in literary analysis, I will explain the following thesis as the chapter unfolds. But for those of my readers who are conversant with this kind of psychoanalytic criticism, my thesis is a rather simple one: I argue that the author of a literary text projects his/her desire (and disgust) for a maternal body/textile onto a female character whose relationship to the text and its characters provides a symbol for the abjected maternal/textile. I furnish examples from selections of "romance" literature, in which a female character (or body) pursues or is pursued by a "desirous" male consciousness. The ambiguous nature of this desire, as will become clear, constitutes the main problem for each story. Beginning with a simplified model of Kristeva's theories of signification, I discuss some of her more complex ideas in terms of the literary texts I have chosen to explicate.

Because Kristeva's theories focus on the relationship of the body to language, her work in semiotics and psychoanalysis provides a lens for understanding the relationship between the textile-body and its text. Since Kristeva's theories also deal with "representations of difference" and with "the logics of power that give rise to women's marginalization,"[1] they provide an interesting model through which to contemplate the recurring association between women and textiles in literature. Although Kristeva does not consider herself a feminist, many of her theories debate (and advance) current ideas in feminist theory.

Time and again, Kristeva turns to literature and art to speculate on certain facets of her own ideas. Indeed, "Kristeva shows that literature and all forms of artistic endeavour fundamentally interpenetrate."[2] Her theories often demonstrate the intimate relationship between artistic production and human psychology, which are both shaped by as well as shape "subjectivity" (or loosely put, a sense of an autonomous self). Although semiotic theory provides only one way in which to speculate on weaving scenes in literature and art, I am convinced that it is an instructive and meaningful tool, particularly because as a theory its ideas derive from so many different disciplines: language theory, psychoanalysis, anthropology, feminism, and history.

For Kristeva, the process by which a child learns to speak (thus signaling that it has conceived of itself as autonomous from the mother and its environment) begins first in the body: "The body, moreover, is the place where we 'are' as speaking beings; it is the place of the material support of the language of communication."[3] I suggest that "the body of the text" to which literary critics refer (the page on which the words are written as well as the agency by which texts cohere) is analogous to the speaking (human) body. To put it more succinctly, the textual body represents the counterpart to the maternal body: the actual text itself—what is written—constitutes the place of the infant. According to Kristeva, "[t]he maternal body prefigures the Law of the Father and the onset of the Symbolic."[4] The relationship between the mother and the child, and the child's "inevitable" separation from the mother, launches the child's entry into the Symbolic. To enter into the Symbolic means to come into language, culture, and the world of representation both as a signifier of this world and as a participant in its signification. Hence, the maternal body "initiates . . . the infant into both language and subjectivity."[5]

I propose that Kristeva's theories provide a working metaphor for the separation between text and textile: the text is likened to the infant, undifferentiated at first from the Mother textile, whereas the textile constitutes the body from which texts issue, from which texts are born. Because the textile depends on a weaver who has already entered into the Symbolic, the textile incarnates the weaver's desire to represent the loss of the pre-oedipal Mother with a maternal-material body to warm and protect it.

At some point in history, a point in time different for every culture, the text separated from the textile through a process of abjection analogous to the infant's abjection of its mother's body and identification with the Law of the Father (or societal law). By "abjection" I mean that which the drives must expel or reject (the Mother for the child, the Textile for the text) in order to gain autonomy. For Kristeva, drives are "'energy' charges as well as 'Psychical' marks [that] articulate what we call a *chora:* a nonexpressive totality formed by the drives and their stases in a motility that is as full of movement as it is regulated."[6] The drives exist in the semiotic realm and "orient the body to the mother."[7] Although the mother's body "mediates the symbolic law" for the infant as well as provides "the ordering principle of the semiotic chora,"[8] the infant must reject this body and its relationship to it so that it can enter into the Symbolic. By abjecting the maternal body, the infant conceives itself as a subject divided from this body, free now to identify with the other, the Law of the Father. The difference between the maternal and the paternal become representations of the difference between the body (textile) and the word (text). "The child abjects the mother's body (milk, warmth, etc.) to take up a relation with the paternal word."[9] Once separation occurs, the child begins a lifelong relationship to longing itself, spending a great deal of its life in an effort to recover (and reject) this body, in particular, the child's undifferentiated relationship with it. In Kristevan terms, the child who fails to abject the

Mother cannot enter into the Symbolic (governed by the Law of the Father).[10] Psychosis then occurs.

For Kristeva, a subject's consciousness is patterned on the relationship between "two heterogeneous realms: the semiotic and the symbolic."[11] An infant's entry into the Symbolic transpires through the development of the *thetic phase* which marks "the point at which the subject takes up a position, an identification."[12] As a psychic membrane, accommodating movement between the semiotic and Symbolic realms, the thetic constantly renegotiates these realms. A subject can neither signify nor function socially without its existence. In metaphoric terms, the thetic functions like a semi-permeable membrane or filter that is constantly negotiated by the semiotic energy that pulses through it. The thetic organizes the semiotic chora that is expressed by a human subject through any signifying activity (although speaking or writing is generally agreed on as being the signifying activity *par excellence* , any activity that seeks to communicate something either to oneself or to someone else is also considered signification within the Symbolic and may include art, dance, music, or even representation through mathematical equations). Energy that cannot be organized by the thetic falls back through this filter to be reorganized later.

The thetic break between the text and textile occurs when the weaver/author, who has already entered into the realm of the Symbolic, abjects the maternal function of the textile—to clothe and protect—in preference for its symbolic material and function. This process of abjection reproduces, metaphorically, the weaver/author's own abjection from the mother. The newly abjected text (as with all texts since) still retains traces of the textile, of this maternal body. These traces are described chiefly in two ways: first, through the author/personae projection of desire for the maternal body, which is somehow veiled, refusing to be captured within the text but always referred to by the text; and secondly, in the text's self-reference to its own "fabrication." I discuss both propositions below.

The first of these "signs" of the "appearance staged as disappearance" of the maternal body arising in the text occurs in what appears to be the author's desire through the process of writing to recover (as well as keep at bay) this body. Remember that the longing to recoup the maternal body is as much feared as it is desired. Theoretically, if one could recover the maternal body and an undifferentiated relationship to it, that person would merge back to a place of shared identity, but one where autonomy was lost and the ability to signify would end. The weaver's desire to articulate autonomy as well as to seek (re)union outside of the self (remember, autonomy is conditioned by a sense of loss and desire for the [M]other) produces a textile which is itself like a veil, another covering, beneath which the maternal body is concealed but never completely revealed.

In literature the author often projects his or her desire for this maternal body in the likeness of a mysterious woman; she is a goddess/enchantress/witch, who is veiled on many levels: by an actual piece of material, through the "veil" of dream or vision, or through the blurred edges of the natural world, such as its mists or the night. She represents both good and evil, being either a fairy-godmother or a Geraldine (see p. 40–41 on Samuel Taylor Coleridge's *Christabel*); her ambiguous nature incarnates the desire/disgust state of abjection.

The Veiled Lady of Nathaniel Hawthorne's novel *The Blithedale Romance,* for example, represents this sought-for maternal body. This novel tells the story of the Veiled Lady who appears both as an actual character within the novel and as a character in a tale told by Zenobia, the female protagonist. The Veiled Lady is a mysterious clairvoyant whose identity is concealed by a white shimmering veil "falling over the wearer, from head to foot . . . to insulate her from the material world, from time and space, and to endow her with many of the privileges of a disembodied spirit."[13] This veiled lady, whose body is replaced by the body of the veil itself, constitutes a perfect metonym for the process by which an author (and text) tries to resurrect the maternal body (the textile) through language. In Zenobia's tale, the Veiled Lady grants Theodore, her would-be lover, three choices when he asks her identity. First, he may leave and forget her altogether; secondly, he may lift her veil out of idle curiosity, but then never again "taste another breath of happiness"; and third, he may kiss her through the veil. The Lady indicates that the third choice is the appropriate one, telling Theodore that from the instant he kisses her "thou shalt be mine, and I thine, with never more a veil between us! And all the felicity of earth and of the future world shall be thine and mine together."[14] Naturally, Theodore mistakes the Lady's offer (after all, what if she were ugly, old, or deformed), and decides instead to lift the veil *first* and to kiss her after he sees her face. His choice represents a desire for, yet another rejection of, the Mother; he wants both—to see her but to withhold himself from her. After all, kissing the Veiled Lady would join him to her forever, "with never more a veil between" them; such an action, though a fulfillment of longing, would also constitute a loss of the autonomy that longing ensures. Predictably, after Theodore lifts the veil and catches a "glimpse of a pale, lovely face beneath," the woman disappears, and the veil falls to the floor. Like Keats's "Knight forlorn," his retribution, is "to pine, forever."[15] The Veiled Lady, like La Belle Dame Sans Merci, haunts her lovers by representing for them the actual condition of abjection.

Furthermore, Percy Bysshe Shelley's poem, "Alastor," explores an author/personae relationship with this veiled maternal body. Again, as with Hawthorne's Veiled Lady, the persona dreams of or imagines an encounter with the Mother, and yet the author postpones, indefinitely, Alastor's meeting with her. Shelley eventually calls this beckoning yet deferred female entity his epipsyche. She is young, beautiful, identical with him; she not only understands all of the poet's and persona's needs and desires, but she can fulfill them as well. Shelley describes this "maternal body" in these terms:

> . . . he dreamed a veiled maid
> Sate near him, talking in low solemn tones.
> Her voice was like the voice of his own soul
> Heard in the calm of thought; its music long,
> Like woven sounds of streams and breezes, held
> His inmost sense suspended in its web
> Of many-colored woof and shifting hues.[16]

She appears as a voice—unseen—a body that produces changes in him.

For Kristeva the child experiences its symbiosis with the mother through an intensification of the senses: "Voice, hearing, and sight are the archaic dispositions where the earliest forms of discreetness emerge. The breast, given and withdrawn; lamplight capturing the gaze; intermittent sounds of voice or music."[17] The mother's body, like Alastor's Veiled Maiden, is but an extension of the child's/poet's (she "Sate near him"). The child/poet sees blurred patches of color and shape spatially undifferentiated ("Of many-colored woof and shifting hues"), and even more importantly, "the 'music' produced" in this symbiotic relationship—the sucking and cooing, the heartbeat and the breath—"is what Kristeva calls the 'voiced breath' that fastens the child to an undifferentiated maternal body," whereas "after the mirror stage the child begins to distinguish its sounds from its mother's."[18] After this time, the "'voiced breath' becomes maternal language, an object for the child."[19] In Shelley's "Alastor," the persona perceives the voice of the veiled maid to be that "of his own soul," indicating his re-experience or desire for the retrieval of the primary mother-child symbiosis.

The sounds he hears are not language per se, but rather constitute sensory and natural sounds like "music," "streams and breezes," the "voiced breath" of the pre-oedipal relationship. They are woven, material, bodily sounds. But more importantly for this analysis, the persona can neither speak nor think independently when in the presence of this voice, for it "held / His inmost sense suspended." The dreamer's "vision" then represents a relationship that exists prior to the mirror stage, before the child differentiates itself from its mother. And yet because the persona only dreams of or envisions this relationship, he speaks of it as a loss he must recover, but he also defers its retrieval for the entire poem. We do not know whether Alastor, at the time of his death, ever unites with his vision, although the author hints at this possibility by describing Alastor's dead face as "faintly smiling," and by telling us that Alastor's "last sight" was "the great [maternal] moon."

Just as "the logic of identification is already operating on the level of the semiotic body prior to the child's entrance into the Symbolic order,"[20] so, too, is a written text encoded with the textile through the semiotic of fiber, structure, pattern, and dye. This semiotic not only constitutes the material out of which meaning is conveyed, but also produces the textile material itself. One way in which an author suggests that a relationship still continues between the text and the textile, between meaning and its body, occurs when the text refers to its own textuality, its own body, or the process by which its narrative thread is woven into meaning. This self-reference occurs as a gap or lacuna in the text's symbolic discourse. Barthes asks, "Is not the most erotic portion of a body *where the garment gapes?* . . . the intermittence of skin flashing between two articles of clothing . . . between two edges."[21] Though not constituted as an erotic moment per se, the text reveals traces of its origins, its body, by flashes; these tactile-textual images represent a metaphor for exposure of the mother's body, through "the staging of an appearance as disappearance."[22] What is "seen"—or imagined—is the phallic mother, "the source of all gratification."[23]

In his poem, "Christabel," Samuel Taylor Coleridge could be imagining this phallic mother in the character of Geraldine. The poem posits Geraldine as (among other things) a maternal figure. The characters—Sir Leoline, Christabel, and Bard Bracy—take up positions toward her, of either desire or fear (or both). The actual nature of her body—what the narrative itself tries to decide—is unknown; even Christabel cannot speak of what she, in flashes, "remembers" about it. Christabel's inability to signify, like Alastor's, always accompanies her recollection of Geraldine's (the Mother's) body. The difference between Alastor's and Christabel's experience, however, seems to be a consequence of gender: Alastor experiences his relationship to the Mother as a desirous one, whereas guilt alone constitutes Christabel's relationship with the maternal figure.[24]

The authors of these poems posit their characters in a strained relationship between autonomy, desire and death; collapsing one's identity into this pre-oedipal world signifies a death of the subjective self. These authors fantasize through their characters how the fulfillment of desire (the end of all desire) would feel. Accordingly, I believe that an author recapitulates his/her own desire (and abhorrence) for the maternal body through the activity of writing.

In this process the author unconsciously inscribes into the text a relationship with the textile which mimics his/her desire. The text's Symbolic always tries to transcend its materiality. The symbolic function weaves together not threads of color and fiber, but ideas and words in an effort to create a fabric of thought suspended outside of the text itself. Consequently, any narrative activity rejects its own materiality in an effort to replace the material of paper and language with that of imagination, to somehow move the reader (or listener) from the paper (or the words) into an imaginative fabric(ation) of the narrator's and reader's own making. Yet a narrative also seems concerned with, simultaneously, the method of its own manufacture, the making of its material body, which it seeks to uncover while objecting it at the same time.[25] In just this way William Blake's *The Four Zoas* explores the process of poetic creation.

Although never completed, and written relatively early in his career, "The Four Zoas" illustrates an epic journey that any individual consciousness may take to recover an experience of its own unfallen innocence. In Blake's poem, which I will treat more fully in a later chapter, the Zoas personify different facets of a united consciousness who is Albion. Albion is both England and the archetypal or "Ancient man," the place—body and mind—in which the Zoas have their being. Although the Zoas exist in the body and "consciousness" of Albion, the "Eternal Man" is relatively unconscious during the poem; in fact, he is asleep. The resulting poem is Albion's dream: he acts as the stage on which the dream unfolds. He is both the dream's author as well as its audience.

A portion of the poem's plot revolves around the Zoas' enslavement to the desire for "progress," particularly Urizen, who characterizes Albion's reasoning function. This "progress" emulates and forms a scathing critique of England's industrialization. Blake's society considered advancement a "good thing," because progress created a strong, competitive nation. Blake sees through this ideal of progress, however, and depicts it in the Zoas as a thinly veiled quest for power at the expense of life itself.

Moreover, the disproportional time or "space" given over to the Zoas' weaving and spinning in their fall from innocence reveals Blake's frustration with the adversarial relationship between body and thought, a struggle symbolized by the aberrant textiles these bodies and thoughts produce. The struggle between the body and its desires (or thoughts), constitutes what Blake tries to reunite. But this furious weaving and spinning of garments, Spectres, plots, and "the Direful Web of Religion" (VIII, 26) also refers to the author's own task, for writing itself marks a fall from unity into duality and despair.

Blake's "Introduction" to the *Songs of Innocence* subtly demonstrates this fall into an experience of duality as the writer's "necessary" predicament. The Piper "Piping down the valleys wild" (l. 1) is asked by a child to sit and write down his songs "that all may read—" (l. 14). To do so, the piper must first put down his pipe, thus stopping his music so that he may record it; this marks the narrator's first separation from nature. Next, he "pluck'd a hollow reed," making from nature an instrument to record experience; here the narrator exploits nature for his own caprice. Third, the Piper "stain'd the water clear" (l. 18) to make ink. The stain itself symbolizes the Piper's compromised innocence, stained in the service of writing. No longer a part of the natural world, he sits down, removed from "the valleys wild." As this poem suggests, the state of innocence cannot represent itself, for innocence is not a state of duality, between subject (narrator) and object (songs), but rather, constitutes a state of undifferentiated unity between singer and song, between the human and the natural worlds—like the bodily territories of mother and child.[26]

As most readers of Blake agree, elements of experience are present or foreshadowed in the *Songs of Innocence* while hints on how to recover innocence are present in *Songs of Experience.* Even as early as these *Songs* were composed, writing and experience often found themselves coupled in Blake's imagination. I suggest here (and pursue more fully in chapter 3) that the Zoas' unceasing weaving of bodies and garments supplies a counterpart to Blake's own activities. While spinning thoughts, Blake is also the weaver; bodies of words fill each page, and his text, like "old England's winding sheet" perpetuates the split between body and mind, between Tharmas (natural instincts) and Urizen. The written text is analogous to a "winding sheet" or shroud in that certain kinds of writing imply a fall into experience which for Blake approximates the death-like state of experience.

Blake seems well aware of his activity, that he must also write the text of *The Four Zoas* and portray "the bitter words / Of Stern Philosophy & knead the bread of knowledge with tears & groans" (IX ll. 818–20) that he may redeem humanity through the language of prophecy. The only way to heal the split and to experience unity is, ironically, to lay down the pen, to let "[h]is crown of thorn [fall] from his head" and to hang "his living Lyre / Behind the seat of the Eternal Man" (IX ll. 710–11). In other words, the writer must renounce the "pleasure/ pain principle" in order to be whole. Thus, Blake's concern with textiles in "The Four Zoas" not only suggests his awareness of industrialization in late eighteenth and early nineteenth-century England, but also represents the author's labor, the making of a material body (the body of the text) and its abjection by the text itself.

II

Perhaps the most significant aspect of Kristeva's theory toward building my argument for the metaphorical relationship between weaving and writing, textile and text, is her concept of the *thetic.* In this section I discuss how a textile inhabits, metaphorically, this position of the thetic—what Kristeva calls "the threshold of language"[27]—and how in some stories the weaving of textiles produces a metaphor for the abjected Mother. The textile, in the process of being woven, represents the thetic phase, the place wherein the Symbolic is established. The thetic "signifies both rupture and boundary. More a filter than a prophylactic barrier, it sustains the symbolic against semiotic drives that would destroy it."[28] Both the weaving process and the textile can represent the thetic function. The textile, as it is woven, constitutes that "place" on the loom wherein disparate fibers (the semiotic) are woven into a fabric whose designs and text "symbolize" the Symbolic. The loom organizes and "beats" the semiotic material/unorganized fibers into place, accommodating them into the artistic/symbolic form of the tapestry.[29]

In this analogy, the textile attempts to introduce the semiotic into the Symbolic realm. When the semiotic energy or material becomes too great for the woven cloth, when the tapestry cannot contain this metaphor for the semiotic, the tapestry's material tears apart from the strain placed on the cloth (and the semiotic material) "to represent." The tapestry/thetic constitutes a psychic webbing, which in the hands of some weavers, continually makes and unmakes itself and those around it.

In order to understand the violent impact of unaccommodated semiotic energy onto the Symbolic, we must first define the chora, which exists prior to language, as an important constituent of the semiotic realm. As defined by Kristeva, the chora compromises the Symbolic, and also, paradoxically, is what this Symbolic rejects: "Our discourse—all discourse—moves with and against the chora in the sense that it simultaneously depends upon and refuses it."[30] It marks that place "where the subject is both generated and negated."[31] The chora does not *signify*. In language, it is "analogous only to vocal or kinetic rhythm."[32] But it contains energy. Though the Symbolic is constructed out of the semiotic energy and pre-oedipal drives that constitute the *chora,* the Symbolic jettisons (or prohibits) everything it cannot accommodate.

Arachne's and Philomela's tapestries, as will be shown, communicate the semiotic chora, a dangerous energy that can, and (in these stories) does destroy both the weaver and those in proximity to her. This semiotic material courses through the textile's designs, signifying its presence in a manner not dissimilar from the semiotic activity or drives; Kristeva explains this as a process that "introduces wandering or fuzziness into language and, a fortiori, into poetic language."[33] The semiotic/pre-symbolic enters language as "the 'materiality' of the symbolic: the voice as rhythm and timbre, the body as movement, gesture, and rhythm. Prosody, word-plays, and especially laughter fall within the ambit of the semiotic."[34]

Excluded from their societies—Philomela is locked away, Arachne refuses to participate in the Olympian tradition, and the Lady of Shalott is immured in a tower—these weavers operate from the margins of the Symbolic order, and weave in their tapestries what is forbidden by their society, what is abject; they weave a metaphor of the semiotic. Oliver writes "[a]lthough every society is founded on the abject—constructing boundaries and jettisoning the antisocial—every society may have its own abject. In all cases, the abject threatens the unity/identity of both society and the subject. It calls into question the boundaries upon which they are constructed."[35] Removed from society and yet an integral part of it, constituting in some sense the abject of their society, these weavers make their tapestries represent their own "location" within the Symbolic. The semiotic chora pulses through the interstices of their weaving and woven tapestries; these tapestries, in turn, convey meaning through a system of signs which, like some poetry, compromises language itself. Laden with semiotic material, the message embodied in these tapestries destroys not only the weaver but those in proximity to her.

An author may demonstrate an abiding relationship between text and textile, as we have seen, through his/her projection of desire in the form of a veiled woman. In such instances the veiled body constitutes a metaphor of Kristeva's thetic in that this veiled body negotiates the semiotic drives and attempts to accommodate them into the Symbolic. In book 2, canto 12 of Edmund Spenser's *The Faerie Queene*, Spenser writes the thetic into Acrasia's body. Adrift on an island, Acrasia of "the Bowre of blis" exists both apart from her society as well as in reach of it. She represents the abject—being both the desired and the repulsed—for the author, characters, and the reader. When Sir Guyon and the reader finally reach Acrasia, we see her in her veil which conceals as it reveals her body. This veil is both a second body (or textile) as well as a text which provides information about her body. Acrasia's body can be viewed as the M(O)ther that can never be recuperated in the Symbolic, but can only be approached through language, through the veil; it can only "expose itself in meaning beneath a veil of words."[36] The message we read or decipher through the veil is janus-like, being both false and true; for though the veil reveals her body, it also shows her body whiter than it really is.

> Vpon a bed of Roses she was layd,
> As faint through heat, or dight to pleasant sin,
> And was arayd, or rather disarayd,
> All in a vele of silk and siluer thin,
> That hid no whit her alablaster skin,
> But rather shewd more white, if more might bee:
> More subtile web Arachne can not spin,
> Nor the fine nets, which oft we wouen see
> Of scorched deaw, do not in thee faire more lightly flee.
>
> (II.xii.77)[37]

Unbeknownst to the Knight of Temperance, Acrasia represents the ultimate goal of his quest, achieved too early for his liking, and therefore threatening the closure of all adventure and signifying pleasure. Sir Guyon first sees Acrasia lying with a young Knight (perhaps a desirous/dreaded projection of himself). As with Alastor, "[t]he young man sleeping by" Acrasia (79:1) has lost his autonomy; his shield and sword "were hong vpon a tree" (80:2), symbolizing the end of his quest. His shield's emblem, "fowly ralst, that none the signes might see" (80:4), indicates that the knight's ability to signify has been lost in his experience of the maternal body. The useless sword implies the knight's castration, for an encounter with Acrasia is an encounter with the phallic Mother: "Her replete body, the receptacle and guarantor of demands, takes the place of all narcissistic, hence imaginary, effects and gratifications; she is, in other words, the phallus."[38] Furthermore, the removal of the shield's emblem indicates the knight's inability to participate in the Symbolic; his is a wretched state, for all of Spenser's knights covet the "signs" that endow them with autonomy, taking great pleasure in defending their own as well as in annihilating those belonging to others. The desecration of the knight's emblem symbolizes his return to the pre-oedipal relationship in which the drives "connect and orient the [knight's] body to the mother,"[39] so that signification becomes impossible.

After glimpsing Acrasia, Sir Guyon violently rejects the invitations of her body by destroying her "Bowre." Before Sir Guyon can vanquish Acrasia, however, he must first confront his own desire for her. After he refuses her "invitations," he must shield himself from her body. With the help of the Palmer (his companion and counselor during this quest), the Knight of Temperance places chains of adamant (an impervious stone) around Acrasia, and then "from the tempest of his wrathfulnesse"

> Their groues he feld, their gardins did deface,
> Their arbers spoyle, their Cabinets suppresses
> Their banket houses burne, their buildings race,
> And of the fairest late, now made the fowlest place.
>
> (II.xii.82)

Stephen Greenblatt suggests that Guyon's destruction of the Bowre reenacts those duties that Spenser himself had to carry out while living, an English noble, in Ireland. I would like to suggest, further, that Guyon's reaction toward Acrasia and the Bowre has a psychic aspect. Consider that Acrasia's veil operates like a thetic membrane, a threshold separating the semiotic realm—Guyon's drives and desires as embodied by Acrasia—and the Symbolic realm of Guyon's autonomy, his shield and his lance not yet "hong vpon a tree." Encountering Acrasia's body overwhelms Sir Guyon—he does not speak, but the pleasure indicated in the mere act of describing her for three cantos suggests the intensity of her attractions, both for the character as well as for the narrator himself. I conceive the knight to be a projection of the narrator's desire for and resistance to the body of Acrasia—a metaphor for Ireland as well as the Mother. Since Ireland is often configured in maternal—usually negative—terms, this multiple symbolism is not at odds.

The energy driving Guyon's journey arises from a consistent attractive/repulsive movement pulling him toward Acrasia's body. The veil lightly covering her body is too porous and thin to shape semiotic energy into a container of language allowing for accommodation into the Symbolic. Therefore, in an attempt at containment, the Palmer and Sir Guyon chain Acrasia in adamant. Here, the adamant replaces the veil as a thetic division, serving as a more efficient and less disturbing substance than the porous fabric. And yet we might as well call out to the Knight "too late!" for even after Acrasia has been bound and the threat of her seduction passes, Sir Guyon embarks on a destruction of the island so thorough and extreme that the act itself suggests his encounter with Acrasia has been unsuccessful, that to some degree he has failed. Sir Guyon's confrontation with Acrasia's body and his own body's desire "contaminates" him, for Guyon's rage indicates a passion equal to lust as well as to madness.

The drives released in the semiotic chora are usually destructive in nature, and Guyon emulates the very nature of these drives. The semiotic energy that escapes from Acrasia's "revealed" body through the thetic threshold of her veil so disturbs the Knight of Temperance that, if judged by the qualities he himself supposedly represents, his quest has ended in failure. Kristeva states that "[d]rives involve pre-Oedipal semiotic functions and energy discharges that connect and orient the body to the mother."[40] And though these drives "have been described as disunited or contradictory structures, simultaneously 'positive' and 'negative,' this doubling is said to generate a dominant 'destructive wave' that is [*sic*] drive's most characteristic trait."[41] Guyon's desire for and repulsion of the maternal body as symbolized by Acrasia's veil results in the rampant destruction of the "Bowre" which, too, symbolizes the body of Acrasia. In a scene that imitates the child's pre-oedipal abjection of the mother and entrance into the Law of the Father, Sir Guyon castrates the phallic mother by rejecting her body and by asserting his own autonomy, his own phallus.

Lord Alfred Tennyson's poem "The Lady of Shalott" illustrates another instance of a textile operating as the thetic threshold between the semiotic and Symbolic. I deal with this poem more fully in chapter 5, as well as with its representations in Pre-Raphaelite art. In my present analysis, I am mainly concerned with the relationship between the textile, the weaver, and the mirror which casts forth "magic sights" from the world of Camelot.

The setting is an island called Shalott past which runs a road to Camelot. A castle on this island "imbowers" the Lady of Shalott, and though no one has ever seen her, she is believed to exist because the "reapers, reaping early" (I.28) have heard her singing. Through night and day she sits at a loom weaving "A magic web with colors gay" (II.38). Her only "window" to the outside world consists of a mirror in which "Shadows of the world appear" (II.48). She will be cursed should she stop gazing through the mirror of representation and choose, instead, to cross her room to an actual window and look out toward Camelot. At first her mirror satisfies her, and on her tapestry she weaves its "magic sights" (II.65). But one day she hears someone singing outside her castle, and as she looks into the mirror the form of Sir Lancelot appears. Unable to resist either his beauty or his song, she goes to her window to look down at him. Within the instant, the poet writes,

> The mirror cracked from side to side;
> "The curse is come upon me," cried
> The Lady of Shalott.
>
> (III.115–17)[42]

From this point on, the lady ceases to weave, and begins her journey toward Camelot, a journey that seems to require her death. As her boat drifts past the towers of Camelot, Lancelot sees her for the first time, and for a brief moment mourns the death of such a lovely face.

This poem has been read as a warning of what awaits women who try to exercise artistic autonomy in a strictly patriarchal culture. It has also been read, on the other hand, as the (non-gendered) artist's struggle between the public and private spheres.[43] This poem seems to suggest that to be an artist you cannot live in Camelot. Toward this view, when the Lady gazes out the forbidden window at Camelot, she chooses against leading her life as an artist in preference for the life of Camelot; therefore, the web of art unravels from the loom, and "the mirror" of creative thought "cracked from side to side" (III.115). Sandra Gilbert and Susan Gubar maintain this interpretation, saying that "the Lady of Shalott seems like the mad, alienated artist" until "she falls in love with a masterful Sir Lancelot, at which point the mirror of her art cracks 'from side to side,'" thereafter "she lapses into a state of depression" from which she eventually dies.[44]

The poem does suggest some of the problems facing the female artist in the early nineteenth century. And although my analysis will move beyond this type of social criticism, I find it of interest how easily the poem lends itself to such an interpretation. For instance, throughout the first half of the poem, the "mirror"—a metaphor for the self-reflective art—alone sustains the Lady of Shalott. This mirror particularly marks an appropriate symbol for the female artist in the early nineteenth century who, as society provides few models, little guidance, and less support, must be sustained by her own work.

Isolation is imperative, for it allows her uninterrupted time and freedom from social constraints; unhindered, she is able to create art.

The Lady of Shalott achieves solitude by immuring herself in a tower and withdrawing from the public life of the court so that she can create, undisturbed, from the reflections of a life that passes by but does not include her. She exists in a world without any referent but herself. There is no "other" whom she can desire or who can desire her; it seems as if she doesn't exist, and yet she is connected to King Arthur's Court by a thread, a road that runs right past her tower to Camelot.

Sequestered in her tower, she is also immured in a phallus-like structure secondary to the primary phallic Castle of Camelot. She appropriates the power of the phallus by creating on a loom a tapestry that signifies her *presence in* as well as her *absence from* this world. The tale her tapestry embodies is neither "new" nor revolutionary; from the point of view of Camelot, the tapestry's story merely represents a society that excludes her. This is the mirror of "primary narcissism", a stage wherein an infant relates to the world as if he/she were its center.[45] It "can do nothing more than to return the gaze."[46] The Lady finds happiness until she perceives the absence of her own reflection: when the mirror projects the scene of "two young lovers lately wed" (1. 70), she then perceives that her own lack of relationship constitutes a loss. No longer satisfied with her narcissistic art, she sighs, "I am half sick of shadows" (1. 71).

Although the foregoing is a popular reading of this poem, I find "The Lady of Shalott" more richly connotative. My reading of Kristeva may elucidate some of the enigma cast over our imagination by this legendary weaver. I propose that the Lady of Shalott's tapestry represents the thetic, a symbolic threshold between two spheres, between Camelot (the Symbolic) and the island of Shalott (the marginalized Symbolic wherein we perceive the presence of the semiotic). The Lady negotiates these two realms, creating a metaphor of both in the body of her tapestry.

Depending on its method of production, the back of a tapestry may show mere traces of the actual design; it is, occasionally, a confusion of threads, colors and knots, whereas, the face of the tapestry articulates and signifies clarity. The difference between the two sides of a tapestry provide a fascinating metaphor for the relationship between the semiotic and Symbolic realms; although separate from each other, they are constituted simultaneously via the operations of the thetic. Earlier in this chapter I suggested that a metaphor for the thetic occurs in the weaving process which organizes the cosmic container of unwoven, unorganized fibers and colors of threads.

These threads and their various colors represent semiotic material waiting to be shaped. Kristeva remarks that "in all painting" (I believe she would allow this for tapestry as well) "color is pulled from the unconscious into a symbolic order."[47] I discuss more fully the semiotic dimension of color in chapter 5, and mention it here only because it is an important element in the metaphoric relationship between semiotic "drives" and unorganized fibers. The weaver arranges these undifferentiated colored fibers in symbolic order on the loom; she places them at the service of the Symbolic, so that they may convey meaning.

When working on certain types of looms, weavers face the back of their tapestries, and weave by consulting a mirror in which the design is reflected back to them. The face of the tapestry (its coherent side) is usually turned down (and scrolled onto a rod). It appears that the Lady of Shalott consults just such a mirror in Tennyson's poem.[48] The mirror not only contains representations of the world outside her tower (also available by looking through the window), but shows her the patterns she weaves.

When not gazing into the mirror, the Lady of Shalott faces the back of her tapestry, the side where the semiotic material is located; she can only ascertain the Symbolic realm (what her art constitutes in the Symbolic) through the device of the mirror. The mirror negotiates the world of Camelot through representation, and constitutes a tool of mediation between the Lady, her tapestry, and Camelot. Because the Lady's function is to signify (through weaving), she must exist in the Symbolic; however, her place within the tower and at the loom situates her in a precarious position between realms, both of which depend on but do not include her as a subject of their domain.

For the Lady of Shalott, the danger lies not only in dealing with the semiotic energy of her art but in facing the Symbolic realm, in gazing through the window toward a world that marginalizes both her and her productions. To those in Camelot, the Lady becomes a metaphor for the abjected maternal body. Although she is sequestered on an island within reach of Camelot, and although the reapers hear her voice at the early dawn, no one ever sees her and therefore no one ever really knows whether or not she exists. The possibility of her existence is important to Camelot, for the conscious is always built on what it abjects. Only when the Lady sends her dead body down the river to Camelot do they realize, however, that she did, in fact, exist. Their curiousity and fear at encountering her dead body originates from this irony—that although she enters Camelot no longer as myth but as a reality, she has already died.

I have more to say on this subject in chapter 5. Let me remark in conclusion, that from the point of view of Camelot, the Lady represents the maternal body beneath the tapestry and beneath all acts of signification. (Her relationship with the tapestry represents a pre-oedipal relationship/identification with the mother.) Thus, while she cannot exist in the Symbolic realm of Camelot (but can only enter as a symbolic element after she has died), all signification done there depends on her ghostly presence, on the longing for and rejection of her body. She cannot be glimpsed alive by the people of Camelot, for she represents the abjected semiotic realm and its *chora,* which cannot be accommodated into the Symbolic.

Elizabeth Grosz writes of the abject, calling it "[a]n unnameable, pre-oppositional, permeable barrier [that] requires some mode of control or exclusion to keep it at a safe distance from the symbolic and its orderly proceedings."[49] The tower of Shalott, the "magic mirror," the window, the tapestry itself all constitute a "permeable barrier" that separates (or excludes) the Lady from Camelot, at the same time that it allows her to establish a place for herself (as an artist). Since both the semiotic and Symbolic realms are co-dependent, the weaving the Lady performs is analogous to the thetic function, which constitutes both realms while it holds them at bay. By weaving representations of Camelot, the Lady sustains herself in terms of, as well as against, the Symbolic.

For Camelot she constitutes the maternal body out of which it has constructed itself; she also represents what society must abject in order to establish autonomy and the signifying function—the phallus. She is analogous to the phallic Mother of the preconscious pre-oedipal relationship; her tower represents this primary phallus. Staring at the (metaphor for the) semiotic side of the tapestry, all day and night, she also could be said to exist in this realm. Since the semiotic and Symbolic are established simultaneously, both towers constitute a mirror or double of both realms—semiotic/Shalott and Symbolic/Camelot.

In the chapters that follow, I discuss stories in which weaving constitutes the active verb for poetic creation, as well as stories in which weaving features the *scene* of poetic creation. I argue that a textile resembles a written text (both exist in the Symbolic), therefore, to equate the textile with the pre-oedipal mother is inaccurate. Since the textile is the result of the weaver's longing to recover the body of the Mother, however, their relationship abides on the level of metaphor. The analogy between text/textile and infant/pre-oedipal mother constitutes a metaphor for desire: The "desire" of the text for the textile metaphorically recapitulates the weaver's desire for the maternal body. Both are failed desires, for the weaver cannot recuperate the Mother any more than the text can recuperate the Textile. The weaver can retrieve from his/her trajectory of desire only a fragment, a piece of cloth, symbolic of the maternal/material body of the Mother. For the writer, desire creates the story itself. A culture records the symbols of its own heritage on the body of a textile, much like a text encodes a page. For the text, however, this trajectory of desire can *only recuperate a discourse of origins.* I isolate this discourse within the literature examined in the following chapters. To do so, I heed Foucault's suggestion that to follow "the thread of analogies and symbols" in a given piece of literature is to "rediscover . . . a meaning that is embodied in various representations, images and metaphors."[50]

3

The Greek Web: Arachne and Philomela, Penelope and Helen of Troy

> Now Peleides set forth the prizes for the third contest,
> for the painful wrestling, at once, and displayed them before the Danaans.
> There was a great tripod, to set over fire, for the winner.
> The Achaians among themselves valued it at the worth of twelve oxen.
> But for the beaten man he set in their midst a woman skilled in much work of her hands, and they rated her at four oxen.
>
> —*Iliad* XXIII.700–705

For women in ancient Greece, weaving constituted their proper activity and sign.[1] Learning to spin and weave marked "a major element in the enculturation of the female . . . second in importance only to that of marriage."[2] Weaving assured that women remain indoors, secure and secured in the *gynaikonitides,* or women's private chambers. These were usually located at the back of the house with no private entry or exit.[3] Immured in the private sphere, women contributed to the public sphere by producing textiles not only for home use but for gifts, religious offerings, and commercial trade.

What we know about weaving during this time derives from literature, archaeological remains, as well as from friezes, wall paintings, and the iconography of vase painting, which record the style of looms and the way wool was carded and spun. Unlike the weaving stories examined here, the way in which women are depicted at their weaving tasks on these vases often suggests "the erotic appeal of the submission and humble labors of women."[4] The female body is often sexualized in these work scenes.

In turn, literature from this culture often illustrates how a woven object embodies the psychology of its weaver, and how weaving itself becomes a metaphor for a woman's thought process. Scenes abound wherein women, like Klytemnestra and Penelope, are depicted weaving plots as well as garments. Even the Greek language links together these two different activities, so that "woven fabric, poetry, and mētis [craftiness]" are all delineated with the verb "'to sew' or 'to weave.'"[5] This term *mētis* "conveys[s] the idea of plotting, planning or meditating," so that "a plot is twined together, *metin plekein* or . . . woven, *metin huphainein*."[6] Occasionally in these myths, poems, and plays, garments or their production function at the level of plot: the shroud woven and unwoven at Penelope's loom grants her time until Odysseus returns; Philomela's tapestry permits her escape; Klytemnestra's robe becomes a net in which she captures Agamemnon; Medea's garment, dipped in dragon's blood, kills her rival, Kreusa.[7] Endowed with agency, these textiles act out the forbidden desires of their weavers as if they were endowed with a life of their own, albeit a life that is predetermined and framed by the weaver's own intent.

In these stories and in this society weaving is almost always performed by women. Although male weavers did exist in Greece, weaving was an activity almost exclusive to women. In literature of this period, to depict a male weaving is to feminize him—Hercules weaves when he is Omphale's slave, and cuckolded Hephaistos weaves a net in which to catch his adulterous wife, Aphrodite, with her lover, Ares.

Weaving by women is also often linked to ideas of enchantment, for the Greeks recurrently associate textiles (and their production) with magic. Marcel Detienne and Jean-Pierre Vernant remark that "before the Hellenistic period, the Orphics used weaving as a model of intelligent activity to give an account of the process of creation," and that "for the Greeks, the destiny which 'binds' men is 'spun' by the Moirai" or Fates, daughters of Zeus and Themis.[8] Weaving magical symbols endows a specific garment with power. This phenomenon occurs in literature when garments (and their production) are attributed with a kind of agency, themselves possessing an uncanny power to curse or to bless, to create life, to prolong or to destroy it. Thus, in the *Iliad,* the scene where Hector dies becomes especially poignant as Homer depicts Andromache in the act of weaving roses, an ancient symbol for protection, onto a garment for her husband at the moment of his death.[9]

In this culture a woman lacked society's permission to speak for herself: she is denied citizenship and has only minimal access to legal recourse. Moreover, only rarely was she taught to read and write. Ann Bergren contends that "[s]emiotic woman is a weaver," and that in Greek culture the woven textile is for women "a silent substitute for (her lack of) verbal art."[10] In accordance with Bergren's claims, I propose that since most of her time was spent weaving or in the related tasks of spinning and carding wool, a woman regarded textiles as a substitute for "written" texts; in textiles women alone could record and read the major events of their lives. In Euripides' *Ion,* for example, the mother, Kreusa, who was impregnated by Apollo, abandons her newborn child in the woods, yet is able to recognize him as a grown man by describing the clothing in which she left him, woven from her own hands.

> This shawl was all I had, girl as I was,
> to wrap you in—a thing I made playing with my loom.[11]

The remembered textile speaks to her a language she had written long ago, one that she alone can read.[12]

Hence in ancient Greece weaving comprised a tool for female signification, but a further distinction can also be made between the *weaving process* and the *woven textile.* Each represent modes of signification quite different from the other. One is process-oriented whereas the other is product-oriented; weaving becomes a metaphor for speech, something occurring in time, whereas the woven material becomes a metaphor for something written, and thus permanent, unchanging.

The rhythmic action of the weaving process—throwing the shuttle and pulling the beater, placing threads one on top of the other—comprises the moment of a fabric's creation, thereby becoming an apt metaphor for speech and poetic composition. Thus, in the following stories when a character is depicted weaving, this weaving will constitute a metaphor for her empowered speech. Indeed, in Greek, "the utterance of poetry or prophecy is described as 'weaving.'"[13] Homer often couples the activities of singing and weaving, wordmaking and cloth-making. For example, when Odysseus's men first glimpse the sea-witch, Kirke, in her hall, Homer tells us,

> They stood there in the forecourt of the goddess with the glorious
> hair, and heard Circe inside singing in a sweet voice as
> she went up and down a great design on a loom, immortal
> such as goddesses have, delicate and lovely and glorious their work.[14]

And when Hermes visits "the lovely haired / nymph," Kalypso, on behalf of Zeus to give Odysseus his freedom,

> She was singing inside the cave with a sweet voice
> as she went up and down the loom and wove with a golden shuttle.[15]

Both Kirke and Kalypso are dangerous in that they are able to speak spells; their words possess an amoral power that can transform the natural world. By depicting these characters singing while weaving, Homer implies their ability to weave subtle webs, plots, spells.

Walter Pater elaborates on this idea of the integral relationship between the activities of poetic composition, singing and weaving in his descriptions of the mythic *nympholepti* of Greece: As nature's weavers, they complete their tasks of "spinning or weaving with . . . many-coloured threads, the foliage of the trees, the petals of flowers, the skins of the fruit" while singing.[16] Like Shelley's Witch of Atlas and Blake's Emanations, the nympholepti weave the corporeal bodies of nature. Considering these close associations among weaving, poetry, and singing (or spell-weaving), we can assert that "the voice of the shuttle" does speak.[17] By working threads back and forth across a warp, the shuttle is comparable to the speaking tongue. This analogy was probably suggested to the Greeks because of the sound a shuttle produces when thrown across a wide warp, a whirring sound suggestive of song. Ann Bergren discusses the problem that occurs in assigning these two activities—weaving threads into cloth and weaving words into spells—to the same verb:

> Greek culture inherits from Indo-European a metaphor by which poets and prophets define themselves as "weaving" or "sewing" words. That is, they describe their activity in terms of what is originally and literally woman's work *par excellence*. They call their product, in effect, a "metaphorical web." But which, then, is the original and which the metaphorical process? Is weaving a figurative speech or is poetry a figurative web? The question cannot be decided. Weaving as the sign-making activity of women is both literal and metaphorical, both original and derived. It is, like the Muses' speech, ambiguously true speech and an imitation of true speech.[18]

This linking of the activities of weaving and speech occurs at the level of grammar. The verb comprises and combines both meanings. On the other hand, the woven textile functions as a written (rather than oral) text.

Now, to connect this idea to the Kristevan analysis and analogy begun in the previous chapter, the meaning of the textile, like a written text, is fixed in the Symbolic, whereas the weaving process illustrates a metaphor for an unmeasured potential that "fabricates" the Symbolic. The weaving function exists, metaphorically, at the threshold between the semiotic and Symbolic realms, in the place of the thetic, negotiating within the loom the transmission and accommodation of energies.

As a finished product, the textile becomes an element of plot in these stories. We gauge the textile's success in conveying its message by the effect this message has on its audience. Conversely, while the textile is being woven, the story's plot becomes suspended, and elements of hope and uncertainty of the story's outcome enter the narrative, for the weaving process constitutes the site of ongoing artistic creation and not—like the textile—its completion. In the production of Penelope's unfinished shroud or Helen's tapestry woven as Homer weaves his poem, the weaving process becomes emblematic of timelessness, or time postponed. As David Jongeward observes,

> The process of weaving inspires a special relationship to time. The rhythmic drumming of thread over thread produces a sense of movement, or flow, quite unlike usual perceptions of time. In tapestry time, a woven design emerges. The design is like a woven net cast out to catch a fleeting image . . . held in time, out of time. Unweaving, however, reverses the flow of water, the flow of time. It's an ominous feeling, unweaving time.[19]

For once the textile is woven, it enters the Symbolic, and must function as a sign, though perhaps a radical one, as in Philomela's tapestry where the text of the textile, its message, invokes violence.[20] On the other hand, Penelope's shroud, because it is never complete, can always suspend the suitors' demand (and the symbolic order) that requires she remarry. Yet, like Philomela's tapestry, her weaving cannot change patriarchal society or her place in it. Weaving as process can only negotiate for her a space, and time, until she can be properly re-accommodated into this society as Odysseus's wife.

In Greek literature these scenes of weaving often depict explosive moments wherein women transform a domestic art into a tool that allows them to write their own texts of resistance. The *grammata* of these textiles, although not necessarily a language per se, represents language (because it is comprised of signs), yet it often conveys meaning in a manner different than "[l]anguage" that is identified completely with the "symbolic function."[21] The tapestry's *grammata,* its signs, function as a poetic language, signifying the presence of the semiotic.[22] Kristeva's conception of poetic language relies on her theory that the semiotic is communicated through language by a "reactivating [of] this repressed instinctual . . . element" to return to the pre-symbolic, symbiotic relationship with the Mother. Although the *grammata* of these textiles does not constitute an agency itself, it conveys a surplus of meaning which then catalyzes the radical action that concludes these tales.[23]

Arachne's and Philomela's textiles seek negotiation with patriarchal society; these textiles represent their effort to bear a new word, a new language and experience, into the world, into the realm of the Symbolic. When their attempts miscarry, their texts fail to recuperate any lasting meaning. Inherent in these two myths abides the notion that any kind of linguistic performance must be communicated within the domain of the Name of the Father, or the message cannot be received or understood. Therefore, the female, who, along with her texts, resists her otherness—her presence-as-absence—cannot be accommodated within this phallogocentric sphere. According to Lacanian theory, all discourse depends on the Name of the Father, therefore, any language that does not support the patriarchal function cannot, in this symbolic realm, exist. In these tales, the gods have the last "word," thereby reestablishing the Name of the Father. They transmogrify the human characters into animals that will no longer be able to signify or transform acts of signification.

In the following sections, I examine four stories wherein weaving signifies revolt against patriarchy as well as acquiescence to it. For the myths of Philomela and Arachne, respectively, I examine how weaving issues a challenge to the patriarchal institution that denies them autonomy. In these stories the weaving process illustrates the moment of creation *par excellence;* weaving constitutes the means whereby each weaver may fashion herself as a subject, as a producer of signs, rather than being cast as an object, embodying the sign of otherness given to her by society.

In the stories of Helen of Troy and Penelope I observe how the weaving process represents, metaphorically, Homer's voice, and how for each tale—whether the emphasis is on the textile or on the process by which it is woven—weaving marks the difference between oral and written poetry. I suggest that although the weaving process becomes central to the stories of all four weavers, Arachne's and Philomela's stories are product-oriented, whereas Helen's and Penelope's stories are process-oriented. Always keeping in mind their purpose, Arachne and Philomela complete their textiles so that these "rebel texts" might rival the script that has been written for them by society. On the other hand, Helen and Penelope defer the realization of their textiles (their texts) in favor of the weaving process; this deferral suggests that their stories are continuous with and perpetuate the story in which they live.

Tereus, Procne, Philomela

The most brutal of all the weaving stories, recent scholarship devotes ample attention to this myth of horror and revenge.[24] Ovid's version divides the story into two parts with the weaving scene poised as a caesura or bridge between each.

In part one the reader encounters Tereus' marriage to Procne, his rape of her sister Philomela, her mutilation (her tongue is cut out), and her imprisonment. As a hero of war, Tereus of Thrace was successful in driving out the barbarians from Greece, while Athens stood by, offering no martial support ("of all cities—who could believe it?—you, Athens, alone did nothing").[25] Nevertheless, by Tereus' victory, Athens is preserved, and so Pandion, the King of Athens, offers the warrior his eldest daughter's hand in marriage. The gods are absent at their wedding, indicating that a crime has already been committed. The narrative never reveals the nature of this crime, whether it constitutes the failure of Athens to defend itself, or its willingness to form an alliance with Thrace. The myth suggests, however, the inevitability of the tragedy that follows, that Athens—by way of Procne and Philomela—will dearly pay for this crime. Thrace and Athens are set up in this myth as contrasting realms: Athens represents the civilized state, whereas Thrace represents a barbaric nation. Rumors that Thracians practiced human sacrifice haunted the Greek imagination.[26] Procne embodies a contract made between these two societies. Procne has no choice but to wed Tereus because to resist would be considered treasonous. Both Procne and Philomela exist as exchangeable property to consolidate relationships between these men and the societies they represent. If we perceive the bodies of the sisters to be a synecdoche for the body of Athens—beautiful, pure, and vulnerable—to wed this body to Thrace is to violate it.[27]

The tragedy begins when, a few years after they have been wed, Procne sends Tereus back to Athens to request of her father, Pandion, that Philomela visit her in Thrace. On beholding Philomela, Tereus finds her irresistible. After obtaining Pandion's permission, Tereus and his sister-in-law sail for Thrace, and the moment the ship lands on alien soil, Tereus drags her off and rapes her. This rape enacts a number of taboos. When Pandion gave Philomela to Tereus, he did so with the injunction that Tereus assume the responsibilities of a father: "I pray you guard her with a father's love."[28] Hence, not only does the rape violate her body, but it constitutes an adulterous and incestuous act. Outraged and defiled, Philomela threatens Tereus that she will reveal what he has done, and so Tereus cuts out her tongue. Then, he locks her in a hut and places a guard outside the door, returns home to Procne, and tells her that Philomela died on the return journey.

In the second part of the myth the sisters avenge Tereus' aberrant brutality by preparing for him an equally obscene fate. Before this occurs, however, Philomela weaves her story. Not only does this weaving scene separate the first and second parts of the story, but it constitutes a site (the only one) of peace. This pause in the violence is also symbolic of the passage of time. Philomela's weaving takes "a whole year's journey" during which time she must recollect the events of her story, inscribe them, and repair them. Although Ovid devotes only three lines to Philomela's weaving, critics view this scene as the most significant in the story.

Whereas feminists regard Philomela's weaving as a uniquely feminist performance, conventional scholars view it as an artistic—human—one; both agree, however, that the weaving is heroic. For these critics, the tapestry becomes emblematic of art arising from, yet surmounting, all obstacles.

Traditionally, tapestries depict scenes from their culture's dominant mythos, reproducing the stories and signs of prerogative. Philomela's tapestry, however, aims at telling the forbidden story of her rape, a tale that refuses to celebrate her culture—Thracian as well as Athenian—one that, instead, undermines the authority on which both cultures are built. Her tapestry represents more than an artistic production or decorative cloth (the function of its material), nor does it merely depict a story of the pathos of abduction and rape (its textual performance). Rather, Philomela's tapestry serves on many different levels, as a message and a map, as a story and a body, delivered to Procne so that Philomela may be discovered and set free. Philomela's achievement consists in her ability to transform wool into an instrument of symbolic and semiotic power.

When Philomela decides to weave her story, she reconstitutes her position in terms of her society, so that instead of remaining an object or body used, silenced, and discarded, she becomes a subject, an artist reclaiming her voice, and her forbidden story. She transforms weaving from an insignificant (female) activity into an act of (female) signification. Her forbidden tapestry speaks what her tongue cannot. And the "safe, feminine, domestic craft of weaving" becomes in her hands a channel for "art as a new means of resistance."[29] Both the decision to act and the action itself constitute the most important event in the text:

> And what shall Philomela do? A guard prevents her flight; stout walls of solid stone fence in the hut; speechless lips can give no token of her wrongs. But grief has sharp wits, and in trouble cunning comes. She hangs a Thracian web on her loom, and skilfully weaving purple signs on a white background, she thus tells the story of her wrongs.[30]

When Philomela begins to weave, the only material available to her consists of crude country wool; its coarseness is emblematic of Thrace, and is inappropriate for her royal status. Wealthy noblewomen in Athens worked in linen or fine wools; coarse wool was for rustics and slaves. Moreover, Philomela has the use of only two colors: purple and white. Each color becomes fittingly symbolic; white signifies her virtue as well as her body, whereas purple represents her royalty as well as her blood. (Purple was sometimes called "the color of congealed blood.")[31] Significantly, this purple indicates not only status as a Princess but also represents the signature of her rape, her broken hymen, her ripped tongue, and the blood that will be spilled in like revenge.

Philomela's only legitimate tool of power consisted in her possessing an unbroken hymen, the sign of her virginity. The intact hymen constituted a potent, though latent, "sign," and as such established her position in this society. Isak Dinesen in "The Blank Page" suggests that "[t]he virgin's hymen must not be ruptured except in some manner that reflects and ensures the health of the existing political hierarchy."[32] Philomela's rape not only violates her body, but it depletes her of worth. She cannot appeal to her father, for she no longer belongs to him. When her hymen is broken, so is her contract with the patriarchal world, because she can no longer operate as a vehicle of power in that world. Her tongue torn from her mouth becomes a symbol of her true status: she is without language.

Exiled and silenced, she now weaves her thoughts into a tapestry; in a sense she replaces herself with her story, her body with that of the text(ile).[33] Once Procne reads the tapestry and interprets the signs, Philomela has achieved her victory. "Her voice," Geoffrey Hartman maintains, "is restored through art."[34] But this tapestry functions not only as art but as a message, a catalyst that not only conveys meaning, but when read by Procne, maddens her. She not only reads this text, but also "identifies with the author's place which is embodied in the *mise en scene* of voices."[35] Like Philomela, Procne too is rendered utterly speechless:

> The savage tyrant's wife unrolls the cloth, reads the pitiable fate of her sister, and (a miracle that she could!) says not a word. Grief chokes the words that rise to her lips, and her questing tongue can find no words

> strong enough to express her outraged feelings. Here is no room for tears, but she hurries on . . . her whole soul bent on the thought of vengeance.[36]

Through the medium of the tapestry and its text, Philomela has communicated herself—her speechlessness, her misery and her rage—by way of an excess (a *jouissance*), a remainder of energy that exists outside language itself. This excess beyond language goads Procne to enact a violent reprisal from which she cannot—even when she desires to do so—abstain.[37] After reading Philomela's tapestry, Procne, overcome by the silence in which Philomela wove her tapestry's designs, contemplates her revenge. The scenario that follows merely attests to the power in the tapestry's message—and, perhaps, within the tapestry itself. The textile communicates not only a message on the symbolic level, but also conveys Philomela's feelings toward her experience.

In Kristevan terms, Philomela weaves a metaphor for the thetic, in which the chora—the intense psychic energies and aggressive drives "where the subject is both generated and negated"—are present within the text itself.[38] Although Kristeva claims that the chora pre-exists language, that it is "lodged within the semiotic as 'energy' charges as well as 'Psychical' marks,"[39] she concedes that within certain artistic productions "the semiotic chora [appears] within the signifying device of language."[40] This creates "a 'second-degree thetic,' "—or, the art itself.[41] The art communicates a message that somehow becomes a catalyst for a subject's own semiotic overload. The drives enter the Symbolic, but not as a message decipherable by a system of signs. The semiotic drives are present in (or create) Procne's maddened silence. They are also conveyed through the sisters' fierce retaliation. The "drives' most characteristic trait," Kristeva states, is a " 'destructive wave.' "[42]

The tapestry as second-degree thetic demonstrates the power and danger latent within the chora; this chora constitutes the place where "[t]he most instinctual of the drives, the death drive [that] threatens thetic foreclosure" resides.[43] The tapestry conveys a destructive message to the culture in which it is read, for its signified unravels and obliterates all other meaning. Once the tapestry is read, no other word or language can be spoken. When Procne reads Philomela's tapestry, she is silenced. Later, even when Procne's son by Tereus pleads with his mother for his life, she cannot hear him, for his language and the tapestry's language cannot coexist. Neither can the tapestry's message be assimilated into either the Greek or Thracian cultures. Because the weaving takes place on a Thracian loom and with Thracian wool, Philomela's Greek *grammata* is, metaphorically, polluted; its signified mutates into an explosive language that cannot be accommodated in the Symbolic sphere. This *grammata* being visual, rather than oral, conveys a continuous message. It cannot be silenced or forgotten.

Philomela sends her weaving not to her father, who has the command of armies and the power of retribution, but to her sister, who is also powerless. Fittingly, the late-born god, Dionysus—the god of revelry and wine who is worshipped in the wild and tolerated only within the margins of Athenian society—becomes the means whereby Procne effects her sister's escape and revenge. Dionysus represents the abject, one who refuses to "respect borders, positions, rules."[44] In Ovid's story, Dionysus substitutes for Philomela's and Procne's father, for it is through his intervention—the occasion of his feast—that the sisters are able to vindicate themselves.

In the revenge sequence, Procne leaves her home on the pretense that she is going to the woods to worship Dionysus. Disguised as a bacchante, she frees her sister. Although Procne is only *disguised* as a maenad, the revenge the sisters enact is peculiarly Dionysian; "the actual sacrifice of a fair boy deliberately torn to pieces" is a relic from this "mystical ceremony."[45] And more importantly, the brutality of the sacrifice is identified with Thrace. According to Pater, it was in the mountain regions of Thrace that the darker elements of the Dionysian rite originated, particularly those elements that included human sacrifice as a component of the mystical rite. Furthermore, the web on which Philomela works has been identified as a "Thracian" web or loom. Although her message resists being framed in a civilized Athenian loom (or language), it conveys a message symbolic of Thrace: however, the message also indicates the presence of the semiotic that cannot be accommodated even by this alien nation.

Interestingly, Ovid's myth presents us with four kinds of female labor—providing sexual pleasure, weaving cloth, cooking food, bearing children—and illustrates Philomela and Procne either violating or violated within each of these spheres. It is natural that Philomela should weave, for in her society weaving constituted women's work, and was as much obligatory as it was compulsory. On the surface, Philomela's weaving represents her acquiescence to the role allotted to her by Tereus—and the society he represents. Weaving signifies, moreover, an activity that cannot possibly threaten Tereus or the power structure that maintains him.[46] And yet it is at the loom that Philomela avenges herself of the rape that comprises the first of these four transgressions. The rape provides the momentum required for the subversion of the remaining three "roles": Philomela transforms the mundane task of weaving into a blood-warrant for revenge, she and Procne cook the forbidden banquet, and Procne—the mother—murders her own son.

Because of their association with Tereus or Thrace, the women appear to morally degenerate on every level. Their reprisal, though perhaps overdetermined by the narrative, becomes tainted with Thracian savagery. Joplin, who praises Philomela's weaving as a form of feminist "resistance," remarks that "the women are remembered as *more* violent than the man."[47] Joplin may correctly characterize the reaction of a modern audience, but for an ancient Athenian audience (Apollodorus is Ovid's source for this myth), the violence may constitute a cleansing demanded by this society.

Whereas the sisters represent Athens, Tereus epitomizes Thrace; Ovid writes "his own fire and his nation's burnt in him."[48] The Athenians would consider Tereus as *allotrion,* "the word for 'foreign,' 'abroad,' which is also often used for 'other' as opposed to 'self.' "[49] And although women are often considered "*allotrion*" within Greek society,[50] in Thrace, the action that Procne and Philomela take could represent Athenian reprisal. Consequently, the text suggests that Procne must take action: before she receives word of Philomela's whereabouts, Procne mistakenly believes that her sister is dead, and so has an alter built to offer prayers and sacrifice. Ovid clearly states that this is not an appropriate activity for Procne: "It was not proper that her sister's fate / Received this kind of honour or its grief."[51] The text condemns Procne for mourning. Athenian society demands revenge.

Although the revenge sequence appears unnaturally barbaric, Procne must sacrifice the son who resembles the father, the child tainted with Thracian blood. Tereus' lineage must thereby end. The death by dismemberment, although gruesome, does not constitute a random choice for the sisters; it stages a murder suitably identified with the darkest aspects of the Bacchic rites, the human sacrifice associated with Thrace. Tereus, who represents Thrace, has been dispensed a punishment appropriate to his country's "crimes." I suggest, then, that although the murder is horrific—especially by modern standards—it would seem ironically appropriate, no matter how ominous, to an Athenian audience. Read in these terms, the story functions as a warning to avoid dependence on, much less treaties with, a foreign nation. What becomes of the sisters symbolizes what would become of Athens should alliance with the "barbarians" (literally, non-Athenians) occur.

The myth concludes even more ominously, for the sisters cannot return to civilization. They have been unalterably transformed by their association with the alien culture and their relationship with Dionysus. Once "hagnos," or sacred, the sisters are violated by Thrace, and so become "agos," a pollution. They cannot return to their original status, and so are transformed into birds—the swallow or thrush (Procne) and the nightingale (Philomela).[52] Tereus becomes the hoopoe, a bird that Ovid describes as having "the look of one armed for war" because on top of his head "a stiff crest appears, and a huge beak stands forth instead of his long sword."[53] Indeed, Philomela's tapestry effects physical as well as psychological transformation.

As stated, weaving constitutes the only scene of peace in this story. Once the textile enters the Symbolic as a second-degree thetic (or in my schema as a metaphor for the thetic), the textile becomes a bridge linking parts one and two of the myth, *thereby erasing the scene of its making.*[54] Twelve months are condensed into three lines, and scenes of violence enacted within a moment or day comprise the rest of the narrative. On the other hand, as examined in the following section, the Arachne myth spotlights the weaving scene that is almost entirely effaced in the Philomela myth.

Arachne and Athena

In this section I offer two readings of the Arachne myth, which, like the Philomela myth, appears in book 6 of Ovid's *Metamorphoses.* Both critiques enrich, rather than contradict, each other. In my first reading, I view Athena as possessor of Olympian prerogative, toward which Arachne "should" acquiesce. Her refusal to do so indicates that her struggle for power, from a position of weakness, is—like Philomela's—a heroic one.

My second reading suggests that the relationship between Arachne and Athena constitutes a struggle between two goddesses—rather than one goddess and one mortal woman. Their competition represents two textile industries competing for reputation in their respective societies. Although seemingly disparate critiques, they each detect a challenge toward Olympian privilege and power through the figure of Arachne. And like Philomela's tapestry, Arachne's signified (in both readings) fragments and collapses beneath the semiotic, which in the Symbolic realm translates into destruction and rage.

Perhaps, for the first time in Greek mythology, does weaving take up so much of the narrative, meticulously illustrating the method by which tapestries are made.

> They both set up the looms in different places without delay and they stretch the fine warp upon them. The web is bound upon the beam, the

> reed separates the threads of the warp, the woof is threaded through them by the sharp shuttles which their busy fingers ply, and when shot through the threads of the warp, the notched teeth of the hammering slay tap it into place. . . . There are inwoven the purple threads dyed in Tyrian kettles. . . . There, too, they weave in pliant threads of gold, and trace in the weft some ancient tale.[55]

The occasion for this scene is the challenge issued by Arachne to Athena. Having developed weaving into a magnificent art form, Arachne is acclaimed throughout the land and honored with a devoted following. She angers Athena by refusing to acknowledge the goddess as her mentor. "Let her but strive with me" taunts Arachne, "and if I lose there is nothing which I would not forfeit."[56] Athena accepts the challenge, and the two women—goddess and mortal—each weave a tapestry depicting the saga of Olympus. At stake here is not only Arachne's unprecedented skill, but also the issue of invention. Whereas Athena claims to have introduced the art of weaving to Greece, Arachne insists that her skill had no teacher but herself.

After the contestants are finished, the narrative then portrays in detail each tapestry's design, as if Ovid himself were reading the text and translating it into language. Athena's tapestry tells the story of "Olympian power" with a clear warning in each corner depicting those mortals who have been punished by the gods for challenging them. On the other hand, Arachne's tapestry signifies a protest against this phallogocentric power; she depicts the stories of women like Antiope, Europa, Leda, and Medusa who were victims of the gods—and of mortals favored by the gods. J. Hillis Miller writes that although "the product is judged flawless in the signifiers of its art—the verisimilitude of its representation . . . its producer must be punished for its signified," that challenges the culture's Symbolic.[57] Therefore, Athena destroys Arachne's tapestry and transforms her into a spider.

Most critics assume that the Arachne myth constitutes yet another Greek story of human pride and immortal retribution, but the more current view treats the myth also as representing a feminist stance, taken by Arachne, against the phallocentric order represented by Athena. Ovid himself seems to support both interpretations. In many of Ovid's stories, the poet ostensibly says one thing, but there is always a submerged text that, like a tapestry, when turned over illustrates the opposite or obverse. Discussions of this myth usually compare it with Ovid's "Philomela" (see note 24). According to a feminist reading, Athena represents the Olympian tradition and its patriarchal prerogative. She is Zeus's own invention, who "sprang, motherless, from her father's head, an enfleshed fantasy." She signifies "the pseudo-woman who tells the tale of right order . . . that resistance to hierarchy and authority is futile."[58] In relation to Athena, Arachne embodies the female position of otherness. Even though her own powers of signification are equal to Athena's, by refusing to identify herself as a subject of this goddess, who is a representative of societal law, Arachne will eventually be ejected by this society and silenced. She cannot at once participate in a discourse sanctioned by the Name of the Father (weaving her tapestry's signified), and refuse to identify with it (via Athena), because any such refusal constitutes herself as absent or silenced. Arachne persists in aligning herself against Athena; her refusal results in her own destruction and that of her tapestry. By transforming her into a spider who will spin meaningless webs, Athena denies her the ability to create art, the ability to signify through weaving.

Before her transmogrification, Arachne tries to undermine the foundation on which Athena's authority is built, by depicting in her tapestry scenes in which gods ravish mortal women. These scenes offend Athena even though they illustrate myths that were quite common, even popular, in Greece. Myths from this period delight in representing mortal heroes of divine ancestry. These men and women possess power and prerogative because they are considered to be half-human and half-divine. However, had Arachne depicted only one or two scenes wherein gods assault and impregnate women, she could merely have been illustrating a famous lineage, or the activities of one god. On the other hand, by weaving eighteen scenes portraying the infidelities of Jove, Neptune, Phoebus, Bacchus, and Saturn, or, in turn, Zeus, Poseidon, Apollo and Mars, Arachne seems to be commenting on the gods' transgressions, how they abuse mortals, particularly mortal women.[59] Because Athena becomes so angered by Arachne's tapestry, and because its pictorial representation contrasts so radically with her own theme, we can surmise that Arachne's tapestry does not constitute an innocent portrayal of the different mortal lineages fathered by the gods.

Most modern critics regard Arachne's tapestry as expressing a negative critique of Olympus and the power Athena represents. By contrast, Athena's own tapestry validates this authority and its prerogative to punish mortals who pose a challenge. Ovid describes the scenes woven in Athena's tapestry as follows:

> There sit twelve heavenly gods on lofty thrones in awful majesty, Jove in their midst; each god she pictures with his own familiar features. . . .

> Victory crowns her work. Then, that her rival may know by pictured warnings what reward she may expect for her mad daring, she weaves in the four corners of the web four scenes of contest.[60]

Athena is deeply offended by Arachne's tapestry because its message challenges the authority of the dominant culture. Her illustrations challenge the patriarchy by representing a popular group of myths—the gods entering the human world by impregnating mortal women—and then undermines the myths' explicit meaning: by depicting eighteen myths of this kind, she emphasizes not the birth of a hero, but the scene of rape.

What occurs, then, is a story of the gods' divine right demystified into a story of the gods' deception and abuse of power. In a Kristevan sense, the tapestry's illustrations create a poetic text wherein "meaning escapes the speaking subject [the weaver] by being a condensation of-meaning-that is, a potential plurality of meanings."[61] Arachne's text constitutes a "*lapsus* linguae—slips over the signified," and as such creates a surplus of meaning that cannot be accommodated into the Symbolic (or one that the Symbolic, in the guise of Athena, refuses to accommodate).[62] Arachne can only threaten the symbolic by couching her tapestry's signified, "innocently," in the proper representations of myths that on the surface merely celebrate the inter-relationship between the divine and mortal worlds. In the Kristevan dialectic, "poetic language, like carnival, is simultaneously a particular speech-act, or particular logic, and its implicit negation."[63] Carnivalization functions in Arachne's tapestry through the pictorial representations, each of which exist like an "'ambivalent' word" retaining its original meaning but also bearing the mark of its opposite, the other of its meaning; "it includes the other of itself within itself."[64] If this is in fact Arachne's intention, then Athena must tear "the embroidered web with its heavenly crimes," so that the tapestry's meaning can no longer challenge Olympian authority nor incite rebellion against it.[65]

The inherent difference between the meaning of the two tapestries is epitomized in their border designs. Athena "wove around her work a border of peaceful olive-wreath."[66] The olive symbolized fertility, "and an olive crown was the highest distinction for those who had served the Athenian state."[67] As the city's patron, Athena bequeathed this tree to Athens. On the other hand, the ivy that appears in the "narrow border" of Arachne's tapestry symbolizes Dionysus. "In Greek it was called *cissos*" and was thought to come from the body of a young dancing girl who died at Dionysus's feet from an excess of joy: "The god was so moved by her performance that he turned her body into the ivy."[68] Arachne appropriates the Dionysian sign for herself. Whereas Athena authorizes herself as the proper patron and inventor of the weaving arts—the olive is a sign of her power to confer honor—Arachne insists that her skill arises from her own "body" like the ivy, like the self-made thread of the spider.

Arachne's tapestry signifies an artistic resistance. The "heavenly crimes" she so painstakingly records represent the victimization of the weakest members of Grecian society. Representing herself as one also victimized, Arachne's tool of resistance—weaving—constitutes the proper medium in which to frame an argument with the power structure, for weaving is "the female's signmaking art *par excellence*."[69]

Athena becomes angry "precisely because she cannot fault Arachne's work."[70] When Ovid describes Arachne's tapestry, he says, "Not Pallas, nor Envy himself, could find a flaw." When "Arachne pictures Europa cheated by the disguise of the bull: a real bull and real waves you would think them."[71] If skill is the challenge, then Arachne's surpasses that of Athena's, for Athena's tapestry is merely emblematic, not realistic.[72] Athena's anger also arises from Arachne's achievement in gaining an immortal reputation derived solely through her own skill. By destroying Arachne's tapestry, Athena proves that it is mortal (like Arachne herself), and by transforming her into a spider, or relegating her weaving to a process empty of signification, Athena disallows Arachne a place or voice in the society she represents.

Moreover, as Mihoko Suzuki suggests, Arachne's tapestry does gain a measure of immortality through Ovid's verse: "Arachne's artistic principles . . . parallel those of Ovid himself" as both are concerned with "the principle of metamorphosis."[73] This theme underlies Arachne's tapestry, which itself occasions the metamorphosis of those who come in contact with it: Athena loses her composure and Arachne becomes a spider.

Athena's destruction of the tapestry and its weaver is too sudden and fierce to merely represent the goddess's resolution to keep Arachne from gaining immortality in competition with her own. Athena destroys the tapestry because she is truly angry. After she tears "the embroidered web," she thrashes her competitor with a shuttle four times. Arachne then hangs herself, indicating that she chooses her own death rather than submitting to Athena's power (albeit hanging was considered an ignomonious death in this society). But Athena's rage is not pacified, and so she revives Arachne only to turn her into a spider. Athena's fury suggests that the tapestry is saturated with semiotic energy. Arachne's verisimilitude is uncanny. Too good, too real, it goes beyond mere representation:

> Europa . . . cheated by the disguise of the bull: a real bull and real waves you would think them. The maid seems to be looking upon the land which she has left, calling on her companions, and, fearful of the touch of the leaping waves, to be drawing back her timid feet.[74]

Not only does Arachne's sea look real, but the girl is depicted in the act of "calling" and "drawing back" her feet from the "leaping" waves. The goddess's reaction is not caused so much by the tapestry's perfection as by the semiotic material overwhelming the tapestry.

The second-degree thetic (represented by this tapestry) insufficiently accommodates the chora, or prelinguistic drives, into the symbolic (the tapestry's illustrations). This cloth conveys the semiotic energy to Athena as if it were itself a "thetic membrane" insufficiently filtering or coding this energy into the symbolic of its designs. The death drive, that "threatens thetic foreclosure"[75] is transmitted through the excessive verisimilitude of the embroidered pictures; these illustrations—the waves that seem to leap up, the girl who calls to her companions, and who draws her feet away from the water—are more than artistic portrayals; their verisimilitude constitute a semiotic overload that is as much responsible for the tapestry's destruction as is Athena who has become infected by these unaccommodated drives.[76]

Nancy Miller remarks that "[w]hen we tear the web of women's texts we discover in the representations of writing itself the marks of the grossly material."[77] Since for Kristeva the body "is the place where we 'are' as speaking beings", the "[b]ody and textuality thus exist together."[78] Athena and Arachne produce representations of their own bodies in the form of textiles; the "grossly material" female body reproduces its "grossly material" as the textile body on which a text is inscribed. Likewise, this works for the previous myth in Philomela's textile which represents her torn hymen that she repairs or revenges by speaking what her tongue cannot. For Arachne, the textile represents her female body on which is inscribed her claim to artistic representation. The tapestry's "grossly material" is inscribed (to different ends) with an Olympian text of male prerogative. Athena's work illustrates the Olympian (male) prerogative as having both the authority to signify as well as the authority to suppress signification. Arachne's representations suggest how divine Olympian prerogative is always already compromised by its desire to enter the natural world; though the gods transforms that world, they are also transformed (into beasts) by coming into contact with that world.

When pursuing mortal women, the gods become animals—a swan, a bull, a dolphin, a hawk—and, losing their divine features, are transfigured into creatures of the natural world, creatures without the power to signify. In this way they become transformed into the "grossly material." When Athena turns Arachne into a spider by "the juices of Hecate's herb," all of her human features vanish and what remains are her fingers and belly. Arachne herself becomes this "grossly material"—also symbolic of *function* (fingers) and *appetite* (belly):

> her hair, touched by the poison, fell off, and with it both nose and ears; and the head shrank up; her whole body also was small; the slender fingers clung to her side as legs; the rest was belly. Still from this she ever spins a thread; and now, as a spider, she exercises her old-time weaver-art.[79]

Thus, Arachne as arachnid is consigned, "driven back into nature," forever weaving "only literal webs, sticky, incomprehensible designs."[80] Her webs will remain textiles without texts, webs without meaning.

To create meaning, to create texts, constitutes the privilege of the Olympian phallogocentric order, an activity usually considered to be outside the domain of weaving. Arachne's contest appropriates weaving from its "ordinary" utilitarian sphere and reconstitutes it as a signifying practice. Both the Arachne and Philomela myths transform the *craft* of weaving into the art of creating meaning. The result is tragic in both instances. These myths propose that if a woman were allowed to speak, she would say the unspeakable, or if a woman were to create texts, she would create dangerous ones. Philomela was imprisoned in a hut and then later transformed into a bird; Arachne is changed into a spider symbolic of weaving in the absence of the signification process. Both transformations are acts of suppression, one devised by a tyrannical king, the other by a tyrannical goddess. Yet despite these suppressions, the stories survive.

In both myths the scene of weaving (and word-weaving) appears as a creative, life-sustaining interval. While they weave, Philomela and Arachne are exalted by their art and become memorable for it; they represent the female artist as long as they operate their looms. Once they cease to weave, however, Arachne and Philomela lose their ability to participate as agents of signification, but are transformed into sub-human creatures without the ability to signify. As long as the story's emphasis is centered on the weaving process, the tale is still evolving, the poet still speaking; but once the emphasis becomes centered on the woven textile, the story completes itself and signification ends.

In my second reading I further elucidate the relationship between Athena and Arachne, and suggest that it derives from an historical situation. This critique may indicate why the myth was so popular and why—according to Virgil—Athena detested the spider.[81]

Henry T. Riley suggests that the competition between Arachne and Athena was, most likely, "for the merit of invention."[82] It was common for goddesses of the ancient world to lay claim to this innovation (see chapter 1). If the "merit of invention" were at stake, then the Arachne myth represents a discourse of origins, for only the most ancient goddess could claim this art, fundamental to the development of civilization, to be her own invention. In such a reading, Arachne's challenge may not merely be one that "challenges the goddess' insistence on the essential identity and dignity of the gods" but one that questions the inherent authority and prerogative of the entire Olympic tradition.[83]

According to James Vogh, both "Ariadne ('spinner') and Arachne ('spider') are . . . Cretan goddesses, and some scholars claim they are two names for the same spider goddess."[84] It could be that Ovid's Arachne myth is but a relic of a more ancient myth, depicting a fierce struggle between Arachne and Athena—both goddesses—for power; most likely the power itself would have been centered in and split between two political/religious institutions that may also have had considerable economic strength as well. Appropriately, in the myth the struggle centers around the loom, an industry that promoted trade and guaranteed economic wealth in the ancient world.[85] And although Arachne is superior to Athena in her workmanship, ironically Athena "wins" the contest because she is able to overcome Arachne through sheer physical strength. If a guild-like religious society represented by Arachne wins the contest of skill, the group represented by Athena wins the contest by force; this myth, then, may be an allegorical representation for two weaving groups or religious cults battling for supremacy—religiously, politically, and economically.[86]

Athena's representation of the founding of Athens (and the punishment of mortals for ignoring the superiority of the gods) as expressions of Olympian power contrasts sharply with Arachne's own illustrations. According to Vogh, the pictures Arachne weaves are not only the crimes of the gods but signs of the zodiac disguised as popular Greek myths.[87] If both religions were vying for favor at the time—the Olympian tradition and a tree-cult-based astrological tradition—the tapestries merely depict the domain each goddess represents.

Interestingly, "in Crete, the ancient mystical tradition that Zeus was born and died annually" informed their religious worship."[88] Perhaps representations of the gods inseminating mortal virgins comments not only on the corruption of Olympus, but refers to the "mysteries" of an agriculturally-based worship founded on the cycle of seasons. In light of Vogh's hypothesis that Arachne's scenes are astrologically derived, it is significant that these "signs" are depicted through scenes of Olympian crimes. By representing her own religious cult through the dominant culture's symbols, Arachne may be commenting on the more unsavory aspects of Olympian power. Arachne's resistance becomes not only a feminist critique but a challenge to Olympian authority, accomplished by effectively imparting symbolic knowledge from her own cult while successfully disparaging those in alliance with Athena.

Ariadne, Artemis, and Helen of the Trees, were worshipped in Crete, Arcadia, and Rhodes, respectively. They were worshipped in forests, forming part of an ancient tree cult, and Arachne may be one of these hanged goddesses, or constitute the archetype of them all.[89]

This myth indicates that at one time the rivalry was one centered on their reputation for excellence. Barber writes specifically about Crete and its highly skilled weaving technology. She states that between 3000 and 1400 B.C.E., "the archaeological finds on Crete and the Aegean islands repeatedly give us solid evidence of a textile industry strong in technology and tradition and closely tied to the women's cultural as well as economic and medical concerns."[90] Volcanic eruptions in the Aegean ended high Minoan civilization, but "in remote areas that the Mycenaeans failed to subjugate, the Minoan women continued to make their elaborate fabrics all the way down into the Iron Age."[91] Minoan textiles were thus produced well into the age of Classical Greece, cloth that would be highly competitive in skill, beauty, and desirability. The story of Athena and Arachne perhaps reproduces the tensions of this artistic warfare. Arachne's defeat may not indicate that Athena won this contest, but only that the myth's true meaning has degenerated over time. In a more ancient telling of this myth Athena's power to change Arachne into a spider, would not necessarily have been a negative transmogrification to an ancient audience. Arachne's transformation might only represent, symbolically, herself, for the spider is Arachne's sign.[92] Arachne's transformation, then, simply indicates her difference from Athena and not Athena's supremacy over her.

The contest may not only hinge on whether Arachne or Athena are equal in skill, but equal in immortality. Clearly, Athena believes her competitor is a mortal woman, but Arachne may have been defending her own right to divinity. That she denies Athena's authority may only indicate that she, too, is claiming that prerogative. Although a goddess like Athena, she is other than Athena; her power is the spider's (whatever that may mean in cult terms), and is not derived from Olympus. Because Arachne's tapestry is more accomplished artistically than Athena's, her work may legitimize her as a goddess, and indicates that she has the right and skill to compete with one of her own kind. And although in Greek mythology no human can withstand the sight of a god or goddess, Arachne remains unmoved when Athena reveals herself to her.

In the following section I turn from the representation of the textile to the scene of its creation, the process of weaving and its relationship to the narrative. Although Ovid highlights the weaving process in the Arachne myth, he does so merely to set the scene for the juxtaposition of the textile's rival texts. He shifts our attention to the illustration of its scenes and not to the relationship between weaving and word-weaving, which, as I proposed in the first part of this chapter and will develop in this final section, marks the difference between written and oral poetry.

Helen and Penelope

> We have known for some time of weaving as an Indo-European metaphor for poetic composition, but have perhaps only begun to realize its implications for Homeric poetics.[93]

Perhaps the most well-known weavers in ancient Greek literature are Helen and Penelope. Homer portrays these women weaving, but each to different ends. With the distaff and loom as her symbol, Penelope's weaving represents wifely virtue as well as cunning, the *mētis* of Athena.[94] Helen's weaving, on the other hand, is not a symbol of chastity or good moral conduct, but rather signifies the poet's art.[95]

In the *Odyssey,* Athena officiates as the patron saint for both Odysseus, the hero, and his wife, Penelope. Unlike the Athena we encounter in Ovid's Roman tale, in Homer's epic Athena represents the positive side of cunning (the most accurate translation for *mētis*). To a modern audience, the term *cunning* carries a negative connotation. To be cunning is to be deceptive, not wise. Its original meaning, however, derives from the Latin verb *cunnen* (to know); it is "the faculty of knowing, wit and wisdom" as well as "skillfulness in deceiving."[96] Like *mētis,* or "transformative intelligience," *cunning* constitutes the ability to "anticipate, escape, elude" as well as the talent for artifice. The Greeks admired this trait because it signified the ability to outwit the opponent; the gods and humans they most esteemed possessed this attribute, using it to negotiate their relationship and destiny with the gods.

To understand how Athena's mētis works through Penelope, the story of Athena's birth deserves telling. Originally, Mētis was a goddess and a Titan (the clan of gods that were eventually deposed by the Olympians). Mētis was known to be a shape-changer. She was very beautiful, and though Zeus lusted after her, she tried to elude him by changing into many different shapes. Eventually, however, she was captured and impregnated with a female child (Athena). Before Mētis gave birth, Zeus consulted an oracle and was told that if Mētis conceived again, a son would be born to her who would depose him, just as Zeus had deposed his own father, Kronus. To prevent this from happening, Zeus coaxed Mētis "with honeyed words" to lay beside him. When she drew near, he opened his mouth and swallowed her. Zeus stated that from thereafter Mētis gave him counsel from inside his belly.

Not long after Zeus had swallowed Mētis, he was seized with a raging headache and began to howl. Hermes found a wedge and whacked open Zeus's skull. Athena sprang out of his head, fully armed and with a mighty shout. Although Athena dedicated herself to serving her father and to remaining a virgin, she exhibits many of her mother's qualities. Like Mētis, Athena, too, is a shape-changer. Odysseus and Penelope, her devotees, are masters of disguise as well.

As the Romans subsumed the Greek gods into their own pantheon, certain qualities and ideas that did not conform to Roman virtues were lost. The meaning of Athena's mētis is no exception. The Romans, whose serious reliance on authority has been documented, considered the quality of mētis or transformative intelligence to be too amoral, and preferred to interpret Athena's chief characteristic as "wisdom." Thus, we have identified her sacred emblem, the owl, as manifesting this quality. I find it interesting that in most native cultures the owl represents occult knowledge, the unknown, as well as death. Because the Romans preferred to tame Athena's nature, the owl came to represent wisdom as knowledge, whereas a more accurate interpretation would be to associate Athena's owl with the ability to apply knowledge in a cunning or transformative way.

Mētis, like cunning, involves a passage from the subconscious to the conscious. By following the route of Athena's birth, we will understand how mētis works. Just as Athena was born from the belly of her mother inside the belly of her father, so, too, mētis resides in the subconscious as an energy waiting to be tapped. In the lives of the three main characters of the *Odyssey* (Odysseus, Penelope, and Telemachus, their son), when they are challenged in life or encounter a difficulty, they swallow that problem (meaning that they accept it as their own). Their subconscious, then, almost instantly formulates a plan. When this occurs in our own life, we often call it intuition, a gut instinct, and the gut is where mētis resides. This plan generally emerges fully formed, like Athena's birth from Zeus's head, attired and ready for action.

Finally, we must acknowledge that mētis as cunning is an amoral agency. Zeus swallowed Mētis for a reason. If he hadn't, she would have killed him—not directly, but through her child. Mētis or cunning generally takes a circuitous path. Mētis is an intelligence that knows context and subtext; it is aware of motive, its own and those of others. It is also aware of the ramifications of its actions. The difference between one who employs mētis or *cunnen* and one who doesn't is the difference between one who acts and one who reacts. Today, mētis as cunning has a negative connotation, but many of the great stories throughout history tell us how to develop this quality. Grimms' fairy tales, for instance, acknowledge that the world is a dangerous place and only those who develop cunning can survive. Likewise, Homer's *Odyssey* illustrates for its audience that the world is a mixed-up place, that evil exists along with pain and misfortune, but that Athena's mētis (or cunning) can be an ally in our quest to lead a life of fulfillment and truth.

Penelope reigns as the most respected heroine in Greek literature because of her mētis. Even though she deceived the suitors for almost four years by weaving a garment and then unweaving it every night, she gains their admiration rather than earning their hatred. Calling Penelope clever and wise, the suitors respect Penelope *because* she has deceived them for so long. No greater epitaph can be given to any heroine than is bestowed on her, "to have good character / and cleverness . . . for none knew thoughts so wise as those Penelope knew."[97] To be cunning in this society is to earn respect, for it constitutes the ability to stay alive.

Helen's weaving in the *Iliad,* the first of the two great epics, represents a different activity altogether. Rather than portraying Athena's mētis, it signifies Homer's. It could be stated that Penelope's cunning helps her to author her own story or destiny, but Helen's weaving becomes an allegory for *the storyteller* himself. Homer shows Helen in Troy weaving a pictorial representation of his poem:

> She [Iris] came on Helen in the chamber; she was weaving a great
> web,
> a red folding robe, and working into it the numerous struggles
> of Trojans, breakers of horses, and bronze-armoured Achaians,
> struggles that they endured for her sake at the hands of the war god.[98]

Helen becomes, as Bergren states, "both woven and the weaver of speech, both subject of the song and figure within the text for the poet's own activity."[99] Her weaving is analogous to Homer's word-weaving; as her shuttle moves across the loom, so do the warriors battle back and forth across the Trojan plain. "Helen depicts the contending armies, but she captures them, so to speak, at a point before either side has finally captured her."[100]

Anthropologist Elizabeth Barber notes that Greek women occasionally did weave large storytelling cloths.[101] The weaving of storytelling cloths was reserved for noblewomen and priestesses. Records indicate a yearly festival commenced in honor of Athena; the presentation of an elaborately woven dress for the life-size statue of Athena on the Acropolis highlighted this occasion: "this robe . . . had woven into it in purple the important story of the battle between the gods and the giants."[102] Homer shows Helen weaving a storytelling cloth of the nine-year war incited by her infidelity. Because she is illustrated in the act of representing her own story, Helen seems praiseworthy.[103] Homer emphatically portrays her in a position of power, for storytelling cloths and their making were of great import; their scenes reproduced signs of political and spiritual prerogative. Barber's research indicates that such storytelling cloths were intended for religious and political festivals and rituals.[104] In this scene, Helen's art is elevated to the level of Homer's, for like poetry, a storytelling cloth bestows honor and "eternal" fame.

The earliest surviving example of a storytelling cloth is the Bayeux tapestry, embroidered between 1067 and 1082 C.E., a cloth that was created many centuries later than Homer's *Iliad*. Separated by space and time, the Bayeux tapestry provides clues to the importance of such cloths as purveyors of history and works insuring that the "right" story is told and immortalized. Their attraction lies in both their decorative use (they can be transported, stored, and hung whenever occasion arises), and their emblemmatic appeal (they could be read and enjoyed by an illiterate audience). Like Helen's cloth, the Bayeux tapestry relies on oral tradition. It tells the story of the conquest of England by William, Duke of Normandy (1066 C.E.), of Harold's treachery and William's hard-won victory. Twenty inches high and two hundred thirty feet long, the tapestry resembles a cloth-like scroll. Referring to this work, Nancy Arthur Hoskins writes that its style "closely resembles drawn and painted manuscript illustrations of the Romanesque period from both sides of the English Channel—a style known as Anglo-Norman."[105] Its style and technique are as significant to the tapestry's meaning as the story it tells.

Although no remnant of Helen's storytelling cloth remains, the fact that Homer depicts her weaving one suggests not only the popularity of such cloths, but their importance as historical and political documents of power and privilege.

As stated, Helen's weaving connotes Homer's voice "telling" the poem. Incidentally, Homer never shows us Helen's completed tapestry. This is in keeping with the analogy Homer makes between the weaver and the speaker. Helen seems to escape the text she is weaving, for as soon as the Greeks capture Helen, the epic will be completed, and the poet silenced.

Linda Lee Clader in her book devoted to the character Helen of Troy, *Helen: the Evolution from Divine to Heroic in Greek Epic Tradition,* states that "Homer himself" suggests the relationship between weaving and poetic composition "for he portrays both Kirke and Kalypso as singing while they weave." Although Helen is not shown singing while she weaves her tapestry, Clader suggests that "[w]herever she appears she is accompanied by poetry or even creates it herself."[106] The process described in the weaving of her unfinished tapestry mirrors the process of poetic composition. By weaving the war heroes in the "red folding robe" (3:126), Helen bestows immortality on the warriors as does Homer by depicting them in his epic poem. Helen's shuttle is analogous to Homer's voice; the pictorial (and symbolic) representations on her tapestry constitute a *grammata* equivalent to the poet's words. Helen as well as Homer tell the tale of the Trojan war.

Emblematic of the story-telling process, Helen's weaving constitutes a metaphor for the timelessness of Homer's art. Conversely, in the *Odyssey,* Penelope's weaving is symbolic of time. As a major element of the *Odyssey*'s plot, weaving epitomizes the element of time against which Odysseus must strive. His journey back to Penelope is constantly beset by temptations to defer. Whether because of Kirke's enticement, the imprisonment by the Kyklops, or the forgetfulness of the Lotus Eaters, Odysseus must continually postpone rest (or death) until he can return. Just as Helen is a fitting counterpart to the poet Homer, so Penelope is the perfect counterpart to her husband, Odysseus; Penelope is "by the grace of Athena, as skilled at weaving cloth as she is at weaving subtle thoughts."[107] Her art/craft/craftiness is analogous to the cunning of her husband, Odysseus. As she weaves Laertes' shroud by day and unravels it by night, Penelope is able to extend time, to hold the suitors and time at bay until Odysseus' return.

At the beginning of this chapter two distinctions were made between the relationship of weaving to speaking and writing. It was suggested that the weaving process was analogous to the spoken word, to poetic composition, whereas the woven textile was akin to a written text. Both Penelope and Helen participate in the weaving process, while the completion of the woven textile, for each, is perpetually postponed. Thus, Bergren states, Helen's tapestry "ever defers the end of the contest, the final capture of herself."[108] Likewise, Penelope's art ever defers the completion of Odysseus's shroud, and "the final capture of herself" by the suitors. Whereas Arachne's and Philomela's lives experience closure following the completion of their tapestries, Helen and Penelope are able to suspend their fate by protracting the weaving process.

For Helen, the shuttle represents an ideal symbol for herself "as pawn to be shuttled back and forth between men,"[109] between two sides, two possibilities, two lives. By keeping the shuttle in action, she suspends certainty, for the tapestry remains incomplete—and her destiny undecided—as long as the war continues. The shuttle also constitutes an apt metaphor for Penelope, as its movement is akin to the flux between day and night, between weaving and unraveling.

If Penelope were to complete the shroud, she would lose the power to create meaning, to weave her own language. She would become just another object of exchange in this society that urges her to choose a second husband from the male suitors who have invaded the "public" rooms of her home. By moving into Penelope's home, the suitors threaten to seize not only the public rooms, but the "private" quarters as well, the *gynaikonitides,* where the loom is located, the symbol of Penelope's virtue. Mihoko Suzuki remarks that "[w]hat sustained Penelope was precisely her vigilant consciousness of the passage of time, her ability to live out the unbearable present by harnessing to it the memory of the past, and hope, however tenuous, for the future."[110] She avoids "Helen's fate as a sign that is exchanged among men."[111] Moreover, I propose that she is able to do so only because she is honoring a previous contract already made between herself and Odysseus. In Penelope's hands, weaving is an agent of the patriarchy and represents its concern with marriage and property, for Penelope is Odysseus' property. The only sign that Penelope's weaving generates is her loyalty to the house of Odysseus, symbolized by the weaving of Laertes' shroud.[112] Albeit, Penelope's cunning suggests the agency of *mētis,* which in its original meaning indicated the presence of an amoral agency which could be used either for or against the patriarchy, but which was reinscribed by Zeus-via-Athena into the patriarchy when Zeus swallowed Mētis and then birthed Athena (see note 88).

Penelope's weaving is a tool that guarantees her freedom, or, rather, her status as Odysseus' property. In her hands weaving constitutes an instrument of resistance; although, what she opposes is also what she endorses—the system of marriage. Her refusal to marry is not a refusal of the social edict, but adherence to it. Her resistance is a form of heroism endorsed by the patriarchy within which she operates:

> Thereby the fame of her virtue shall never
> die away, but the immortals will make for the people of
> earth a thing of grace in the song for prudent Penelope.[113]

I have already discussed the important role of weaving for women in Greek society. She who weaves, like Penelope, fulfills her capacity as a woman; her weaving is as important to her as her roles of wife and mother. Many of the stories critiqued in this study illustrate women transgressing this sphere by using weaving for revolutionary and/or subversive ends. Euripides' *The Bacchae* demonstrates the view held by society at that time of the catastrophic results that occur when a woman turns aside from her proper place at the loom. In the play's climactic scene, Agaue presents her son's head—believing it to be that of a lion's—to her father, Cadmus, and delivers an arrogant speech how she has rejected weaving in favor of hunting:

> Father! Now you may boast as loudly as you will
> That you have sired the noblest daughters of this age!
> I speak of all three, but myself especially.
> I have left weaving at the loom for greater things,
> For hunting wild beasts with my bare hands. See this prize,
> Here in my arms; I won it, and it shall be hung
> On your palace wall.[114]

The hunting trophy usurps the place on the wall that should have been designated for Agaue's tapestry. In this scene Euripides clearly suggests that Agaue—and therefore all the maenads—has stepped outside her proper sphere; she has failed as a huntress and, instead, has become a murderess.

In his figure of Penelope, Homer persists in the Greek view that weaving constitutes womanhood. However, Homer seems aware of the possibility that weaving can just as well represent a sinister activity when undertaken by a sinister weaver. Whereas Penelope's weaving symbolizes her chastity, her refusal to take a lover from the suitors who solicit her, Homer offers his readers another picture of Penelope and the possibility that her weaving suggests otherwise. In this scene, Telemachus (Odysseus's son), questions his mother's celibacy in the presence of Odysseus (disguised as a beggar):

> but it was for your sake I came here, to look upon you with my eyes, and to hear a word from you, whether my mother endures still in the halls, or whether some other man has married her, and the bed of Odysseus lies forlorn of sleepers with spider webs grown upon it.[115]

Telemachus imagines that the bedclothes—symbolic of the cloth of Penelope's loom—have been covered or replaced with spider webs, signifying a very different kind of weaving performed by this imagined Penelope. The supposed presence of spider webs signifies not only the absence of a "constant Penelope" but the presence, instead, of a personality resembling the inconstant Klytemnestra.

As stated, weaving and cunning were indicated by the verb, *mētis,* in the Greek language. Penelope's weaving represents cunning in that it tricks the suitors and thus keeps her chaste. In the *Odyssey* when Odysseus is stranded in the land of the Phaiakians and still in disguise in the court of Alkinoos, he listens to the bard, Demodokos, sing of the adulterous affair between Ares, the god of war, and Aphrodite, the goddess of love. In this way weaving is again depicted as a cunning art. The cuckolded husband, Hephaistos, parallels the "wily Odysseus" and his wife Penelope, in that Hephaistos, too, is crafty; he weaves a plot as well as a net in which to catch his adulterous wife:

> Now when, in his anger against Ares, he had made this treacherous
> snare, he went to his chamber where his own dear bed lay,
> and spun his fastenings around the posts from every direction,
> while many more were suspended overhead, from the roof beams,
> thin, like spider webs, which not even one of the blessed
> gods could see. He had fashioned it to be very deceptive.[116]

In this scene, Hephaistos weaves plots for the practical purpose of discovery. But by depicting for Odysseus a scene of adultery, the poet performs a double action, entertaining the possibility of Penelope's unfaithfulness, while at the same time celebrating her chastity. She, like Hephaistos, weaves a plot in the service of virtue.

For most of the *Odyssey* Penelope is embowered in her private chambers, weaving. Her seclusion indicates both that she is chaste and that Odysseus's lineage remains pure. Many critics have suggested that "the uncertainty of fatherhood is . . . the reason for the male desire exclusively to possess semiotic power."[117] Through weaving, women in this culture generate signs. From the seclusion of the *gynaikonitides* we hear their voice. For Penelope, however, the text she weaves is one that indicates her refusal to speak; it is a blank text, as far as we know, on which she declines to write anything. She weaves a shroud that is silent, on which no tale is told.

Homer never describes scenes on her cloth, but it has been suggested that Penelope's textile is not merely a shroud but a detailed funerary cloth. Barber suggests that "Homer's audience would have known that only the weaving of a non-repetitious pattern such as a story which is so very time-consuming" and its nightly unraveling could only have fooled the suitors for so long.[118] But since Homer never describes what kind of scenes Penelope could be weaving, we realize that her text is unimportant, and that the process of its manufacture constitutes a figure for time and craftiness that is so very important to the *Odyssey*'s plot. Like the Sioux Indian woman who must not complete her rug or the end of the world will come, Penelope must defer the completion of her burial cloth, or she will be forced to wed one of the suitors. Not only would Penelope commit adultery, but her son by Odysseus would lose his status in Ithaka as his father's heir.

Penelope does not epitomize Homer, as does Helen, through her weaving. Even though Penelope's weaving is representative of oral poetry, of the activity of storytelling, Homer gives us no indication that her cloth tells a story important to or analogous with the poem he is composing himself. Penelope's weaving concerns a textile, not a text. The shroud she weaves, as far as the audience is concerned, is blank. Her weaving does not attempt to tell a story, for she is not a story-teller. By weaving and then unraveling what has been woven, Penelope's work does not represent Homer's voice, for the very activity it suggests (the poet's voice as it composes a story) is canceled out by the opposite activity of unraveling. All that remains, then, is silence, the stillness of the loom at dawn, when Penelope must begin her task all over again. Jane Marcus observes that "Penelope's art is work, as women cook food that is eaten, weave cloth that is worn, clean houses that are dirtied. Transformation, rather than permanence, is at the heart of this aesthetic."[119] And for Penelope, the work of transforming constitutes a perpetual task, whereas transformation itself is continually postponed. The shroud will always be woven but never completed.

Although Penelope represents the "good, loyal spouse" and Helen "the false wife" we might ask if their weaving is so radically different as their reputations indicate. Is not their weaving joined in service to the same authority? Both Penelope and Helen can weave (or speak) without consequence to the patriarchal order because they do not threaten it. Although they speak, they are also "spoken for." Helen speaks (or weaves) because she is already spoken by Homer—her words are constituted by his, her threads depicting the body of his poem.

Shortly after Iris summons Helen from her loom, Helen joins the Trojan King, Priam, to gaze down upon the battlefield that she had just been weaving in her tapestry. This is a significant point in the story because "the weaving she is doing has direct reference to the very scene about to be enacted outside the walls, the duel between Paris and Menelaos for possession of her."[120] The weaving scene that follows so closely the *teichoscopia* indicates the mimetic relation of Helen's art to Homer's poem. And yet Helen's verisimilitude does not constitute the semiotic overload witnessed in Arachne's and Philomela's tapestry. Helen's tapestry neither speaks against nor resists her fate or the hierarchy that has ordained it. Penelope, too, speaks, while at the same time she is "spoken for" by Odysseus, her husband. Unlike Philomela and Arachne, Penelope and Helen perform weaving that is endorsed by the dominant culture. Their weaving may indicate resistance—Helen's tapestry defies her own capture, Penelope's shroud frustrates the suitors who pursue her—yet one could say that not only is their weaving condoned by the patriarchy but also that their weaving creates and sustains it as well.

The difference between the weaving of Arachne and Philomela and that of Helen and Penelope constitutes a distinction between the oral and written word. As Bruno Gentili points out, "Greek poetry in general, up to the end of the fifth century . . . [was] not written but oral communication. It was a poetry that appealed to the ear, as Plato described it in contrast to painting, which appeals to the eye."[121] Thus, for Helen and Penelope, process is of primary concern: Their texts imitate the manner of oral poetry, where significance (signification) lies not in product (textile) but in the flow of the story's language, in the whir of the shuttle, or tongue, thrown across the story's warp or plot. The weaving of Helen and Penelope exists in the service of a larger text, the epic (oral) poem. And though Penelope is not representative of Homer as is Helen, her weaving functions as a figure for the poet's own narrative process. Conversely, with its emphasis on product, the stories of Arachne and Philomela represent a culture rooted more deeply in the written tradition, reflecting the storywriter Ovid rather than the story-teller, Homer.

Written texts are not necessarily more subversive of patriarchal order, but, if not destroyed, they constitute more "permanent" and subtle challenges to that order. Unlike spoken imputations, they can not be as easily dismissed or forgotten. Oral speeches and certain kinds of oral poetry, however, can also incite a crowd to political revolt against the patriarchal system. And yet this crowd will most likely replace their newly toppled government with a system that merely reproduces the one they destroyed. Written (or woven) texts can be circulated and stored over time, and as such, may provide a more useful critique of dysfunctional political and social systems, and more effectively incite their change.

Each of these tales focuses on the power of cloth to convey meaning. We have already discussed how Philomela's tapestry is a story created from the place of her torn hymen, a reparation that is accomplished by the act of remembering. Her shuttle weaves the story her tongue cannot tell, while recreating out of its meaning a material wholeness to replace what was torn open and destroyed. Arachne's tapestry also represents her body, embroidered with her refusal to acknowledge the supremacy (or infallibility) of the Olympian gods. On her body she weaves the stories of those mortal women victimized by this hierarchy. By weaving this veil, she becomes transformed into its image; the message of Arachne's text includes her in its story, as her body becomes sacrificed (signified by the tearing of her tapestry) to the gods.

In the Arachne myth, Athena's anger derives not so much from the offensive nature of Arachne's signs or from her superb artistry, but from the important nature of the storytelling cloth. Representing a subversive theme is not a matter of expressing a "different" point of view, but of immortalizing it. Thus, Athena shreds the tapestry to protect the Olympians, and turns Arachne into a spider so that she will never tell such a story again.

And what of Penelope's text(ile)? We have already concluded that it does not constitute a text, for it tells us no story but is made and unmade with the passing of each day. The absence of a text can also become emblematic of Penelope's body, particularly because her body is one on which nothing new has been written; her absent text represents the story of her constancy, her celibacy, and her unwillingness to engage in the social life (illustrated by the feasting and drinking done by the suitors). As an apt symbol for Penelope's body, the "blank page" of her textile represents a story perpetually deferred until Odysseus returns.

Helen's tapestry, too, represents her body, embroidered with this conquest. Her body is, arguably, the text of this war; metaphorically, it constitutes the "ground" on which the war is fought as well as the goal for which this war is waged.

When describing her tapestry, translations differ as to whether Helen weaves the battle on a red or purple background. Because of the Greeks' great love of purple, I am inclined to believe that Homer meant the tapestry's background to be woven in this color. Purple was difficult to find, costly to manufacture, and it was at all times the color of royalty.[122] Purple would be the most fitting background for these immortal scenes as well as an indication of Helen's status. This background constitutes the one place where Helen's weaving becomes nonrepresentational; "the semiotic dimension" permeates the space around its symbolic content, and challenges our assumption that Helen's weaving merely reproduces Homer's art.[123] Purple is not the literal color of the atmosphere or background in which these battles are fought. Purple indicates something else: more than anything it indicates the immortality that these warriors strive for, occasioned by Helen; it is, as well, Helen's color for she is a queen. Moreover her continuous interaction with the immortal world bestows on her an immortal presence, which she confers in the storytelling cloth. This color also connotes ideas of royal fame and honor that she will confer on those persons she has chosen to embroider onto the cloth. In this sense, Helen's tapestry—particularly its purple background—*represents* her body. Moreover, it has been suggested (arguably) that the Greeks literally fought for Helen's body because "the right to the throne of Sparta passed through her female bloodline, not his. Without Helen, Menelaos could not be king."[124]

Signification is the province of weaving. Barber suggests the different ways in which societies dealt with their desire and anxiety to leave marks of immortality on the landscape and in the minds of those who remained after their passing. She states that whereas "the Indo-European men raised (burial) mounds and composed oral epics to try to attain immortality for their names and deeds, during long periods when writing was not widespread . . . the women turned to their textiles to portray the deeds of their families."[125] Or, as in the case of some of the stories here, the women turned to their textiles to illustrate their society's crimes. Whereas Homer depicts his weavers rightfully using the loom—particularly, Helen, whose storytelling cloth bestows meaning and honor on a war that suffered so many losses; Ovid imagines his weavers subverting authority from their "territory" at the loom. Whereas Helen confers immortality on the warriors questing after her elusive body, Philomela immortalizes the story of her subjugation. Like Agaue, Philomela and Arachne stray outside their proper sphere: Arachne does so willingly, whereas Philomela is forced into her position by Tereus. Hence, their textiles reflect their defiance of power.

The challenge their tapestries embody actually began the moment they turned their looms against the establishment. As we shall see in the following chapter, weaving constitutes a powerful tool that reflects the weaver's mind as well as her position in society.

4

The Loom of Language and the Garment of Words in William Blake's *The Four Zoas*

> The harlot's cry from street to street
> Will weave old England's winding sheet . . .
> —William Blake, "Auguries of Innocence"

IN THE PREVIOUS CHAPTER I DEMONSTRATED HOW WEAVING FUNCtions as a female semiotre analogous to the male activity of writing texts. Through the stories of Philomela, Arachne, Helen of Troy, and Penelope, I contrasted the textile and the weaving process, suggesting they represent the difference between written and oral poetry. In *The Four Zoas,* William Blake also depicts weaving as an almost exclusively female performance, which is somewhat surprising since weaving had been produced in England almost entirely by men (via guilds) for over two hundred years.[1] It no longer functioned as a female semiotics, for women performed only ancillary roles in cloth production, like spinning and carding. Blake ignores the "conventional" view that weaving comprised a male activity. Instead, he reestablishes the ancient link between women and weaving. A close reader of Greek literature, philosophy, and mythology, Blake chooses to ally the task of weaving to the ancient, Indo-European definition of the verb "to weave," particularly its correlation with the weaving of poetry, spells, and prophecy. As discussed earlier throughout the book, the Greek language links together these two different activities, so that woven fabric, poetry, and *mētis* are all delineated with the verb "to sew" or to weave. Blake explores the linguistic dimension of the weaving metaphor and consistently equates weaving with the speech act. He further distinguishes between the weaving process and the woven product as marking the difference between artistic creativity (or imagination) and the generated body (or senses).

In Blake's reading of Greek literature and mythology, the great weavers—Athena, Helen, Andromache, Penelope, Medea, Arachne, Philomela, Klytemnestra, Kirke and Kalypso—became models for the female aspects of his Zoas. By examining the weaving these characters engaged in, Blake made the link between two very different notions of weaving: first, weaving created textiles that, like independent bodies, had a will all their own, and secondly that weaving was coterminous with language and the imagination. Blake incorporates both of these ideas in his weaving metaphor.

As a process, weaving fascinates Blake; he uses it as an allegorical tool demonstrating and contrasting two kinds of activities: physical generation (of the body) and the imaginative process (the word). Weaving always accompanies a vocal moment in the *Zoas,* so that rather than producing cloth, the weaver creates with language a body, an incarnation of the word-made-flesh. In this study I explore the role of weaving in *The Four Zoas* in an attempt to understand why Blake places such an important activity (and metaphor) for creativity almost exclusively in the hands of his female characters.[2] Remember, the four Zoas personify for Blake four different aspects of a human being. They actually reside within each human being. Blake calls the archetypal "Man" by the name of Albion. Within him the Zoas reside. Hence, Urizen is the character that allegorizes the reasoning function or intellect; Tharmas represents the senses; Luvah personifies the emotions; and Urthona is the imagination. In their unfallen state when they are functioning at their highest potential, the Zoas are neither male nor female, but when a Zoa "falls" from Eternity into Experience, the world of time and space, then it splits into male and female counterparts. Blake calls the male part by its original name, a Zoa, whereas he calls the Zoa's female companion an Emanation. Thus, for Urizen (intellect), his female counterpart or Emanation is called Ahania; for Luvah (emotion), she is named Vala; for Urthona (imagination), she is Enitharmon; and for Tharmas (the senses), she is called Enion. The moment a Zoa splits into male and female, that Zoa has fallen into the realm Blake terms Experience. This world is marked by duality, strife and discord, pleasure and pain.

Feminist criticism on Blake often concurs with Irene Tayler that "the 'female,'" constitutes a "metaphor for fallen creation."[3] Although this metaphor "will pass," Tayler remarks, it is one that operates throughout Blake's oeuvre.[4] Why, then, does Blake assign weaving to the Emanations, when it represents one of Blake's most consistent and significant analogies for artistic (and poetic) creativity in *The Four Zoas?* Blake could have just as easily placed this powerful metaphoric activity in the hands of the male Zoas, for as I've stated already, during his time weaving in England had been considered an exclusively male vocation.[5] I suggest that the limitations placed on gender are inscribed in the weaving process (Nights I–VIII), but as the Emanations become restored in Eden (Night IX), so is their weaving reconstituted to reflect their new condition. Like an engine, weaving in Eden generates and organizes the different worlds.

The Four Zoas dates from around 1796, and even though the text is unfinished and not formally rendered pictorially (i.e., not engraved), it is often considered to be the foundation on which Blake conceived his two great works, *Milton* and *Jerusalem*.[6] Northrop Frye has called it "the greatest abortive masterpiece in English literature."[7] Although Frye intended his remark as a compliment, like many other critics of this poem, I think that *The Four Zoas* resists the implication that it has miscarried or failed the author in some way. So often read as a finished composition, *The Four Zoas* lends itself easily to interpretation because it illustrates a unified vision.[8] Weaving comprises one of the epic's major unifying symbols: it initiates the action of Night the First and contributes to the Apocalypse of Night the Ninth.

Unfolding in Nine Nights, the plot forms an allegory in two parts: first, it enacts a psychological drama of a paradise lost, beginning concomitantly with the poem; and second, it regains this paradise in the final night. The first movement enacts at a psychic level the fall of Albion, the universal man, when his four Zoas (the four faculties of the human soul) fall into disunity. The second movement depicts the Zoas' struggle toward unity, culminating in a celebratory feast in which Albion, who has been sleeping for most of the poem, participates. Once more regaining the throne he had abandoned to Urizen, Albion relegates the Zoas to their subservient but equal positions as attendants to Man. Blake links the poem's interior action, which takes place at the level of dream, to an historical landscape, wherein Albion represents all of England as well as the Englishman who needs to undergo a similar process of spiritual redemption.[9] Blake's language and imagery imply that Albion's transformations fulfill Biblical prophecy, and the heaven-on-earth the Eternal Man achieves represents England's goal and destiny. I suggest that *The Four Zoas* illustrates a personal Apocalypse, whereas *Milton* and *Jerusalem* enact a national one.[10] The way in which Blake employs his weaving symbolism in *The Four Zoas* differs dramatically from his use of it in *Milton* or *Jerusalem*. This difference, I will demonstrate, characterizes the main distinction between personal and national apocalypse.

Disunity occurs when the Zoas split from their Emanations, and enter a gendered state. In Nights One through Eight, Blake represents their condition as a battleground wherein "female" and "male" identities engage in a struggle for dominance and power. Night Nine represents the reconciliation between the Zoas and Emanations, as well as Albion's return to the throne he had abandoned to Urizen. Although the Zoas and their Emanations are not always depicted at war during the first eight Nights, Blake inscribes each gender with notions of difference that become catalysts for misunderstanding and further conflict.

Occupation constitutes one of the main differences between the Zoas and their Emanations. For example, while Enitharmon, Los's (female) Emanation, weaves, Los himself works, Vulcan-like, forging tools in the furnaces of Luvah. Enion's weaving initiates the "first" sin in Night I, and for most of the first six Nights continues to create division (and disharmony) between the Zoas and their Emanations.[11]

Most of the important sources for Blake's weaving symbolism were first noted by Kathleen Raine, particularly, the Greek, Biblical, and Hindu sources. Nelson Hilton broadened this research, suggesting that this extensive image of weaving done exclusively by female weavers derives as much from Teutonic mythology as from the Greek.[12] He views, as well, Blake's female weavers to be representations of those women suffering in the textile factories prevalent in the early stages of the Industrial Revolution.[13] And yet I argue, along with Jane Schneider and Annette Weiner, that the meaning of cloth altered with the advent of capitalism. Blake would have been alert to how industrialization alters the meaning of any activity. Through mass production, the meaning of work as a personal and spiritual mode of expression is lost.[14]

Nevertheless, industrial exploitation did outrage Blake, but the poet would have encountered this kind of symbolism in his literary studies as well. The depictions of women suffering physically and mentally from abuse in the textile trade was not a recent phenomenon. Chrétien de Troyes, in his poem *Yvain: The Knight of the Lion* (c. 1177–81), for example, illustrates the misery of women exploited in this way:

> He [Yvain] saw three hundred girls
> All sewing away some working
> With golden thread, some silk,
> Working as hard as they could.
> But their wretched poverty was such
> That they sat there bareheaded, many
> So poor that they wore no sash,
> And their dresses were torn at the breast
> And out at the elbows, and their shifts
> Were dirty around the neck.

When Yvain asks these women to tell him their story, after some length they lament:

> "None of us will ever leave.
> We'll spend our days weaving
> Silk, and wearing rags.
> We'll spend our days poor
> And naked and hungry and thirsty,
> For they'll never pay us what we earn."[15]

Blake's "enslav'd Daughters of Albion" are as much counterparts to Yvain's laborers as they are personifications of the industrial revolution.

Although Erdman, like Hilton, suggests that weavers in *The Four Zoas* sometimes "appear as the textile trades whose 'needlework' is sold throughout the earth"[16] I suggest, rather, that *Jerusalem* more fully realizes this socioeconomic symbolism in the portrayal of weaving women: There "The Daughters Weave their Work in loud cries over the Rock / Of Horeb!"[17] In *The Four Zoas,* on the other hand, weaving is never obligatory. Instead, it comprises a mimetic activity: when weaving is accompanied by expressions of sorrow, this sorrow derives not from weaving, but from the weaver's loss of a unifying vision. Because each Emanation creates her own state of disunity, weaving does not mark enslavement; rather, it comprises action, which for the Zoas is located almost entirely in thought and speech. First, I will explore how the weaving Emanations derive from Blake's encounter with myth, and then demonstrate the relationship between weaving and language.

Morton D. Paley first noted the significance of weaving in Blake's literature. Although Paley intended to understand the development of "the figure of the garment" in Blake's major poems, he discussed this development in terms of Blake's weavers and weaving plots. He remarked how Blake spotlighted weaving for the first time in the *Zoas:* "even the word 'loom,' of which the *Concordance* lists sixty-eight occurrences, is not to be found in Blake's writing before *The Four Zoas!*"[18] Paley suggests that the weaving metaphor "for the most part (is) added to the poem's original structure" whereas it finds permanent symbolic expression in *Milton* and *Jerusalem.*[19] I argue, instead, that the dissimilarity between the weaving scenes in the *Zoas* and those in his later masterpieces indicates a difference in each poem's purpose. *The Four Zoas* represents a highly personalized model for transformation, whereas social revolution occurs more significantly in *Milton* and *Jerusalem.* This difference conforms to my earlier suggestion that whereas weaving functions as a metaphor for socioeconomic exploitation in Blake's later works, it constitutes a mimetic (and linguistic) activity in the *Zoas.*

I mentioned in previous chapters that for the Greeks the natural world was thought to be created in the looms of the nymphs. These *nympholepti* wove the fabric of nature—trees, flowers, fruit—with "many-coloured threads."[20] Blake, likewise, depicts in *Jerusalem* his "Daughters of Los" weaving nature's garments. He characterizes them as beings who weave less cheerfully than their Greek sisters, as they "Create the Silk-worm & the Spider & the Catterpiller / . . . the wooly Lamb & the downy Fowl / . . . Weaving in bitter tears / The Veil of Goats-hair & Purple & Scarlet & fine twined Linen."[21] The "Purple & Scarlet" are undoubtedly the blood and organs, whereas the "fine twined Linen" constitutes the skin that clothes it all.

Porphyry similarly depicts these nymphs weaving "garment[s] with which the soul is invested."[22] Thomas Taylor's translation of Porphyry must have further suggested to Blake the idea that weaving produces the body of nature, when Taylor wrote that "according to Orpheus, Proserpine, presides over every thing generated from seed, [and so] is represented weaving a web . . . which is as it were the veil or *tegument* of the celestial gods."[23] Blake's descriptions of Enitharmon's daughters closely resemble Porphyry's Prosperine, for they, too, "weave the ovarium & the *integument* / In soft silk drawn from their own bowels in lascivious delight."[24]

The idea that the body comprises a garment or veil extends far back in Greek cosmogony. Marcel Detienne and Jean-Pierre Vernant write: "Zeus weaves a multi-coloured veil (pharos) which he offers, on the third day of his marriage, to his companion so that, once she has donned it, she wears embroidered on her apparel [body] the entire range of forms which constitute the organized world."[25] On her body/veil Zeus begets and masters the natural world. By wearing the veil of creation, she is reduced to a sign of that creation, possessed by Zeus.

The textile has long been accepted as a symbol for the phenomenal world (see chapter 1). Blake's poem is consonant with this idea that the textile comprises a body or covering "proper to souls descending into generation."[26] The body/veil/shroud conceals from the soul the vision of Eternity, and reveals instead the duality of the mind and senses. Hilton states that this veil of illusion divides "inside from outside, mind from brain and body, I from us, good from evil, woman from man."[27]

More than any other of the Emanations, Vala embodies Blake's notion of the "veil of illusion" (a Hindu definition for Maya). I am aware that in reference to my second chapter, her presence in this poem raises issues about veiling and the body. Like Hawthorne's "Veiled Lady" and Alastor's "Maid," Vala represents the maternal body. Unlike them, however, her veil conceals no transcendent qualities. Blake defines Vala in terms of nature and sexuality because, as the veil, she constitutes the body in all its materiality. His as well as the *Zoas*' ambivalence toward her recapitulates the process of abjection that I have defined in chapter 2.[28]

Blake's Emanations do not weave mere inanimate fabrications. Rather, they create conscious entities that transform the Zoas' universe. For example, in the First Night when Enion weaves the Spectre of Tharmas "in her shining loom / Of Vegetation"[29] it comes alive, and has "a will of its own"[30]:

> . . . he
> Reard up a form of gold & stood upon the glittering rock
> A shadowy human form winged.[31]

In the hands of the Emanations, weaving is analogous to human reproduction. The bodies represent, on one hand, the horror of the female principle in the fallen worlds. As products of the natural world, the bodies incarnate the negative aspect of the female principle within that world; each body constitutes a mundane shell that clothes, suffocates, and imprisons the "male" soul. On the other hand, these bodies can also form "a Vast family wondrous in beauty & love."[32] Blake inscribes this contradictory attitude as abjection, or desire for, yet rejection of, the body, and invests it into the structure of his poem. Weaving embodies this very contradiction, so that while weaving creates division, it mends division at the same time.

Blake epitomizes the multiple perspective of these alternating views in the weaving performances of Enion and Enitharmon. Whereas it is Enion's weaving that creates division and despair, and perpetuates the fallen world of the Zoas, Enitharmon's weaving (like Helen's and Penelope's) literally embodies the artistic principle, thus redeeming the world. Enitharmon's weaving enacts an important Blakean premise, that the idea must embody form, otherwise it exists merely as unrealized potential. Enitharmon's weaving also comprises the only means by which the fallen spectres—created by Enion's weaving—may be redeemed. As bodiless forms of longing, the spectres must first pass through Enitharmon's looms and enter into generation. They must incarnate. Once they are clothed in the garments of the body, they may then take their first step in the journey to Eden.

Although textile production can symbolize the positive aspects of creativity, during the first six nights of the *Zoas,* weaving comprises an activity corresponding to the Zoas' fall into experience. Imbued by Blake with almost god-like powers, these female Emanations and their spectres spin and weave in the tradition of the Greek Moirai or Fates who, too, have power over mortal life and death.[33] As stated previously, desire pulls the Zoas into the world of generation, and Blake characterizes this fall by representing it as a lapse into gender—and, I would add, language. Recall that in Lacanian and Kristevan theory, "desire and language . . . locate the subject as split and divided."[34] When a Zoa divides into its male/female counterparts, Blake represents this split as one occurring simultaneous with language. The female character, more than the male, incarnates difference: Although the male counterparts to the female Emanations are equally fallen, Alicia Ostriker points out that Blake "can ultimately imagine human unity only by imagining that the female is reabsorbed by the male."[35]

Whereas the male Zoas represent fallenness in and through their activities, the Emanations, who symbolize nature, often generate this "fallen" principle in their weaving. By creating bodies, coverings, veils, mantles, the illusion of death, the illusion of separateness, they weave representations of what they themselves are. In other words, they fabricate duplications of their own bodies, "fallen" forms of nature. In this sense, weaving comprises a debased occupation.

Yet as stated earlier Blake envisages another, broader possibility, for the weaving process. Not only functioning as an analogy for procreation, weaving represents the imaginative process as well. This "imaginative" moment is consonant, I believe, with the incantations or songs, the sighs, and musical accompaniment made by the weavers while weaving. Thus, Enitharmon's weaving in book 8 of *The Four Zoas* is accompanied by her muse-like inspiration, in the etymological sense of "breathing in" or "filling with life."[36] She "sighed forth on the wind the spectres / And wove them bodies"[37] and Enitharmon's "Silver looms" are described as "singing lulling cadences on the wind."[38] Like the *nympholepti,* Enitharmon weaves more than bodies. She invests these bodies, through the power of her voice, with life. Blake exploits this linguistic dimension of the weaving metaphor by consistently equating weaving with the speech act. Taylor's translation of Porphyry also suggests this connection: "[O]n these stony beams, the nymphs should weave purple garments is wonderful not only to the sight, but to the auditory sense."[39] The sound of the nymphs singing, the whir of the shuttle, the rhythm of the beater, please the senses no less than the sight of these material bodies.

Homer depicted his nymphs, Kalypso and Kirke, singing while they wove their immortal tapestries. Blake, too, links the weaving process to language and sound: To mourn and to weave, to curse and to weave, or to pray and to weave all comprise the same activity; to speak and to weave constitute the same action.

Whereas weaving occurs simultaneous with the fall (elaborated on momentarily), Blake depicts the Zoas' fall into disunity as, also, a fall into language. Each time a Zoa speaks, it becomes more severed, more estranged from its original form.[40] Helen McNeil elaborates on the important relationship between language and division: "Words are as irrevocable as incidents" she contends; for the Zoas, "[t]he destructive thought is the destructive act."[41] Not only does language coincide with the Zoas' fall, but I suggest weaving is constitutive of language, and cannot be separated from it.

Significant to our discussion, in Lacanian (and Kristevan) theory, gender and language are inseparable. Language creates gender. Jacqueline Rose remarks: "For Lacan the subject is constituted through language" and "[l]anguage can only operate by designating an object in its absence."[42] When Enion "absences" herself from Tharmas, her departure initiates loss, hence, speech.

Non-linguistic utterances are constituents of the Zoas' language, signifying the semiotic. These sighs and groans indicate the presence of "nonverbal signifying systems" that Julia Kristeva suggests "are constructed exclusively on the basis of the semiotic (music, for example)."[43] I suggest that the relationship between these sounds and the weaving process constitute an even tighter link as they both produce or reveal the presence of the semiotic through *jouissance,* or excess. Hence, weaving produces a metaphor for *jouissance;* it literally embodies this quality, already signaled as entering the Emanations' speech through these non-linguistic sounds. Kristeva describes *jouissance* as "cracking the sociosymbolic order, splitting it open, changing vocabulary, syntax, the word itself, and releasing from beneath the drives borne by vocalic or kinetic difference"; thus, "*jouissance* works its way into the social and symbolic."[44] Even the bodies created from the Emanations' looms indicate semiotic excess; Blake describes them in terms of excess: they are either immoderately bright, like the Spectre, or extremely anguished and wailing creatures. The sorrowing bodies and spectres produced in the Emanations' looms introduce—like the Zoas' emotional excess—the semiotic drives into this symbolic/social realm; they strain against the Symbolic, threatening its utter collapse.

Enion's Spectre is wrought, like Arachne's web, into a piece of art. I will demonstrate how the bodies woven by the Emanations—analogous to the tapestries of Philomela and Arachne—introduce revolution and the semiotic into the symbolic-social realm. Verisimilitude exists at the heart of the Emanations' weaving (as it does for Arachne and Philomela). Their textile/bodies manifest the semiotic energy flowing through, around, and against the Symbolic. Kristeva calls this kind of art the "semiotization of the symbolic" that "represents the flow of *jouissance* into Language."[45] In like manner, weaving constitutes a metaphor for this semiotic excess.

Whereas *The Four Zoas* begins *in medias res,* no definitive narrative exists to explain the events that lead up to the fall of Albion (this fall is also connected to the inexplicable argument between Tharmas and Enion). No single motive drives the action. Plot is premised on the violent rantings and ravings of the Zoas that occur throughout most of the poem. The only element of plot consistent in the *Zoas* is Action predicated by speech. Action and reaction comprise the various scenes in the poem, and language (as well as weaving) precludes and coexists with action. In this plot that seems based entirely on the spoken word, on lamentations and groans, on shrieks and sighs, the Zoas speak their condition which, in turn, conditions their speech. This interlocking transference between speech-performance and action is strikingly rendered in the weaving episodes of Enion and Enitharmon, Rahab and Tirzah.[46]

Night the First constitutes one of many scenes in which weaving comprises the main action. Before Enion, the weaver, creates in her loom the appalling Spectre, she first weaves a place to hide from her beloved Tharmas, her Zoic counterpart. This hideout indicates Enion's first step towards physical division and eventual alienation from him:

> I hide from thy searching eyes
> *So saying—From her bosom weaving soft in Sinewy threads*
> A tabernacle for Jerusalem she sat among the Rocks
> *Singing her lamentation. Tharmas groand* among his Clouds.[47]

In this scene speech and weaving are not consecutive but simultaneous acts. "Saying," "Weaving," "Singing" and "Groaning" take place at the same moment and constitute synonymous actions.

In a truly Lacanian moment, while Enion speaks her loss, her language (and weaving) creates this separation/loss at the *same time.*[48] Donald Ault observes that "the conversation [between Enion and Tharmas] and the weaving are *spoken* and *bodily* versions of an action that comes into existence . . . through the poem's narrative sequence."[49] Weaving performs the action that "Saying" announces. Enion's singing eerily accompanies her weaving, as if she is engaged in the ancient art of cursing. The tabernacle for Jerusalem embodies this curse, comprising a twofold symbol in Blake's cosmology for the religious rite and the sex act "done in secret, dark, covert places, incensed and perfumed."[50] The tabernacle for Jerusalem mystifies the problem between Tharmas and Enion, and plays an important role in Urizen's Religion of Mystery in Blake's later works.

Although not made explicit, Enion seems to be weaving from within the enclosure of the tabernacle; the threads she weaves are drawn forth from both her bosom and from Tharmas's nerves and veins, drawing enough life out of her own being and Tharmas to weave "A Frowning Continent," a false version of reality—Ulro—in which the Spectre (the false form of Tharmas) appears. The Spectre's life signals, in typical Blakean irony, the presence of "Eternal Death." Although the Spectre is not "woven subservient to her hands but [has] a will / Of its own,"[51] it depends on Enion for its subsequent speech and action:

> Listning to her soft lamentations soon his tongue began
> To Lisp out words.[52]

Brought to life only after hearing her words, the Spectre's own speech mirrors Enion's now fallen consciousness.

The Spectre's relationship to language and the mother enacts the process of abjection that Julia Kristeva describes as a condition for an infant's entry into the Symbolic. According to her schema, the child first experiences itself through the linguistic and bodily sounds produced by the mother; when the infant can imitate these sounds on its own, it soon acquires a separate identity. Similarly, when Enion gives birth to the Spectre by weaving it into existence, the Spectre first hears its "mother's" "soft lamentations" before it can "lisp out words" itself; even after the Spectre begins to speak, his words merely imitate Enion's own language (that has made the state of Ulro possible). The Spectre tells Enion that the "Frowning Continent" she has woven resulted from her own thoughts (and, consequently, her language):

> This world is Thine in which thou dwellest that within thy soul
> That dark & dismal infinite where Thought roams up & down
> Is Mine & there thou goest when with one Sting of my tongue
> Envenomed thou rollst inwards to the place whence I emergd.[53]

Hence, the curse Enion weaves returns on herself. As the poem progresses through the first eight Nights, Enion falls farther into her filmy woof—the place into which Tharmas has disappeared and from which the Spectre has emerged.

The bizarre but unmistakable sexual encounter between Enion and the Spectre comprises an important scene toward understanding the ubiquitous presence of weaving in Night I. Enion's intercourse with her own creation, a degenerate form of Tharmas, constitutes an incestuous encounter reminiscent of the scene in Milton's *Paradise Lost* wherein Satan and his daughter, Sin, copulate to give birth to Death.[54] In Blake's version, however, Enion joins with Death (the Spectre) and gives birth to Los and Enitharmon. These children of the "first fall" will liberate their parents from "original sin."

The ravishment becomes important to our discussion because the union between Enitharmon and Tharmas's Spectre, as Donald Ault suggests, "is also a version of weaving."[55] Both beings are physically and psychologically transformed; in the Blakean terminology, their "garments" or bodies become so altered that "a 'softning' of the rocky inorganic form of the Spectre and a deepening of color in the 'crystal clear' Enion . . . ends in a near-total union."[56] Enion herself becomes monstrous by assimilating part of the Spectre's "scaly armour"; the transformation of her body's texture marks her transformation of vision, and of consciousness, for everywhere in Blake's poetry characters can only "see" what they already are.

Blake parallels Enion's features to her Miltonic counterpart, Sin. Whereas John Milton regards Sin in *Paradise Lost* as a being who "seemed woman to the waist, and fair, / But ended foul in many a scaly fold,"[57] Blake likewise characterizes his Enion as "Half Woman and half Spectre," a "monster lovely in the heavens or wandering on the earth."[58] When Enion mingles her essence with the Spectre, she becomes enmeshed in the very being who personifies the hellish garment woven from her own hands. She becomes entangled in this garment like a spider caught in her own web. Enion, the weaver-artisan, who should be able to dominate or control her own creation, becomes enmeshed in her own devising, helpless to stop it.

Weaving creates a tangible world (Ulro) and its first inhabitant (the Spectre), and also creates the psychic state necessary to fall into the world it has created. To paraphrase what was said of Los in the Fourth Night, "She became what she was doing she was herself transformd."[59] Enion's weaving, then, incarnates language, becoming the bodily form of those words spoken by the characters in this scene. This cosmic lover's quarrel between Enion and Tharmas, results in accusatory speeches and curses that weave a world "dark & dismal," a veil that constitutes a labyrinth of fallen language, a terrified space "where [obsessive] Thought roams up & down."[60]

The first female character to divide herself from the male principle with whom she shares her existence, Enion represents, more than any other weaver in *The Four Zoas,* Blake's ambivalence toward the female body; hers epitomizes the body of the phallic Mother. The

Spectre reproduces Enion's own femaleness (her body), for he is likewise characterized as a body *excessive* in its own making: "a form of gold," a "human form winged" and immoderately bright "as of gems shone clear." Enion weaves this body from threads drawn forth from her own bosom. These threads represent the emotional and physical pleasure of the nurturing mother's body. Whereas the bosom signifies the region of the breasts, it also denotes the heart. Hence, from these "Sinewy threads" the Spectre feeds his body, while her heart broods over him with obsessive care. On the other hand, the "vein & lacteal threading" drawn from Tharmas "issuing from his feet in flames of fire"[61] indicate the pain and terror of the mother's body, which threatens existence at the same time it creates life. In this manner the very properties of abjection are woven into the body of the Spectre so that it abhors its mother and consort (calling her "thou Diminutive husk & shell")[62] while at the same time he desires to have intercourse with her, "Mingling his horrible brightness with her tender limbs."[63]

Blake associates Enion's weaving with the plane of generation, and generation constitutes Vala's world of vegetation; when portrayed in her fallen form, Vala represents the phallic mother, who is:

> . . . *the Worm Weaving* in the *Ground*
> Thou'rt my mother from the Womb
> Wife, Sister, Daughter to the Tomb
> Weaving to Dreams the Sexual Strife
> And weeping over the Web of Life.[64]

Blake characterizes Enion's weaving as being even more hideous and unnatural than Vala's, for the Daughters of Beulah are unable to weave a body for her Spectre; without a new body, the Spectre cannot be reborn, will never again "revive in spring."

Blake balances this negative picture of weaving with an equally positive one: Enitharmon's weaving reverses the process of degeneration that Enion's began. Enitharmon succeeds where the Daughters of Beulah have failed, perfecting the mode of regeneration, clothing those souls who have fallen into Ulro with bodies necessary for redemption. Like Enion's, Enitharmon's creations possess life of their own. But unlike Enion's "insane & most / Deformd"[65] creatures, hers are clothed "With gifts & gold of Eden."[66]

Paul de Man views one of the central paradoxes in the poetics of romanticism as "the theme of imagination linked . . . to the theme of nature."[67] Blake's distinction between the woven textile and the weaving process constitutes just such a dialectic. In the words of Northrop Frye, when "the artist is . . . woven in the looms of

Cathedron [he] feels a correspondence between his imagination and nature."[68] The textile synthesizes what de Man saw as the central paradox in romantic poetry, the convergence of two worlds—the natural and the imaginative. Ironically, these worlds are often spoken of in terms of gender; Blake equates the "natural" realm with the female principle and the imaginative world with the male. Blake's weaving scenes, however, often consolidate representations of the imaginative (male) process within representations of the natural (female) process, primarily when weaving occurs during language, and is portrayed as an activity that is constituted through language. As already mentioned, the verb "to weave" connects with ideas of poetry and prophecy, constituting a metaphor for creativity and the imagination. Blake juxtaposes the weaving (of nature) done by Enion and Enitharmon with song (the imagination) so that textile-weaving and spell-weaving exist simultaneously.

Whereas the mother, "Singing her lamentation"[69] uses her voice as a loom to divide her beloved Tharmas into a Spectre, her daughter weaves new bodies from her "Songs of Lamentations."[70] Enion's singing arises from self-pity; her lamentations constitute a song and state of consciousness that created Tharmas's Spectre in the first place. Enitharmon's lamentations originate otherwise. Arising from her feelings of pity and compassion for the fallen spectres, Enitharmon's weaving does not separate or differentiate like Enion's; instead, it reverses Enion's action, and becomes for Enitharmon a task that makes whole. She clothes the Spectres in bodies, weaving into being "a Vast family wondrous in beauty & love."[71] Rahab and Tirzah, on the other hand, continue to work in place of Enion, weaving those devastating veils of ignorance and bodies of death that perpetuate the existence of this lowest world, Ulro.

Tharmas first instructs "Enitharmons hands / [to] Weave soft delusive forms of Man above my watry world."[72] Ault reminds us that though Enitharmon's weaving "seems to be associated by the narrator and several of the other characters with some hope of redemption, Tharmas's original command (as well as Enion's initial weaving) was intertwined with suppression, enclosure, and delusion."[73] I would qualify Ault's remark by reminding the reader that at the time Tharmas commands Enitharmon to weave "delusive forms," he has deteriorated so far from his original nature that he cannot remember or conceive of the kind of weaving in which Enitharmon will actually engage. All Tharmas hopes to gain by Los's and Enitharmon's labor is a glimpse of Enion: "To ease my pangs of heart & restore some peace to Tharmas."[74] Little does this Zoa know that his charge to Los and Enitharmon to "Go forth [and] Rebuild this Universe"[75] will eventually return him to his companion, Enion, as well as transform them both back to their primal innocence, to live once again in "the Gardens of Vala."[76]

At the end of the Seventh Night, Los tells Enitharmon that he feels inspired

> . . . to fabricate embodied semblances in which the dead
> May live before us in our palaces & in our gardens of labour
> Which now opend within the Center we behold spread abroad
> To form a world of Sacrifice of brothers & sons & daughters
> To comfort Orc in his dire sufferings.[77]

Enitharmon agrees, but once Los sees the spectres "Embodied & Lovely / In youth & beauty in the arms of Enitharmon,"[78] he changes his mind. Both Enitharmon and Los decide, rather, that they themselves "meet Eternal death than to destroy / The offspring of their Care & Pity."[79] This is the first sacrifice of *self* that any of the Zoas make, and it constitutes the first step toward their reunion.

A war ensues between the powers of Light ("the Divine Countenance shown in Golgonooza")[80] and the powers of Darkness ("the Synagogue of Satan in dark Sanhedrim")[81] which is Urizen's domain. Enitharmon's looms "erected . . . in Luban's Gate / And calld the Looms Cathedron"[82] comprise the heart of Golgonooza, around which the battle rages. The narrative suggests that whosoever controls these looms will win. We must remember, however, that this view constitutes Blake's vision of duality, wherein light and darkness, love and hate, life and death invent each other and coexist.

S. Foster Damon's *Blake Dictionary* defines "Lubans Gate" with the vaginal opening (Catherine's/Enitharmon's), signifying that the looms operate at the place where generation occurs.[83] Blake indicates through a series of allusions, however, that Lubans Gate is "the Gate of Pity / The broken heart Gate of Enitharmon."[84] The breaking of Enitharmon's heart allows her to perform a merciful kind of weaving, one that repairs and reverses the consequences of Ulro, which was woven by her mother in the epic's opening scene. Remember, Enion wove a tabernacle to hide Jerusalem from Tharmas's prying eyes. Now Enitharmon's broken heart is equivalent to the rending of this secret place. Although the broken heart may signify the vaginal opening which Los is now free to explore, I think this suggestion a tentative one, for Blake himself specifies that Los enters through *"Enitharmons bosom"* to "explore / Its intricate Labyrinths."[85] This comprises the same exact location from which Enion first drew threads of her own being to create the body of the Spectre. It is a place of psychic wounding. In this scene, Los's entrance into the bosom of Enitharmon heals the wound of separation made by Tharmas when he tore Los from his Emanation. A penetration that is sexually and spiritually intimate, Los's entry into her heart signifies that the time for reunion between the Zoas and their Emanations is nigh.

Enitharmon's final act of reparation for her mother's sin occurs when she weaves a body for Jerusalem. Afterward, from within "Jerusalems Veil" Enitharmon "Wondring . . . saw the Lamb of God."[86] She sees for the first time "The divine Vision . . . within the inmost deep recess / Of fair Jerusalems bosom in a gently beaming fire."[87] Enitharmon, apparently, has fulfilled her destiny, the task for which she was born. She has begun a new kind of weaving, one that regenerates fallen souls. She has allowed her heart to be broken by the pity and compassion from which her mother's heart had been sealed. As a result, her weaving once again reveals Jerusalem's presence to those eyes who had been blinded to it ever since Enion first wove the tabernacle or thick veil concealing Jerusalem from sight.

Because Enitharmon and her daughters still exist in a world of duality and psychic disrepair, Rahab and Tirzah counter their activity by unravelling all they have woven. The daughters of Urizen then create "far different mantles"[88] for the spectres, weaving them "Veils of ignorance covering from head to feet with a cold web."[89] Rahab and Tirzah practice an even more degenerative form of weaving than introduced by Enion. Blake suggests, however, that both kinds of weaving are mutually dependent: Rahab and Tirzah's looms epitomize how weaving both imitates and initiates the fallen consciousness in(to) Ulro—for, like language, weaving can pave a path toward further fall into disunity; in contrast, Enitharmon's loom epitomizes how weaving repairs this split and restores not only the spectres but the Zoas themselves, initiating their recovery toward primal unity. Yet even here the Zoas still exist in the realm of duality.

As we have seen through close examination of these scenes in Nights I through VIII, weaving functions as a product as well as a producer of language. Weaving also produces bodies that fall into language: Through tears (the water necessary for generation), songs (of lamentation), and sighs (of breath), "the Vegetated bodies" for the Spectres are woven. Enitharmon is pictured, time and again, *"Singing lulling Cadences,"* weaving "in tears *singing Songs of Lamentation," "singing lulling cadences on the wind,"* and with her daughters singing *"songs of sweetest cadence* to the turning spindle & reel / Lulling the weeping spectres of the dead."[90] Weaving always accompanies a vocal moment, in which the *body* is created simultaneous with the *word.*

Consonant with my analysis, Morton Paley has suggested that two incompatible forms of weaving find mutual expression in Blake's poetry (the weaving that redeems and the weaving that enslaves) because Blake himself was ambivalent about the nature of the body and the soul. And yet Paley notes a central ambiguity about this body. On one hand, it constitutes a vegetated body that dies, a mundane cocoon that entraps the soul, and a veil that obscures the eternal vision to keep the soul in ignorance. On the other hand, this body-garment redeems the soul, and is absolutely necessary for entry into Eternity: "If the vegetated body is a garment which is finally to be 'cut off,'" Paley asks, "what is the spiritual body but another kind of garment?"[91] In other words, if two different kinds of garments are being woven in these poems—the bodily garment and the spiritual/eternal garment—Blake would be indirectly claiming that a fundamental difference exists between the body and the soul, that they are not one and the same. And yet, in *The Marriage of Heaven and Hell,* Paley reminds us, "Blake had affirmed through the voice of the Devil that 'Man has no Body distinct from his Soul.'"[92]

If we accept Paley's reading, one way of resolving this seeming duality in Blake (particularly when Blake himself resists it) is to perceive weaving as an activity, Rieger states, as one "which exists on four levels of discourse, corresponding to the four worlds of Blake's myth."[93] When the Zoas, their Emanations, and Spectres fall from Eden to Beulah, from Beulah to Babylon, and from Babylon to Ulro, weaving represents a mimetic device that, like language, weaves texts appropriate to the consciousness into which the weaver has fallen. As a metaphor for the imaginative process, weaving mirrors to Blake's readers the difference between "true" and "false" creativity: The woven product duplicates the mind of the weaver by literally embodying in the textile the language/sounds spoken by her when weaving. This textile/body reads like a text, demonstrating the clarity of the weaver's vision, whether her imaginative process is in keeping with a vision of Eternity, or if it has gone awry.

Hilton, Paley, Raine, and Frye among others have all noted that Blake's "weaving" constitutes an anomalous symbol, representing two disparate processes: In the hands of a positively creative character, it signifies a redemptive enterprise transforming death into life. Enitharmon performs this kind of weaving, wherein shapeless Spectres are woven bodies from "the Looms of Cathedron" by "The Daughters of Enitharmon":

> Lulling the weeping spectres of the dead. Clothing their limbs
> With gifts & gold of Eden. Astonishd stupefied with delight

> The terrors put on their sweet clothing on the banks of Arnon
> Whence they plunge into the river of space for a period till
> The dread Sleep of Ulro is past.[94]

Enitharmon's weaving is reminiscent of the artist's task. Northrop Frye has remarked that the poet and artist must "use natural images . . . to give body to" their ideas.[95]

Toward this analogy, "[a]n abstract idea is a spectre, a collapsing skeleton" for which a body must be woven to give it shape and meaning.[96] Weaving without the imaginative principle represents the thoughtless manufacturing of the natural world where nothing but the lifeless "mundane shell" is created. The artistic principle, then, incarnates a picture or a poem that it may enter and exist in the natural world.[97]

Conversely, should a weaver fall into duality, she will weave garments that perpetuate this condition. From the fallen state, she can only produce material signifying sorrow and death. Thus, Rahab & Tirzah weave the spectres "anew in the forms / Of dark death & despair & none from Eternity to Eternity could Escape."[98]

The Zoas' fall into Blake's four possible worlds of consciousness is not always so clearly demarcated. For example, when Enion in Night I weaves a song of lamentation that draws from Tharmas his Spectre, we can not be certain whether Enion exists in Babylon and is about to fall into Ulro, or whether she has fallen into Ulro already. By weaving the Spectre of Tharmas, however, Enion most definitely has cast herself from the "Great Eternity," the "mild & pleasant rest / Namd Beulah"[99] which represents for Blake "the married state, the last station on the way to eternal bliss."[100] On the other hand, if the weaving of and divesting of bodies also takes place in Eternity, as Paley himself suggests, none of the characters in *The Four Zoas* or in *Jerusalem,* for that matter, has ever been able to envision what it would look like. Enitharmon remarks toward the end of *Jerusalem,* before she merges with Los, "if he be that Albion I can never weave him in my Looms / But when he touches the first fibrous thread, like filmy dew / My Looms will be no more & I annihilate vanish for ever."[101] She can not imagine (or weave) a text which is appropriate for the Eternal Man.

Important to the manufacture of bodies and veils from these four psychic "places" is the possibility of "casting off" the bodies and material coverings in each of these psychic realms. According to James Rieger, the leaving of bodies represents "the self-annihilation that leads to salvation . . . which (Blake) expresses by the metaphor of divestment," and, I would add, reinvestment.[102] Projected onto each pair of Zoa and Emanation are four different states of renewal. The final night illustrates these four different ways of "casting off" the body of experience and entering into a renewed body of innocence: First, the formless Enion and Tharmas are recast in the bodies of children. Second, Urizen and Ahania are envisaged as beautiful youths: The ancient patriarch shakes "his aged mantles off / Into the fires" and rises "into the heavens in naked majesty / In radiant Youth";[103] his counterpart, Ahania, parallels this process of rebirth by similarly casting "off her death clothes" like "the harvest Moon."[104] Third, Vala and Luvah are renewed through their veils or garments: Luvah's veil is a "golden Cloud upon the breath of morning,"[105] and Vala's garments constitute the vegetated earth. Fourth and finally, Los and Enitharmon, depicted throughout the entire poem as naked, "without a covering veil,"[106] almost entirely disappear from the poem. They are, in a sense, renewed through their absence.[107] Blake's deliberate ommission of Los and Enitharmon in the final section of his narrative implies the importance of self-sacrifice in this poem. The only evil in *The Four Zoas* constitutes the Zoas' desire for separation, their yearning to establish the ego (epitomized by Urizen's "Am I not God . . . Who is Equal to me")[108] as a quality distinguishable from the cooperative "we." Los and Enitharmon first act selflessly by refusing to sacrifice their children to comfort Orc, and their ensuing actions motivate the other characters' transformations. At the beginning of the final night, Los tears down his own world in sorrow; in this scene he refuses to replace Urizen's "Golden World" as first envisioned in Night the Second, with a world of his own making. Clearly, Los's best quality is his ability to sacrifice himself for the lives of those around him. After providing the catalyst for the Zoas' psychic reparation and unity, Blake sacrifices Los and Enitharmon for the "benefit" of the poem's progress, hence their disappearance from the narrative. We could say that Blake has sacrificed them to Albion's well-being.

Blake's portrayal of weaving so far can not possibly represent a process consonant with Eternity, because it epitomizes duality and difference (between Enion's and Enitharmon's looms). In the final weaving scene at the end of Night the Ninth, however, Blake unites the seemingly antagonistic oppositions of duality by illustrating a very different kind of weaving, one that apparently holds together the different worlds—Ulro, Babylon, Beulah, and perhaps Eternity. This marks a novel form of weaving in which all four Emanations take part.

The Emanations are united in this scene, and Blake depicts them on the threshold of Eternity, working joyously at their Golden Looms:

Enion & Ahania & Vala & the wife of Dark Urthona
Rose from the feast in joy ascending to their Golden Looms
There the wingd shuttle Sang the spindle & the distaff & the Reel
Rang sweet the praise of industry. Thro all the golden rooms
Heaven rang with winged Exultation All beneath howld loud
With tenfold rout & desolation roard the Chasms beneath
Where the wide woof flowd down & where the Nations are gatherd
together.[109]

The looms—their shuttles, spindles, distaffs and reels—generate song and praise. This music embodies "the wide woof" that flows down through the worlds; as the "garment" descends, the music changes into howls and roars. The vast machinery of the looms generate movement and activity, from "Eternity" (if this is indeed the place where the Emanations exist in this scene) on down through Beulah, Babylon, and Ulro. "[T]he wide woof" apparently represents the material embodiment of a river of flowing language, with the eternal Word becoming more opaque and distorted as it flows through the lower worlds or "Chasms" "where the Nations are gathered."

The weft woven by the Emanations in this final scene trails through the worlds; the material itself functions like a Jacob's ladder that the spectres ascend and descend at will. This material ladder also embodies discourse; churned out by the Golden Looms, this language/garment keeps the worlds in activity—defines and sustains them. Donald Ault suggests, likewise, that "The musical weaving of the females . . . breaches the gap between the lower and upper worlds, making it seem as if the weaving is implicated in the woe and opening the possibility that the 'Nations' beneath might ascend to the upper world by means of this connection."[110] The weaving sustains both weal and woe, Beulah and Ulro, because in this scene weaving performs a very different function: it no longer constitutes the positive/negative traits of duality.

The scene in Night IX wherein Luvah rises from the feast epitomizes a repudiation of duality by the Zoas who are now linked with their Emanations. Blake depicts Luvah's "crown of thorns" falling from his head, as he hangs "his living Lyre / Behind the seat of the Eternal Man."[111] I suggest that when Luvah relinquishes both the crown of thorns and the lyre, he is casting aside the pleasure/pain principle that has kept the Zoas in action. By returning the lyre to the Eternal Man, Luvah restores the vision of primal unity to Albion, and, hence, to the Zoas themselves.

Immediately following this scene, Blake portrays weaving as the embodiment of the entire creation. Neither Enitharmon's nor Enion's performance is given preference in the final scene because both types of weaving find expression in the weft that flows down through the different worlds. Like Rieger says of language, weaving, too, "exists on four levels of discourse."[112] In Blake's epic poem, it comprises a "passive" symbol that merely reflects back these different worlds of discourse, and it also constitutes an active agent that produces these four discourses and worlds.

The Emanations correlate with the weaving goddesses and gods discussed in chapter 1, such as Spider Woman, Brahma/Maya, and Nummo. The weaving all these creator figures engage in, like that of the Emanations, produces both thoughts and things, texts as well as bodies, the corporeal world as textile on which a text or thought is inscribed. Likewise, the Emanations correlate with Helen of Troy and Penelope in that their weaving, at times, represents the author, Blake's, creativity: as the Emanations weave together the worlds and clothe the Spectres of spirits, the poet, too, clothes his thought and inspiration with the body of words.

In Blake's *The Four Zoas* we once again encounter a situation in which female weavers, occupied in their mundane tasks at the loom, participate in the creation of a culture by authoring its texts. I would be naïve to argue that Blake believed the female (whether human or Emanation) equal to the task of artistic creativity as a male (whether human or Zoa). In *The Four Zoas,* however, Blake stumbles onto the powerful metaphor of weaving which has buried in its history the privilege of female divinity. In other words, in this epic alone, Blake raises the status of his Emanations to one which vies with the Zoas, through the weaving metaphor which becomes allegorical of the *poet* (or Creator) as well as the *poem* (or his World).

5

"A Magic Web with Colors Gay": Representations of the Lady of Shalott in Pre-Raphaelite Art

Who is to blame? The Weaver?
Ah, the bewildering thread!
—Emily Dickinson, "A Shady Friend—for Torrid days—"

I

IN THIS CHAPTER I TURN AWAY FROM THE RATHER EXCLUSIVE TASK OF showing how weaving in literature functions as a metaphor for linguistic or textual production, and instead to the representation of weaving in art through the character of Lord Alfred Tennyson's The Lady of Shalott.

The scene of a woman engaged in textile production—spinning, sewing, weaving, or embroidery—recurs frequently in the history of art. Through scenes of textile manufacture, the artist conveys to the viewer ideas of womanly virtue or promiscuity by portraying the order or disorder of her threads, the relaxed or rigid posture of her body poised over her work—whether her body opens to or resists the penetrating male gaze.[1] By painting on a *lecythos*[2] a woman's bared leg while she is carding wool, or painting on a canvas, as does Velázquez, a woman's bared leg while she leans back from the labor of pumping her spinning wheel (*Las Hilanderas*),[3] the artist illustrates not only a scene of female labor but another spectacle (in a long history of spectacles) that reiterates the pleasures of the female body. The activity of weaving only frames her body and is incidental to the painting; in this category of pictures, the artist's main subject is always bodily display.

The most popular representation of a woman weaver occurred during the Pre-Raphaelite period (c. 1848 in London, England) when *The Lady of Shalott* was illustrated by at least seven different artists: Dante Gabriel Rossetti, Elizabeth Siddal, John Millais, Sidney

Meteyard, John William Waterhouse, Edward Burne-Jones, and William Holman Hunt. Extreme differences exist among these paintings and drawings, yet their common subject indicates that these artists shared an obsession for this doomed weaver who first appeared in Tennyson's poem.

These artists, however, did not limit their representations merely to illustrating Tennyson's poem. Choosing different incidents from the poem to depict, and then introducing details into their work not present in the poem itself, these painters produce variations on Tennyson's narrative, constituting what I would call meta-texts. The relationship between the poem and its multiple representations creates a supplementary dialogue: these texts (in this sense, a painting constitutes a text) interact with each other creating several meanings that no one text, particularly that of the poem, can resolve.[4]

These pictorial variations represent a visual counterpart to oral storytelling: no two stories (or pictures) are ever told (or drawn) the same way twice. Painting may constitute a static medium, but when we examine these paintings together, we sense a kind of movement, a dialogue between continuity and change. This interchange becomes even more interesting when we juxtapose the poem with its pictorial representations. Using Tennyson's text as a starting point, we see that these artists go beyond language, constituting what Julia Kristeva calls "something that is more-than-speech, a meaning to which space and color have been added."[5] Although in this sense each painting or drawing constitutes what Kristeva calls a "'sign'" and "is its own reality," or a "separate referent" the relationship among these illustrations, as well as between them and the poem itself, sets up a fantastic dialogue between language and its representation. After considering the various illustrations of the Lady of Shalott, I propose that pictorial variation and reproduction have both expanded and yet diminished the meaning of Tennyson's text.

A painting or drawing can stand on its own, and an artist need not feel compelled to render faithfully his or her source. Yet, when more than one artist becomes captivated with the same motif or image, their works form a compelling dialogue. By analyzing, collectively, such representations, we may begin to understand what these images tell us about the artists as well as their audience. Margaret Miles suggests that "a visual image, repeatedly depicted, may be assumed to have popular attraction for people of its original culture" because it addresses "the strong anxieties, interests, and longings common to all or most people of that society."[6] Similarly, Kristeva describes repeated images or ideas in painting as an "unfolding narrative" and constitutive of symbolic Law.[7] Pre-Raphaelite artists emphasized verisimilitude (truth to the subject) as a hallmark of their paintings. Hence, as Pre-Raphaelite pictures, each of these representations will exhibit an important relationship to its source.

The Pre-Raphaelite Brotherhood was formed in 1848. Dante Gabriel Rossetti, William Holman Hunt, and John Everett Millais comprised, initially, the most important (and influential) of its seven members. Their title derives from their common belief that art declined after Raphael. Although the artists had distinct preferences in subject matter (Hunt became known for his religious themes, Millais for his literary subjects, and Rossetti for his mystical paintings) they each exhibit a common approach. Jerome Buckley writes, "Each sought to recover the sense of wonder and mystery, the dream beyond the commonplaces of an order [the Industrial Age] which was increasingly devoted to the mechanization of human life."[8] The Pre-Raphaelites sought to escape their society's emphasis on "progress" and the future, by focusing nostalgically on an idealized past. And yet they did so with a peculiar Victorian flavor, an emphasis on reproducing details with an almost scientific energy.

The rendering of natural details [verisimilitude] became a hallmark of Pre-Raphaelite art, even when the artist used nature as a vehicle for symbolic expression. So insistent were these artists on reproducing, exactly, the details of their subject, that they often went to peculiar extremes. For example, when Elizabeth Siddal posed for Millais's famous painting, "Ophelia," [1851–52], she had to lie in a tub of water, fully clothed, for hours on end so that Millais could accurately portray the hair and gown of a drowning woman.[9]

In the pages that follow I examine the similarities and differences among six separate representations of the Lady of Shalott. I suggest how these portrayals revise or reenact passages from the poem, and I explore the relationship between these artists and their subject, in order that we may come to a closer understanding of why the Lady of Shalott marked such a popular subject for artists of this particular age.

Tennyson first published his poem in 1832, but ten years later revised it substantially for a second publication. The author claims that an Italian novella gave him the idea for the poem, but he invented the setting, the weaving plot, and the mirror. The first section of the four-part poem describes the pastoral landscape in which this poem is cast. The Lady's castle, built on a small island and surrounded by lilies, connects to Camelot both by a road that winds along the mainland shore and by the traffic of boats that sail past the island. Though the castle is plainly seen, no one has ever glimpsed its inhabitant. Because they sometimes hear her singing from the tower in the early morning, only the farmers can attest to the Lady's presence. Her existence, however, is only conjectured, for they call her a "fairy."

The second section moves away from the external landscape and focuses on the tower's interior; here, the Lady is described as weaving a wonderful web, working into its design scenes from Camelot, which are shown to her by a magic mirror. We are told that she must look at Camelot only through the mediation of the mirror; if, instead, she gazes out the window toward Camelot, she will be cursed. This section ends with the Lady admitting for the first time that she is unhappy to merely weave the mirror's scenes: "'I am half-sick of shadows.'"

The prohibition placed on the Lady seems to derive from the ancient Irish *geasa.* Functioning more like a taboo or something forbidden than a curse, the *geasa* was usually "imposed by formula and was either injunctional or prohibitive in character."[10] According to ancient Irish mythology and literature, before a warrior or hero entered a sacred order or obtained supernatural favors, it was not unusual to have gaesa imposed on him. These taboos were often idiosyncratic, yet they were also a form of empowerment. The warrior received something by losing something else. The geasa imposed on the legendary Irish hero, Cuchulain, offers a fine example of the nature of the geasa from which his exceptional powers derive. "It was geis [geasa] or tabu to him to narrate his genealogy to one champion . . . to refuse combat to any one man, to look upon the exposed bosom of a woman, to come into company without a second invitation, to accept the hospitality of virgins, to boast to a woman, to let the sun rise before him on the fields of Emain . . . " etc.[11] Hence, as each geasa is broken, Cuchulain loses a corresponding power. Finally, the last geasa broken signals the end of Cuchulain's career. With this realization comes an acceptance, if not longing, for death: "'I have no reason for preserving my life long,' said Cuchulain, 'for the end of my time is come and all my *geasa* [tabus] are lost.'"[12]

Grimm's fairy tales also employ the concept of geasa without naming it directly. In "Rumplestiltskin," for example, the farmer's daughter wins a kingdom and crown (via the supernatural intervention of Rumplestiltskin himself) at the price of her first-born son. Charles Perrault's version of "Bluebeard" even better illustrates the geasa: Bluebeard tells his wife that she may have everything she desires as long as she does not open one particular door. Likewise, the Lady of Shalott may work "happily" at her loom, weaving a magic web as long as she avoids looking out a certain window. Her power of weaving this "magic web" undoubtedly derives from this notion of geasa. Although the poem never addresses who or what gives her this gift, like Coleridge's "Kubla Khan," the mystery and lure of "The Lady of Shalott" is attributed in part to this fragmentary quality.

The third section of Tennyson's poem introduces Lancelot. Paralleling the movement of the narrative, Lancelot moves first in the landscape outside the tower and then "flashes" into the private, enclosed space of the tower through the Lady's mirror. Simultaneous with his entry into the tower via this mirror, the Lady hears him singing outside her window. Leaving her loom, she walks over to the window to gaze down upon him. As she breaks her *geasa*, the mirror cracks and her tapestry unravels; when she violates her taboo, her magical powers—if, indeed, she possessed them—desert her.

In the fourth section, the poem's action once again moves beyond the magical interior of Shalott, and into the public landscape. Once the lady leaves her tower, she lies down in a boat on which she has inscribed her name, sings her last song, and dies as her sloop drifts into Camelot. Lancelot glimpses her as she glides by, and dwelling for a moment on the sight of her lovely, dead face, he consigns her soul to God.

The Lady of Shalott begins as a lighthearted, romantic tale that turns, two-thirds into the poem, into a story of inexplicable longing and unavoidable death. I will explicate this process in terms of the paintings I have selected. I propose that when these painters choose to illustrate a particular scene from "The Lady of Shalott," they inadvertently efface another equally important scene. For instance, instead of emphasizing the Lady's artistry as Tennyson portrays it in the poem's first two sections, these artists prefer to illustrate the last portion of the text. As we shall see, they focus on the weaver, not on the enjoyment of her art, but at the moment when her art can no longer sustain her or be sustained by her—at the moment either of artistic failure or at the moment of her death. Even criticism of this poem tends to focus on the last portion of the text. And although this is clearly the most dramatic sequence in the story, such an emphasis effaces the first half of the poem in which a perfect equilibrium and harmony are established between the mysterious world of the Lady in her tower and the agrarian world of commerce—peasants, squires, knights, and friars—that surrounds her.

Like the paintings we will examine, literary criticism tends to deemphasize the Lady's artistry and highlight, instead, her "inevitable" death. To do so, the criticism either glosses over the weaving scene, or represents it as compulsory.[13] In her important essay, "Tennyson's 'The Lady of Shalott': Victorian Mythography and the Politics of Narcissism," Isobel Armstrong reasons that "The Lady of Shalott *seems* to be at play, weaving an aesthetic web of many colours. But she is actually imprisoned and just as certainly she is at *work.*"[14] Armstrong's emphasis depends on the assumption that this "work" constitutes a forced activity, suggestive of exploitation. I disagree with this interpretation, and maintain, instead, that what these artists and many literary critics consistently efface is the positive scene of artistic creation in Tennyson's poem.

Another commonplace reading construes the Lady of Shalott as an infantile, sexually immature female whose crisis entails her failure to enter the public world of Camelot, and her death of unrequited love as an inevitability from which the poem cannot escape. Armstrong demonstrates that this kind of interpretation comes from Tennyson himself, who "implied that the Lady simply dies of a broken heart and [that] this is still the most important thing to say about 'The Lady of Shalott', which describes a woman who cannot come into sexuality or language except by dying."[15]

The poem's surface action easily lends itself to such an exegesis, and yet the prolific reproduction of this poem in drawings and paintings testifies to a surplus of meaning that cannot be so easily explained. Medieval and Romantic texts feature many *femmes fatales,* whose failed relationships and deaths constitute more drama than the one enacted by the Lady of Shalott. This weaver, however, signifies a departure from the tribe of Romantic heroines not because she is located in an Arthurian context, nor because of the spectacle of her death, but because her role as weaver derives from ancient Greek and Teutonic mythology. Her death resonates because it conveys to Camelot, to the sphere of consciousness, a message about art itself, about how it works, how it sustains itself, how it can flourish, and when it will die. Finally, her presence in so much art strongly suggests that the artists' identify with her story and with their own representations of her.

Joseph Chadwick points out that Tennyson modeled his poetry on the "Romantic aesthetic ideal" that—according to Arthur Hallam's famous review of Tennyson's *Poems, Chiefly Lyrical*—identified "the artwork with femininity."[16] The Lady of Shalott, however, occupies a sexually ambiguous position: although she gives the poem its title and is its female subject, her activity as an artist places her in the male position as the artist and her "magic web with colors gay" (2.38) occupies the feminized position of the art object or poem itself.[17] She is both the artist and the work of art, both subject and object.[18]

It was not uncommon for this milieu to feminize their identities as artists. In a passage from *Praeteria,* the autobiography of the famous nineteenth-century art critic, John Ruskin, which describes his writing method, Ruskin feminizes his activity and compares his literary work to a young girl's embroidery. He states that his writing was accomplished

> as quietly and methodically as a piece of tapestry. I knew exactly what I had got to say, put the words firmly in their places like so many stitches, hemmed the edges of chapters round with what seemed to me graceful flourishes, touched them finally with my cunningest points of color, and read the work to papa and mama at breakfast next morning, as a girl shows her sampler.[19]

The Lady's position as both subject and object contributes to the poem's popularity, suggesting why so many artists became preoccupied with this theme. Her position as an artist allows male artists to identify with her, whereas her status as a woman decides her fate—a death which, ironically, constitutes the subject of most of the art about her.[20]

For my discussion of the poem and its representation in art, I will again turn to Kristeva, who also investigates the role of semiotics in literature and painting. These two vocations, writes Lechte, have "always featured prominently in Julia Kristeva's writing, because for Kristeva . . . there is no fundamental discontinuity between the production of a work of art and the life of the individual."[21] In works like "Motherhood According to Giovanni Bellini," and "Giotto's Joy," Kristeva focuses on painting, proposing that semiotic elements enter the Symbolic through an artist's use of color and space. Through these two means artists can work within the Law of the Father and at the same time "show their independence of symbolic Law *by pitting themselves* against the represented narrative."[22] Kristeva's work provides a lens for exploring the "unfolding narrative" of the Lady of Shalott in art and poetry.

The paintings and drawings I examine fall into two groups. The first group includes those portraits wherein the Lady is shown at work within the tower, at a moment just before the curse (Sidney Harold Meteyard's painting [1913]) or subject to the curse itself (William Holman Hunt's drawing [c. 1857] and painting [c. 1886–1905] and Elizabeth Siddal's drawing [1853]). The second group includes two works, both depicting the Lady of Shalott in her barge: John William Waterhouse's painting (© 1888) portrays the Lady singing her final song as she unties the boat from its anchor; Dante Gabriel Rossetti's drawing (1858–59) shows Lancelot gazing down at the dead body of the Lady as her boat floats beneath the towers of Camelot. Both groups of painters similarly efface the positive artistic activity in which this weaver engages at the beginning of Tennyson's poem. By examining each group of paintings separately, I will consider why the Lady of Shalott constitutes such an important subject for these artists. At one time a storyteller who "weaveth steadily" (1.43) scenes from her mirror, the Lady becomes in these pictures the story itself, silenced, mute, who dies, inevitably, and sends her own body down a river and into the world to be gazed on—made a spectacle—by men.

II

Of the first group of paintings examined, the drawing by William Holman Hunt represents the most elaborate effort to accurately portray Tennyson's poem. Ironically, the drawing angered Tennyson because the poet thought it too unlike the poem. Hunt depicted the Lady of Shalott standing inside a round frame loom, supported a foot or so off the floor. The tapestry itself gives the effect of a giant spider's web, with its circular mass bisected in triangles from the center. Hunt's illustration positions the Lady inside this frame, caught within a tangle of threads that wind tightly about her as if she, the spider, has become the fly.

Behind her head hangs a large round mirror, below which the round tapestry is suspended like a perfect reflection or shadow of the glass. The mirror reflects the scene in which Sir Lancelot first "flash'd into the crystal mirror" (3.106), before the Lady looks "down to Camelot" (3.113); yet we realize that the curse is now unfolding because the Lady is entangled in her own threads. Surrounding this mirror appear a group of eight roundels, each reflecting a different scene within the poem, in an endeavor made by the artist to illustrate the entire poem in one scene.

Tennyson took great interest in the drawing because it was supposed to illustrate the 1857 Moxon edition of his poems.[23] He objected to Hunt's central scene, because it did not exactly follow the lines: "She left the web, she left the loom, / She made three paces thro' the room" (II.109–10). Instead, Hunt depicts the Lady of Shalott standing *inside* the frame of her own loom as the curse is triggered, rather than looking out the window as the poem indicates. Hunt defended his work, saying, "'I had only half a page on which to convey the impression of weird fate, whereas you use about fifteen pages to give expression to the complete idea.'"[24] Hunt's effort to transpose narrative, to give the effect of movement and time in a medium that by its very nature celebrates stasis, forced him to alter the very text he had hoped to accurately reproduce.

William Holman Hunt (1827–1910), English. *The Lady of Shalott* 1850, black chalk, pen and ink. 23.5 × 14.2 cm; Felton Bequest, 1921; National Gallery of Victoria, Melbourne, Australia.

Hunt's final portrait of the Lady of Shalott, perhaps the most well-known painting on the subject, retained many of the features first sketched in the 1850 drawing: the Lady is shown inside the frame of her loom, trying to disentangle the threads from the lower half of her body.[25] Although in the earlier drawing a shawl is tied around the Lady's hip, which "adds a touch of sensuality" and "emphasizes that part of her nature vulnerable to the dazzling sight of Sir Lancelot,"[26] Hunt chooses not to include the shawl in his painting (he may have thought it derivative of "The Awakening Conscience" [1854]). Nevertheless, Hunt draws the audience's attention to the Lady's lower body by depicting the threads more tightly wound around her hips and legs than in the earlier drawing. Instead of emphasizing her hips with a red scarf, Hunt paints her skirt a dark rose and pink. Drawn up into the tapestry's entangling threads, this skirt reveals a white slip hanging underneath. By exposing her white undergarments, Hunt indicates the Lady's arousal as well as her virginity.

In keeping with his desire to capture the essence of Tennyson's poem in painting, Hunt develops a dialectic between captivity and release in symbolic motifs throughout the painting. In fact, this tension constitutes the painting's leitmotif. For example, the shoes that the Lady of Shalott has removed from her feet lie both within and without the parameters of the sacred circle; one is "caught" within the work space wherein the curse circulates, whereas the other shoe remains outside the loom, turned towards the window that faces Camelot. Rather than depicting the tapestry ripped from its frame (a symbol within the poem signifying the devastation of the curse), the Lady's hair, shaken loose and blown across most of the upper part of the canvas, substitutes also for this effect, signifying something torn apart and "floating wide" (3.114). Furthermore, Hunt portrays her hair streaming up toward the ceiling where a few wisps escape outside the window above her mirror, along with the body of a dove. The flowing hair gives the impression of abandonment or release, which Hunt strongly curtails by fettering the Lady's body. Yet the most vivid expression of this tension between captivity and escape is portrayed in the flight of two doves, soaring just above the loom: one directly above the tapestry, and the other at the same level but just outside the frame. Although flying parallel to each other, one of the doves enters the snare of threads unravelling from the fabric, while the other, flying outside the cursed circle, escapes these swirling threads.

Since the fifteenth century turtledoves were a common motif in European art. Almost always painted or carved together, their union symbolized "true love." They frequently decorated marriage and courting mirrors, which were fashionable gifts throughout the eighteenth and nineteenth centuries.[27] Hunt's turtledoves likewise symbolize the relationship between the Lady and Sir Lancelot: just as these doves are separated by the tapestry's curse, so, too, are Lancelot and the Lady divided from each other. The doves fly side-by-side, although the bird who flies outside the loom is positioned a bit lower and ahead of the bird caught within the threads; similarly, Lancelot's reflection in the mirror parallels the Lady's body, but his back is turned away from her (and the castle) as he freely rides away.

Finally, Hunt illustrates this struggle between captivity and freedom not only through the painting's symbolism, but also through the spatial setting of the scene itself, the tension between inner and outer space. The magic mirror reflects the outside portals of the tower, below which we glimpse Lancelot riding away. On one hand, these columns and arches lend an oriental flavor to what must be the tower's architecture; on the other hand, these columns look like the bars of an exquisite cage. Although the doves entering her tower from a high window are free to leave, the Lady clothed in her rare costume and working at her rare art must always remain imprisoned. In this sense, she represents a caged bird, an idea suggested when the reapers hear her in the early morning (a time for birds) singing "a song that echoes cheerily / From the river winding clearly, / Down to tower'd Camelot" (1.30–32). The first two sections of the poem depict the tower as a place in which the Lady can freely work "by night and day" (1.37), to "weave[th] steadily" (1.43) with "little other care" (1.44). In Hunt's painting, however, the tower represents imprisonment and terror. In contrast, the outside world symbolizes liberty and the possibility of love; in this landscape Lancelot rides (and the dove flies) free. Yet Tennyson's poem indicates that the Lady seals her fate by leaving this tower, and because of this act also destroys the possibility of freedom, both to live and to work.

Armstrong suggests ambiguity in Tennyson's line, "And little other care hath she." She proposes that this line implies that the Lady of Shalott is not "careless and carefree" but "is actually careful or full of care."[28] Yet the Lady freely leaves the tower at the end of the poem, and nothing in the narrative suggests that she lives there as the tower's unwilling victim. Moreover, the poem states that the lady sings "cheerily," and "delights / To weave the mirror's magic sights" (2.64–65), implying her own satisfaction with her life at the loom.

The last lines of part 2, in which she laments "'I am half sick of shadows'" (2.71), portend the second half of the poem in which the Lady will neglect her loom for a glance at Lancelot. These lines set up the poem's moment of crisis, but in no way suggest that this has been the Lady's attitude toward her situation all along. Instead, these lines constitute for the Lady of Shalott a new way of envisioning her life that will determine her fate and the rest of the narrative. Hunt's painting, however, suggests otherwise. His emphasis on the tower and the world beyond suggests a dialogue between confinement and release. Hunt bases this dialectic on two different kinds of space: the relatively claustrophobic tower chamber (comprising most of the painting), and the open countryside reflected in the mirror that lies beyond. The presence of birds trapped and/or flying free reiterates the significance of this theme. Like the dove within the loom, the warp threads, too, bind the Lady's body; like this dove her body constitutes the subject of (and is subject to) the tapestry's "drives," unleashed through the curse. Hunt's painting emphasizes the horror of the weaver's situation, her defenselessness against the terms of her fate, and the misogyny that so isolates her from community with the world beyond the tower window. Hunt accomplishes this, however, only by emphasizing that moment in which the Lady's delight in weaving has ceased.

I now turn to two more pictures that portray the Lady of Shalott working within her tower room: Elizabeth Siddal's drawing (1853) illustrates the moment the Lady looks out her window at Sir Lancelot, and Sidney Harold Meteyard's painting (1913) illustrates the lines "'I am half-sick of shadows,' said the Lady of Shalott." In both pictures the Lady has ceased to work. In Siddal's drawing, though the Lady's hands still rest on the upright frame loom, she has turned herself away from her work to gaze at the figure of Lancelot outside her window, and the warp is already torn off the frame. Deborah Cherry writes that Siddal's "narrative" creates "another story to that told in the poem or in those drawings by Hunt, Millais, and Rossetti which claim the poem as their subject"; Siddal's drawing, "resists the ending in death. . . . The Lady is represented at the moment of her look. She is not offered as a victim or a spectacle for the masculine gaze, nor does she attain visibility within its relays of power."[29]

Although the Lady of Shalott, in glancing outward, follows her own desire rather than the decrees of her imprisonment, this glance and its consequences work to victimize her. The drawing presents too much evidence supporting this view: the cracked mirror in which Lancelot is reflected, the warp torn from the loom, the long shadow of the crucifix behind her all suggest powerlessness, doom and, particularly in terms of the crucifix that stands between her gaze and the window, sacrifice.

Siddal emphasizes the pleasure of work, however. She portrays a sparse yet large room with the Lady's loom situated at its center. Sitting straight on the stool before her frame, Siddal dismisses the mythic dimensions that Tennyson's poem suggests, by casting the Lady of Shalott as anything but a "fairy" or mystic weaving "magic sights" (2.65). Instead, Siddal sets the scene in an austere room, feminized or adorned only by the presence of the Lady. Cherry comments that "We are offered an interior which is cool, airy and spacious: a work-room with evidence of past labours in the tapestry hanging on the far wall, a sanctuary with a crucifix for devotional use."[30] Here, Siddal resists the magical and mythic qualities of the Tennyson poem in preference for an austere, even ascetic, setting. Siddal also avoids the sensuality she would have seen in Hunt's, Rossetti's, and Millais's illustrations that constitute a more simplistic view of the poem as another anecdote in the annals of medieval chivalry. Siddal's performance refrains from pandering to the male gaze.

As in the previous three illustrations, Meteyard's painting represents artistic closure; the Lady's signifying activity has ceased. In his work, the Lady leans away from her tapestry loom against a pillow, her eyes closed, one hand gripping the frame of her tapestry and the other hanging idly at her side. Meteyard so indulges in his use of the color blue that, as I will later explain, color, alone, seems to be the painting's subject. Furthermore, Meteyard introduces details into the pictorial narrative that are wholly incongruous with Tennyson's poem. The pillow against which the Lady leans, the crystal ball that stands behind her seat, the curtained walls, and the white camellias (a common hothouse flower, indicating that the Lady cannot survive in the harsh soil or reality outside her room) communicate an atmosphere of mystery and death. The most noticeable discrepancy between Meteyard's painting and Tennyson's poem is the fact that he paints the Lady *embroidering* rather than weaving. Embroidery does not carry with it any mythic implications: in Greek and Teutonic mythology goddesses do not embroider, they weave; they do not merely decorate cloth, they create it. Embroidery, however, was a common pastime for the leisured nineteenth-century woman. Meteyard trivializes the Lady of Shalott by painting her at an embroidery frame rather than at a loom. Thus, the pictorial narrative emphasizes not the magical quality of her work, but instead creates an atmosphere of time passing, of hours wasted as she waits for Lancelot to appear in her glass so that she may fulfill her role as another victim of unrequited love.

These illustrations all depict a theme: the Lady within the tower in a failed relationship to her work. Hunt and Siddal portray the Lady at the moment the curse violently halts her work. Meteyard illustrates the Lady resting from her labor, a scene that occurs in Tennyson's poem to indicate the Lady's dissatisfaction with her life in the tower, as well as to foreshadow the release of the curse. Hunt's painting and drawing, more than Siddal's and Meteyard's work, give the impression that the Lady of Shalott represents a supreme artist who "weaves by night and day / A magic web with colors gay" (2.37–38). Siddal does not even represent the Lady's work, whereas Meteyard portrays her embroidering on a small frame rather than weaving a magical web. In all four pictorial narratives, the artists refrain from depicting her industry, her creativity, and her song, but instead illustrate the moment when she becomes helpless to forces outside her own control, when she ceases to speak or to act.

Meteyard displaces the lady's creative magic, indicated in the poem as her weaving, onto external objects to represent the supernatural. The crystal ball standing beside her right elbow echoes in color and shape the large convex mirror in which the lady gazes. The figure on her tapestry, embroidered in gold thread, on one level represents Sir Lancelot, but also illustrates the tarot card figure, Death. Indeed, his horse is black, and the sheaves of wheat clustered around the horseman's image indicate that he is "the Harvester," another name for Death. The red roses punctuating the embroidery suggest that the image derives from the Rosicrucians. The painting conflates two ideas: death (the embroidered figure) and passion (the lovers who appear in the mirror).[31]

In choosing to portray the Lady inside the tower, the artists orient our gaze away from her work and onto her body by showing her either entangled in or turned away from her activity. The Lady's struggle against the threads in Hunt's painting, more so than in his drawing, produces an undulating flow of sensual curves. This movement begins at her breasts, gathers momentum at the hips, and as the gaze travels down below the knees, rewards the onlooker with a glimpse of a chastely white slip.

Bodily display may indeed be the sole justification for Meteyard's painting. Beside a large deep blue mirror, framed by blue-black curtains and clusters of flowers, and languishing against a blue silk pillow, the Lady seems to be asleep or resting. Meteyard's painting is gratuitous, sensual; here, the Lady leans back in her chair with her head turned away from the observer, arms apart, opening up her body to the onlooker's gaze. Although she wears a high-necked, long-sleeved gown, the material clings to her figure, revealing every curve that it "apparently" conceals.

Helena Michie discusses this Pre-Raphaelite tendency to clothe female figures in such a way that though on "the one hand [they are] flamboyantly sexual, on the other, [they are] cloaked—even smothered—in layers of clothing, figuration and myth" so that "the body itself . . . titillates by its absence."[32] The clothing worn by these female figures swells not only with an elaborate design but with the elaborate curves and power of the body beneath the garment, so that the effect is not one of erasure, but of manifold (many-folds of) presence.

Comparisons between these paintings and Tennyson's poem are so easily drawn because one of the most important objectives of Pre-Raphaelite art was "truth to nature," which, in this case, would translate as representing the subject (or poem) as closely as possible. Although Meteyard champions the Pre-Raphaelite style, he neglects to adhere to the ideal of verisimilitude. In Meteyard's defense, he was never an "official" member of the Pre-Raphaelite Brotherhood; he painted his "Lady of Shalott" over thirty years after Rossetti's death. His subject matter, however, is definitely Pre-Raphaelite, and so is his depiction of mood. The fact that he takes liberty with Tennyson's poem only distinguishes him from those predecessors with whom he aligns himself.

Siddal's drawing is the least sensual of this group; Siddal represents the Lady's body as slight, without ornament, and lacking any curvature. Although the Lady's head is uncovered, the hair is pulled behind so that even this aspect of her femininity is withheld from sight. In fact, Siddal's *Lady of Shalott* closely resembles Hunt's drawing of her, except that no scarf accents her hips, and the sleeves of her high-necked gown are straight and without adornment. Whereas in Hunt's drawing the neckline of the Lady's gown falls to her shoulders, her neck is accented with a strand of beads or pearls, and the sleeves are drawn more elaborately. Siddal's refusal to sexualize the Lady, then, makes the Lady's glance toward Lancelot all the more curious since her body's attitude appears to resist desire. Moreover, the crucifix standing between her gaze and the window would interfere with this look, or at least temper it. Finally, the observer stands in an entirely different position within Siddal's picture than s/he does within Hunt's or Meteyard's work. In Siddal's drawing, the audience is obviously inside the tower room with the Lady; one can observe both the window (through which the curse enters) and the magic mirror (reflecting Lancelot's figure). In the works by Hunt and Meteyard, the audience is located outside the tower, gazing on the scene *through* the window which stands opposite the magic mirror, thus implicating the audience in the position of Lancelot. On the other hand, Siddal includes the audience in the Lady's experience; by rendering them more like participants than observers, Siddal places her audience in a feminine position rather than a masculine one. Siddal's drawing constitutes an act of resistance toward the poem and toward the art of her contemporaries that insistently enshrines and lingers over the female body.

According to Kristeva, paintings or drawings can loose (and lose) themselves from the constraints of narrative by *"pitting themselves* against the represented narrative . . . as well as against the very economy of symbolization (color form-representation). Thus, pictorial practice fulfills itself as freedom—a process of liberation *through and against the norm.*"[33] Kristeva would probably not consider Pre-Raphaelite paintings, with their emphasis on realism, as the kind of art that clashes against the Symbolic.[34] Yet those very characteristics of Pre-Raphaelite art that herald its imitation of reality also compromise this reality, through a jouissance that manifests through brilliant color, overly intricate (even ostentatious) designs of fabrics and architecture, and more particularly, through their voluptuous subjects and postures.[35]

William Holman Hunt's drawing, the most conscientious attempt at verisimilitude of the four works discussed, contends with the Symbolic: its elaborate and painstaking details compromise the very stability of the narrative from which his drawing derives. In order to represent the poem and its movement from past, present, to future, Hunt changed the Lady's action and hence the meaning of the poem itself. To do so he compromised the "reality" of his drawing by cluttering it with the various roundels and their scenes surrounding the mirror. Consequently, his drawing needs to be read as a narrative. Although, on the one hand, his attempts at verisimilitude are successful, they also represent failure, for they violate the very text he had hoped to represent.

Kristeva maintains that because of the factor of color "the language/painting analogy . . . becomes untenable."[36] Through an artist's use of color and what Kristeva calls "pictorial *space,*" a painter experiences that freedom from the narrative that is (and is not) the painting's subject. Meteyard's painting, more than any other considered here, indulges in color; the excessive presence of color constitutes this painting's meaning because it evokes a particular mood. Buckley writes that "a close analysis of moods—the peculiar heightening of individual impression and emotion")[37] constituted an important element and subject of Pre-Raphaelite art. Unlike Hunt, Waterhouse, and Rossetti, Meteyard does not care to render accurately Tennyson's poem. He invents the pillow, the crystal ball, the tapestry frame, and the great quantity of flowers. His particular concern seems to be with illustrating (or, through the figure of the Lady, embodying) one line of the poem: "'I am half-sick of shadows,' said

The Lady of Shalott." The shades of blue are essential to conveying the "feeling" of malaise. Meteyard focuses so much attention on color that it becomes the painting's main subject, connoting an atmosphere so rich and mysterious that even the Lady's body becomes subordinate to it.

These shades of blue are both oppressive and enigmatic. The gown she wears is a continuous blue, broken only by a purple belt tied at her waist. The profusion of blue emphasizes the languor of the Lady's body, and is echoed in various shades throughout the rest of the painting. The pillow she leans against is of a shade slightly darker than her gown, a shade intensified in the curtains behind her. Finally, the painter renders the face of the mirror—in which the Lady has ceased to gaze—in his deepest blue. The Lady clutches a cluster of dark blue threads in one hand, which she unconsciously draws out from the basket at her side.

Perhaps most unsettling is the tapestry's blue background, for it is embroidered with the same blue as the color of her gown. The tapestry frame is propped against her knee, and but for a shadow indicating where her lap ends and the frame begins, the color of the Lady's clothing flows right into the tapestry in one continuous motion. The Lady's body appears to be framed by the tapestry she embroiders, her body constituting the material on which these scenes of courtly life are inscribed, for her blue gown is of the same color as the tapestry's background. In addition, a mass of loose threads pinned onto the frame and waiting to be sewn flows down the embroidery and spills onto the Lady's lap, suggesting, symbolically, that the Lady and her work are not separate, but one and the same.

The identical color of the Lady's gown and the tapestry's background could represent, by analogy, not only the Lady's body but also the place where the pre-oedipal Mother exists, for the background marks a formless space, existing only in the atmosphere, the margins; it demarcates the Real that encompasses Camelot, sustaining but not comprising its existence. Meteyard's excessive use of the color blue indicates, metaphorically, an immoderate presence of semiotic material pulsing throughout the canvas, threatening even to swallow up the signified in the obvious enjoyment of abundance. This enjoyment is epitomized in the silken blue folds of material that reveal for the spectator the enticing contours of the Lady's body, but her body represents perhaps only the climax of blue that elsewhere distributes its own body across the canvas in a seemingly endless variety of shades. The color effaces its own subject and absolutely threatens the balance between subject and form.

Kristeva's theory of color provides insight into the effects of Meteyard's painting on the viewer. Based on research in visual perception, Kristeva's theory posits that colors are perceived by an infant before self-identification, but blue, having the shortest wave-lengths, constitutes the first perceived color. "Thus all colors, but blue in particular, would have a noncentered or decentering effect, lessening both object identification and phenomenal fixation. They thereby return the subject to the archaic moment of its dialectic, that is, before the fixed, specular 'I,' but while in the process of becoming this 'I' by breaking away from instinctual, biological (and also maternal) dependence."[38] In other words, blue represents the color of abjection, the place in which the infant realizes the presence of the mother as well as the presence of itself as separate from the mother; it is the color of melancholy, of loss, when the infant abjects its "instinctual, biological and maternal dependence"[39] in a bid for autonomy. The melancholic atmosphere surrounding Metayard's painting distinguishes it from the other Pre-Raphaelite efforts at accurately rendering details from Tennyson's poem. Meteyard's portrayal is one wherein mood or being prevails.

As indicated, Hunt's two pictures along with Siddal's and Meteyard's work, depict the Lady of Shalott at a moment in which her work is arrested, in which her body expresses either weariness (Meteyard), entanglement in fate (Hunt), or acquiescence to fate (Siddal). In all cases, the artists illustrate the moment when her body no longer belongs to her, but is imposed on and controlled by a power greater than her own will. By depicting the curse, these artists choose to render the moment of her helplessness, when she succumbs to forces or imperatives outside herself; they illustrate (perhaps with the exception of Siddal) the moment when the narrative shifts from the weaver at her loom to the weaver's body. By focusing on the Lady's failed autonomy, these paintings commemorate that moment in the narrative when her body acquiesces to the male gaze.

In the second half of the poem (when the curse is activated) and in the above referenced pictures, time, movement, action, and fate enter the hermetically sealed tower—its inner chamber. Weaving, then, becomes secondary or incidental to the poem and its representations. And yet, Tennyson's poem captured these artists' imagination because the Lady was a weaver, an artisan, a magician of sorts. The myriad colors of her tapestry as well as her song represent her exceptional art. By linking weaving and singing at the poem's outset, Tennyson presents us with a mythical subject whose industry also constitutes the presence of mētis—crafting plots, poetry, and spells.

The tapestry constitutes a "magic web" (1.39), and yet neither this textile nor the weaver are able to contain the curse. Mythic weavers are often depicted as agents creating spells or curses to cast on others, but Tennyson imagines his weaver otherwise. She is helpless before the curse that destroys both her and her beautiful tapestry. The torn warp and threads no longer signify a story but instead suggest artistic failure, uncompromising fate, and death. In both groups of illustrations, the artists portray that moment in the poem where the Lady's activity halts entirely and the poem's attention shifts to her body. Although this shift occurs at the end of the third section, more than halfway into the narrative, it is this moment the artists commemorate.

III

The fourth and final section of the poem comprises the subject of this next group of portraits in which the Lady carefully prepares her body for its final scene when the "Knight and burgher, lord and dame" (4.160) will leave their castle to gaze on her. John William Waterhouse and Dante Gabriel Rossetti portray the Lady of Shalott outside her tower, far away from her loom, gliding down the river to Camelot. Waterhouse illustrates the Lady sitting upright in the canoe, her eyes beginning to close as one of the three candles beside the crucifix, although still lit, is about to be extinguished by the wind. She rests on an elaborate cloth, which, we may presume, is the tapestry she had been weaving in her tower, for it is woven with "colors gay" (1.38). On one panel a scene illustrates the lines, "The knights come riding two and two" (1.61), while another shows a figure, perhaps the "abbot on an ambling pad" (1.56) riding beneath the towers of Camelot. Waterhouse portrays the Lady leaning forward "[l]ike some bold seer in a trance" (1.129) as she "loosed the chain" (1.133) to set the boat free; her unbound hair flows over her shoulders, her garments are gold and "snowy white" (1.136), and we can imagine that when she dies, the tapestry on which she now sits will become her shroud.

Both Waterhouse and Hunt situate the Lady of Shalott in the middle of her web: in Hunt's painting she stands inside the loom, caught in the threads, and in Waterhouse's version she is about to recline on this web and die within its meshes. The image of the spider spinning out her web has always been a metaphor for creativity (in both its positive and negative aspects); Asian-Indian myths often cast the spider in the role of "Maya, the eternal weaver of the web of

Dante Gabriel Rossetti, *The Lady of Shalott* (1858–59), Wood Engraving, 10″ × 8″, Illustration for Moxon's *Poems of Alfred Tennyson* (1859).

illusion."[40] In Tennyson's poem, as well as in its illustration by Hunt and Waterhouse, the weaver becomes caught in this "web of illusion" and is eventually destroyed by the illusion she had been weaving all along—an eerie reversal that presents the artist enmeshed in her own art, killing rather than sustaining her.[41]

Rossetti's drawing illustrates the last two stanzas of Tennyson's poem, and is the most enigmatic of all the portraits discussed. Here, the Lady of Shalott occupies the least amount of physical space in the picture, whereas those leaning over her boat to peer by torchlight upon her body are drawn full view, particularly Lancelot, who scrutinizes the curious cipher of her dead face.

Significantly, the Lady's face turned towards us reveals nothing but beauty and silence. Although a cloak shrouds the Lady's body, Rossetti places it under direct scrutiny from all sides, by four men gazing down from above, and by our gaze toward which her body is turned. Only her face is discernible, however; no other part is made visible. Rossetti suggests this bodily presence through the textured folds of her cloak and gown; below her hips, the cloak falls aside to reveal her dress, and within the gowns' creases appears the shape of a vulva. This uterine shape within the folds implicitly sexualizes the Lady's body. And yet her face invites prolonged contemplation. The energy and expectation focused on her face demands that it speak or reveal something about her presence here. Her eyes are closed, her lips are parted, and though she is compared to a visionary earlier in the poem, this sibyl cannot speak. Her presence, however, demands interpretation.

Although the reader of the poem would be aware of her past, Rossetti's drawing provides no clues that the Lady was a weaver. Even though it illustrates the Moxon edition of Tennyson's poems, the drawing's context is not evident. The onlooker would not necessarily be able to discern what poem it supposedly illustrates. Rossetti's drawing does not even incorporate the Lady's name that, according to the poem, she had written on the prow of her boat. The illustration refrains from linking her to a particular past, as if she had no existence before this moment when she floats into Camelot, to lie beneath the gaze of Lancelot. It as if the entire action of the poem before this moment were effaced.

The drawing seems to be a highly personalized, visual epithet, illustrating the relationship not only between Lancelot and the Lady of Shalott, but between Rossetti and Siddal. Certainly, the faces are those of the artist and his favorite model. The drawing constitutes a visual narrative of their relationship. It documents Rossetti's gaze, and Siddal's acquiescence to it—her posing and his immortalization of her face by obsessively painting it. Interestingly, Rossetti draws the Lady's face so that it turns away from Lancelot (Rossetti's self-representation) in deference to the artist's gaze.

The intensity of looking and gazing that Tennyson describes in his poem and that Rossetti illustrates so well demands an interpretation that Lancelot's epitaph simply does not provide: "'She has a lovely face; / God in his mercy lend her grace, / The Lady of Shalott'" (4.169–71). Since "God" and "mercy" have not entered the poem

William Holman Hunt (c. 1886–1905), oil on canvas, 74 × 57 in. WADSWORTH ATHENEUM, HARTFORD. The Ella Gallup Sumner and Mary Catlin Sumner Collection Fund.

Sidney Harold Meteyard, *"I am half sick of shadows," said the Lady of Shalott* (1913), The Pre-Raphaelite Trust, Paris.

John William Waterhouse, *The Lady of Shalott* (c. 1888). Oil on canvas, 60¼ × 78¾ in. The Tate Gallery, London.

until this point, to introduce them here seems irrelevant. Looking at both Lancelot and the Lady, we confront a feeling not of cursory blessing but of romantic haunting.

The Lady's curse is not, simply, that she dies, but that she must stop weaving, stop signifying; it forces a suspension of the artistic function. Although her death prevents her from sexual intimacy and relationship, on the other hand—because her relationship with Lancelot remains unconsummated—it also represents an ideal relationship and the highest form of Romantic love. In keeping with the Romantic tradition, Rossetti represents Lancelot gazing lovingly and longingly at the pale and silent face of the Lady of Shalott. Whatever feelings her beauty evokes in him, they will always remain idealized because her ability to act, move, live, speak, or change has been arrested; therefore, she is incapable of altering his feelings for her. Her dead face symbolizes what Eric Newton called "the romanticism of mystery"; such impassioned worship comprises "the essence of Tennyson's *Idylls of the King* . . . the ardent pursuit of a dream."[42]

After she dies, the Lady's body floats into Camelot. Typically, she enters into this public, albeit fabled, realm at night, a time, according to Newton, when "imagination is awakened."[43] The Lady's presence in Camelot constitutes a two-fold sign that both inspires and warns. On one hand, her silent, beautiful face represents the goal of the Romantic quest: its silence indicates that the goal has not been achieved; its beauty suggests that the quest is worthy of continuing. On the other hand, though her face represents the ideal that has inspired all activity in Arthur's court, her dead body suggests that such quests end in death, both for those who seek and for those who are sought. Although the presence of the Lady's body indicates that unearthly beauty and poetic (or artistic) inspiration do exist in the domain of Camelot, the fact that the body is hidden from us (and that she is dead) suggests the elusive nature of these qualities. Finally, the Lady's beautiful but dead face would imply that to find beauty of this kind is to kill it at the same time. Her dead body represents the art object itself.

By contrasting the two very different worlds of Camelot and the Isle of Shalott, the poem suggests that these two worlds cannot converge. Although these spheres appear to exist in terms of each other, they can only be mediated by a "third term." The Lady has access to Camelot only through the mediation of the mirror, whereas Camelot can approach the Lady only through the mediation of her song. The Lady's corpse incites fear in the citizens of Camelot as well as a sense of impending doom, for it is through her corpse that these two worlds meet.[44]

Who is this? and what is here?
And in the lighted palace near
Died the sound of royal cheer;
And they cross'd themselves for fear,
All the knights at Camelot

(2.163–67)

She constitutes a sign that signals an ending. Her tapestry has miscarried; her life is cut short. Whatever her purpose may have been prior to the curse, the moment the curse is set into action, she embodies it and passes it on to Camelot. Neither the Lady nor the citizens know the nature of this curse (the Lady "knows not what the curse may be" [1.41]), but those in Camelot are frightened and confused by her presence there. She was only a myth while she was alive, but with her death she becomes real. And yet because she has died, her very corporeality endows her with more mystery than when she had been alive.

Kristeva's theories may offer insight into the relationship between the Isle of Shalott and Camelot, two separate spheres that converge when the Lady's corpse drifts into Camelot. Kristeva's theory of signification constructs itself on the relationship between two realms, the semiotic and the Symbolic. Both realms establish themselves through the expulsion of the maternal body. The return of the (M)Other (conveyed, metaphorically, through the Lady of Shalott's body) to the Symbolic would indicate rupture, psychosis, and madness. When the Lady enters Camelot in her sloop, she enters as a sign from the unconscious, "disruptive of the symbolic, as death is disruptive of life."[45] Her presence interrupts the "sound of royal cheer" (1.165) that has been resounding throughout Camelot, and arrests the activity of the court. Prior to this scene, her body was sequestered in a tower (or phallus) that represented, perhaps, her presence as the Phallic Mother (see chapter 2).

Note that her existence could only be verified by hearing the sound or music of her voice—not its words, or signified, but its *sound;* one way in which the pre-oedipal child experiences the mother is through the vocalizations of her body and her throat. Kristeva distinguishes music that avoids "overloading sequences with narrative" and whose logic constitutes a "permanent awakening in the very drift of syllables" as lying "within the domain of the Phallic Mother."[46] The subject registers this kind of "sound," according to Kaja Silverman, as a "maternal voice fantasy."[47] This fantasy always constitutes a moment of desire as well as a recognition of loss; by hearing the "maternal voice," the subject (in this case, either the reapers in the fields hearing the Lady, or the Lady hearing the song of Lancelot), imagines the primal mother-infant dyad.[48]

As Lancelot unwittingly passes by her tower, his singing absorbs this quality, and words become the light and enchantingly rhythmic "'Tirra lirra,'" wherein signification drops in preference for a *jouissance,* always indicating the presence of the semiotic. If the Lady of Shalott, indeed, represents the Phallic Mother, then her death would acquire a new meaning, for with it she pays the tribute necessary to enter Camelot—wherein the Law of the Father resides. The tension and dependence between these two realms illustrate Jacques Derrida's idea of *différance,* "as the displaced and equivocal passage of one different thing to another."[49] So that as long as the realm of Camelot and the Isle of Shalott remain linked but separate, each will "appear as the *différance* of the other, as the other different and deferred in the economy of the same."[50] But once the Lady of Shalott looks out her window to an actual, unmediated Camelot, and similarly once her body enters unmediated into Camelot, the equilibrium between these two realms ruptures. This process of mediation by both spheres could be called unravelling "the double-bind between completely inhabiting the Symbolic—and thereby taking up a rigid unified subject position—and refusing the Symbolic—and thereby inhabiting psychosis."[51] The (M)Other can only exist in terms of Camelot but not within its walls. She must exist, however; otherwise Camelot as the Symbolic would have no terrain, no space on which to establish its foundation, for the Law of the Father organizes itself on the outcast body of the Mother.

Consequently, the Lady of Shalott signifies two different possibilities: as an "actual" autonomous being, she weaves on the margins of the Symbolic, producing a tapestry that constitutes a metaphor for the semiotic, or more particularly, for the maternal body. On the other hand, the Lady of Shalott represents, metaphorically, this abjected maternal body, who, mediated by the mirror of representation, weaves a tapestry—constituting the thetic position—that is woven on one side with representations of Camelot, and on the other side (the side on which the Lady sits) with the semiotic material of loose, undifferentiated colors and threads.

Ironically, as Lancelot casts his gaze toward her little boat drifting past, this bearer of the Name-of-the-Father refuses to confront her as anything but a body, consigning her soul to the great Father of Camelot who is "God." She has traveled from the unconscious realm, outside the boundaries of Camelot, on the stream of the unconscious, to the highly conscious world of Camelot. No one can interpret her presence correctly, least of all Lancelot (although unlike the others he is not afraid of her, merely curious), for the symbolic of Camelot cannot have direct access to the pre-Symbolic from whence the Lady comes; in Camelot, she immediately enters the Symbolic either as a disembodied voice or a disembodied "face" (1.169).

Furthermore, if the Lady of Shalott no longer lives, if she can no longer weave the "Shadows of the world" (1.48) from the unconscious realm in which she abides, will Camelot continue to exist? Perhaps her art, woven from the reflection of her mirror images of the life of Camelot, sustains that world. Perhaps she is a necessary counterpart to the psychological stability of this society. For, as I have suggested, language itself consists of the precarious balance between the unconscious and conscious realms; this balance—which prevents the two realms from collapsing—is negotiated by the thetic.[52] Instead, in this poem and its pictorial representations, the thetic would be represented by the tower in which she is immured, the tapestry she weaves on her loom, as well as the "mirror clear" (2.46) from which she gathers information about the world in Camelot.[53] Gazing directly through the window onto this world, rather than through the mirror of representation, she confronts her own expulsion from this world, and therefore her own death. Her presence in Camelot signifies that a rupture between the two worlds or two realms, between the conscious and unconscious, has occurred. Essentially, her presence indicates that Camelot, too, will end.

The only way that the Lady could enter into Camelot alive was through the mediation of her song. The reapers overheard her singing in the early morning and late evening; like her corpse, her music enters Camelot during that familiar time in Romantic settings when "nothing is completely revealed."[54] Her voice constitutes the only evidence of her existence for the people of Camelot. And as she floats down the river to Camelot, she is heard "[s]inging her last song" (4.152), as she died, so that her presence as well as her departure are registered or inscribed through song. Moreover, it is the sound of Sir Lancelot's voice singing "'Tirra lirra' " as he "flash'd into the crystal mirror" (3.107) that confirms his presence to the Lady of Shalott. What makes these scenes significant is that her voice is heard. Even Lancelot's words seem trivial to the conscious mind; they are meaningless, nonsensical, and gratuitous in that they revel merely in sound.

Sir Lancelot's singing, and presumably that of the Lady of Shalott, enact what Kristeva would call a "'fundamental language' that is quite simply rhythm."[55] Kristeva describes the musical quality of language, the "'tirra lirra' " of language, as that which

> asks for nothing—no deciphering, at any rate, no commentaries, no philosophical, theoretical, or political complement that might have been left in abeyance, unseen and forgotten. . . . It whisks you from your comfortable position; it breathes a gust of dizziness into you, but lucidity returns at once, along with music, and you can watch your opacity being dissolved—into sounds.[56]

This quality in Lancelot's song is precisely what beckons the Lady of Shalott from her loom to the window. Whereas Lancelot's presence represents a sign from the Symbolic, once he enters the realm of Shalott, his song absorbs the same semiotic qualities that she weaves into her tapestry. Ironically, instead of injuring Lancelot with her own voice (like Alastor's maid or Keats's La Belle Dame Sans Merci), he, as bearer of the Law of the Father, wounds her. The presence of the semiotic in Lancelot's song unleashes the curse, inaugurating that moment when all conscious signification represented by the mirror becomes overcharged with semiotic drives so murderous that the Lady of Shalott cannot withstand them, so that her tapestry-as-metaphor for the semiotic becomes overcharged, and thus annihilates the tapestry-as-thetic threshold. "For what you take to be a shattering of language is really a shattering of the body" says Kristeva.[57] The "'Tirra lirra'" of Lancelot's song comprises the tear in the signified, the crack in the mirror, and the entrance of death.

Although Lancelot seems to dispense this semiotic overload, the poem itself indicates—in its elaborate description of his image in the mirror—that Lancelot provides a catalyst for the Lady's repressed desire (which Tennyson earlier suggests in her lament "'I am half-sick of shadows'"). He embodies the desire already existing within her psyche. This surplus of energy is represented in Hunt's painting and Siddal's drawing by the suggestion that a great wind has entered her tower chamber; in Hunt's painting the Lady's hair is blown across the canvas, and in Siddal's illustration the foliage on the trees beside her window enter through the casement, a door on her work table is blown open, a bird perched on her loom leans forward in struggle against this wind, and the tapestry's warp is blown off the frame.

The Lady's silence conveys the most meaning in the poem; this silence indicates, through the beautiful lineaments of her body, presence as well as absence. Elaine Scarry, in her introduction to *Literature and the Body: Essays on Populations and Persons,* confronts the very idea of what she calls "the 'materiality' of language" that is often "portrayed by directly tying language to the body itself."[58] In this poem and more particularly in Rossetti's drawing, the figure of the dead Lady embodies the absence of language, but this absence signifies loudly and itself constitutes a sign, a cipher, the meaning of which cannot be articulated by language but which desires interpretation nevertheless. Kristeva calls this a *lapsus lingua* or "slips over the signified," carrying with it an excessive amount of drive or semiotic material; in this poem, the presence of the semiotic registers through the silence with which the people greet her body: "And in the lighted palace near / Died the sound of royal cheer" (4.164–65), as well as in the fear her body inspires: "And they cross'd themselves for fear, / All the knights at Camelot" (4.166–67).

Curiously, these paintings and drawings emphasize those moments when she ceases to act but is acted on by outside forces. If pictured within the tower, she is either entangled in her own threads or leaning away from her work; when portrayed outside her tower, she is either about to die or dead already. Each of these drawings and paintings suggest that her curse is not death, but a demand that she cease working at her magical web, that she leave aside the creative life she has heretofore enjoyed, and that her work —her text or textile— will never be seen by the world because it unravels before its completion. The curse does not necessitate her death, but like Cuchulain, who chooses his death after he realizes all his geasa are broken, she resolves to die.

By illustrating the lady's death or her curse, these artists seem to identify with the Lady of Shalott's predicament by expressing their own fears regarding the nature of art: its fragile quality, the artist's tendency toward antisocial behavior, the problem of reaching an audience, and the anxiety of adequately imitating (or completing the imitation of) the vision; this latter concern is particularly fitting for a Pre-Raphaelite artist who had spent time and energy painting realistic details.

On the other hand, these artists also disassociate themselves from the Lady by overtly sexualizing her in their paintings.[59] Meteyard's constitutes the most excessively erotic work, but Hunt's also expresses *jouissance* of the Lady's body, particularly through the luxurious folds of her scarlet skirt drawn up over the white slip. Consequently, both Waterhouse and Rossetti become fascinated at how her body can represent an economy of death: Waterhouse portrays her "singing" before she dies, whereas Rossetti's illustration resonates with the silence surrounding the Lady's dead face. Although these artists may have originally identified with the Lady's position as artist, once they began to illustrate her, they seem unable to escape both their own history (as male painters) as well as the history of art that fosters representations of the female body as containers for (male) desire. Even in Velázquez's realistic painting of the portrayal of women's work, *The Weavers,* the weaving scene is withheld (located obscurely in the background), and those women who are engaged in work (the carding and spinning of wool) are represented to us in attitudes that focus our gaze on their bodies and not on their work.

If the pictures examined here had instead focused on the creative scene, they would merely reflect back to the artists their own scene of labor. Those pictures that depict the curse, however, illustrate the actual moment in which she loses possession of the phallus, the *moment of castration.*

According to this study, the Lady of Shalott constitutes an enigma primarily because she represents so many different things: the (male) artist, the desirous female body, and the phallic (pre-oedipal) mother. In all cases, however, these pictures represent her castration, and so illustrate, as well, the artist's fear of "lack." With the exception of Siddal, these artists represent her body as a male fantasy of desire; at the same time, because she is either depicted ensnared in a curse or at the moment of death, they posit this desire in terms of its inaccessibility. Even when her body arrives in Camelot, the citizens have no clue what to do with it; Lancelot assumes the role of "Master of Cememonies," and acknowledges her "presence"—"She has a lovely face" (1.169)—and then deftly consigns the rest to God. Presumably, her little boat continues to drift down the river, past the world of romance and desire, the "tower and balcony" of Camelot.

6

Uniquely Feminine Productions

The wheel of ecstatic love
turns around in the sky,
and the spinning seat is made
of the sapphires
of work and study.
This woman weaves threads
that are subtle,
and the intensity of her praise
makes them fine.
Kabir says, I am that woman.
I am weaving the linen
of night and day.

—Kabir, *The Kabir Book*

WEAVING THE WORD CONCERNS THE RECOVERY OF A LOST TRADITION, weaving, and its relationship to textual practices. Although we tend to regard literary history and textile history as separate disciplines, my intention in this study has been to reestablish the link between them, particularly since they each contribute significantly to the organization and evolution of culture through the transmission of knowledge.

In many of the tales I've focused on in this study, women manufacture at their looms stories as well as garments signifying their personal and societal repression. I have suggested that some of these artists were particularly effective in communicating their condition to those around them because of their "handling" of the semiotic: "[T]he artist," Kristeva remarks, "introduces into the symbolic order an asocial drive" that seeks to alter or transform the societal realm.[1] Arachne, Philomela, and the Emanations express "impermissible" tales (or in the case of the Emanations, impermissible bodies) in an appeal for change. Their textiles/texts—representations of revolution—convey the asocial/semiotic drive into the symbolic arena at the cost of their own destruction.

This kind of weaving is analogous to what Elizabeth Meese terms the foremost problem for women writers who try to express themselves within language; their weaving represents a kind of writing that "constitutes a challenge to the boundaries of difference, writing that consciously attempts to traverse the limitations erected by phallocentric discourse."[2] Although their textiles/texts fail to effect change within the limitations of their personal histories, the fact that these stories exist affirms the possibility (and necessity) of change within the social realm and its discourse.

Self-expression exists at the heart of all these weavers' stories: The Lady of Shalott creates the myth of Camelot at her loom; Helen textualizes the war that Homer will eventually tell; Enion voices her vexation with Tharmas by weaving the body of the Spectre; Arachne's tapestry expresses her dissatisfaction with Olympian prerogative; Penelope weaves and unravels skeins and skeins of thread in an effort to write her own story against the one already written for her (the social imperative requiring she remarry); whereas Philomela's tapestry communicates her tale and reveals the exact location of her imprisonment. Each of these stories demonstrates how weaving represents a revolutionary signifying practice. As women, these weavers constitute the suppressed subjects of their society, and are doubly so when weaving from a "place" of suppression—Philomela's hut, the tower of Shalott, or Penelope's chamber. These artists often *express* the very qualities of repression (via the semiotic) within the symbolic elements of their design.

Each of these weavers is an artist, and as artists the ultimate product of their labor is themselves. On their loom they weave their own destiny in the realm of time. Time is their enemy as well as their ally; as long as they are weaving, they are involved in the realm of possibility, crafting their lives, creating a world. But once their weaving is completed, they must submit to the text they have created. Hence, each weaver shifts out of the position of a Creator to become created by her own text or world. Interestingly, the definition of a creator is "one who creates out of nothing." Likewise, these weavers create something out of undifferentiated fibers and threads, and engage in an active (rather than submissive) life by assuming the position of a Creator only to end up relinquishing their will and allowing themselves "to be created" by the very text they have woven.

The weavers here compare to the Greek Moirai or Fates. Like the Fates, they weave and determine destinies, not for others, but for themselves. As long as they are weaving, they can still negotiate with fate, but once the weaving is complete, their destiny is sealed. Interestingly, the Fates are represented by three women: Klotho, the youngest, spins the thread of a person's life; Lachesis, a middle-aged woman, measures the thread. Finally, Atropos, a crone, cuts the thread with her shears. These women depict three stages of life, and together they represent a complete perspective of human experience. They also represent how something as imperceptible as an idea can take a form (or body) and manifest in the world.

Klotho's energetic spinning symbolizes the creative process; she spins the thread of thought that constitutes the very material out of which our lives are created. Like Penelope's weaving and unravelling, Klotho's spinning is a reminder that the future is determined by how we engage in the present. The next fate is the matron, Lachesis, who measures and delineates the length or lot of a person's life and destiny. She sees the pattern that has emerged. Her vision is broader than Klotho's, but more limited than Klotho in that the destiny has already been determined. The story of Arachne illustrates this aspect of fate; once Arachne completes her tapestry, she has committed to its message and intent. She can admire her work, but she can alter it no longer. Interestingly, *fate* means "that which has been spoken" or "that which can not be recalled." Both Arachne and Penelope's tapestry, like a woven fate, snare the weavers in their own web. In these stories, fate expresses not only what "has been spoken," but also what "has been woven."

Finally, Atropos, the crone, symbolizes an end, which most often is interpreted as a death. With her shears she divides the product from process and separates the creation from its creator. Atropos is a positive figure in that she liberates the creator from her successes as well as her failures. Hence, for Enion and Enitharmon, Atropos signifies release, the ability to move on and beyond the past, to create anew.

For these weavers, the loom can be viewed as a symbol for harnessed, focused attention. By concentrating on the present, these weavers influence the future and thereby shape and determine their own destinies. Philosopher Jacob Needleman calls this kind of freedom "the choice to be aware of the life you're living and the self that's living it."[3] Although these women are cast as second-class citizens and servants to and within their patriarchal societies, when weaving at the loom, they come in full command of their own lives. And even though the only overt action they take is to sit faithfully and quietly in one spot every day and throw the shuttle of their attention back and forth across the loom of their mind, this action powerfully affects those with whom they associate.

How, then, can weaving represent a revolutionary activity? As Sir Phillip Sidney has said, "Truly a needle [or shuttle] cannot do much hurt, and as truly . . . it cannot do much good. With a sword thou mayest kill thy father, and with a sword thou mayest defend thy prince and country."[4] Certainly, Penelope's weaving—like a weapon—defended her own king, Odysseus, and the fate of her country, Ithaka. Philomela's weaving, too, constituted an outcry against Thrace and a fierce Athenian revenge.

Throughout this book we have regarded the energy unleashed by these tapestries and their texts as embodying a semiotic overload. Yet another way of understanding how weaving endows textiles and their texts with such power is to examine the connection these textiles have with their creators. What these female weavers demonstrate is the power that exists when engaging attentively to one's work. In Africa, the term *mana* defines the power of transformation that occurs when performing daily work. "Energy is directed and flows toward and into the material" at hand.[5] This work can be as simple as pouring sugar into a bowl, dabbing paint on a canvas, smoothing a wrinkle from a jacket, dropping a seed into a hole. *Mana* infuses that sugar or canvas, that jacket or seed. It becomes energized by human attention. *Mana* occurs when there is a belief that "creation is an interaction between the creator and the medium, a oneness between the two."[6] This is another way of describing why and how the textiles woven by these weavers seem to act out the weaver's own will, even when that will becomes destructive to the weaver herself so that the textiles function not only as texts but as independent bodies as well.

Those weavers who seek to initiate change by weaving this "forbidden" discourse are usually scapegoated by their society. We see this even in the case of Helen of Troy and the Lady of Shalott, whose weaving, unlike Arachne's and Philomela's, serves the Symbolic (Helen's creates a representation of Homer's epic poem, and the Lady of Shalott's either mirrors or produces Camelot.) The Lady of Shalott is sacrificed to Camelot, whereas Helen of Troy is scapegoated by the poem.[7]

Helen's scapegoating occurs not because she weaves a forbidden representation, but because she has initiated the scene that she herself weaves. This battle scene illustrates, symbolically, the devastating effects of the death drive—the dominant drive activating the semiotic chora. According to Kristeva, the release of the death drive into the sphere constitutes, perhaps, the artist's most significant "role." When Homer depicts Helen busy at her womanly art, he radically contrasts this image of the demure, feminine weaver with the scene of death and destruction that she weaves (as well as the one Homer describes happening concurrently outside the walls of Troy). Kristeva remarks that art distinguishes itself by introducing the death drive—what she calls "murder"—into the Symbolic:

> opposite religion or alongside it, "art" takes on murder and moves through it. It assumes murder insofar as artistic practice considers death

> the inner boundary of the signifying process. Crossing that boundary is precisely what constitutes "art." In other words, it is as if death becomes interiorized by the subject of such a practice; in order to function, he must make himself the bearer of death. In this sense, the artist is comparable to all other figures of the "scapegoat." But he is not just a scapegoat; in fact, what makes him an artist radically distinguishes him from all other sacrificial murders and victims.[8]

Arachne and Philomela likewise design tapestries that "bear death," literally, to themselves and those around them. Arachne is victimized when Athena administers social and divine punishment by transforming her into a spider. Philomela's tapestry, which constitutes a metaphor of the semiotic chora, "weaves" or implicates both Procne and Philomela into its design; the sisters embody this drive, and so convey its destructive message to those around them. They, too, are punished by the gods, who turn them into birds; their feathers are brushed with (symbolic) stains of blood, and their species will be "forever" pursued by Tereus, the hoopoe.

Significantly, Helen of Troy and the Lady of Shalott are absent from the scenes they weave; their bodies exist elsewhere. Helen declines to weave herself in the storytelling cloth, even though she is both the author of the cloth and of the story it depicts. The Lady of Shalott cannot weave herself into her tapestry of Camelot, for she does not reside in that realm except as a "possibility," as *"hearsay"* (she is called a fairy, has never been seen, and only "exists" because some farmers attest to hearing her sing).

These two weavers, in particular, represent the spectral fantasy of the pre-oedipal mother, whose absent body initiates loss and, therefore, all categories of signification. The societies in which both weavers exist require that each "remain perpetually out of reach in order for . . . [society] to speculate forever on how to reach her, or to replace her with [its] own abstractions."[9] The tapestries they weave, ironically, symbolize their absence; the textiles constitute a metaphor for their bodies that the scenes woven into their designs fail to represent.

Whereas I have posited the relationship between women, weaving, and writing, Rozsika Parker has traced the "notions of femininity" through the representations of women embroidering. All aspects of textile manufacture—embroidery, weaving, and sewing—have at one time or another constituted female activity, and therefore, embodied notions of femininity. Parker's remarks about the relationship between textile work and a doctrine of femininity has particular bearing to this study. She states: "[T]he conviction that femininity is natural to women is a crucial aspect of patriarchal ideology."[10] The weaving stories I have examined exemplify the tension between notions of femininity and masculinity.

Whereas society sanctions their use of the loom, these women convert its original function into a tool for rebelling against their society (signifying male aggression); yet, simultaneously, by operating the loom, they maintain their essentially feminine identities. Parker suggests that "[t]he development of an ideology of femininity coincided historically with the emergence of a clearly defined separation of art and craft."[11] And although Parker believes this specific distinction to have occurred during the European Renaissance, notions of difference between male and female activities began much earlier.

The stories I have examined are embedded in this ideology of difference. These weavers transgress the boundaries and limitations placed on (female) "craft" by invading the realm of (male) art and signification. Their textiles express both masculine and feminine qualities because they embody forms of masculine discourse and still retain their signs as uniquely feminine productions.

Notes

Introduction

1. An old French poem by Chretien de Troyes, *Yvain, the Knight of the Lion,* 155–60, translated by Burton Raffel (New Haven and London: Yale University Press, 1987), portrays a scene wherein a knight stumbles on three hundred noblewomen who had been sent by their king to pay for his ransom. Held against their will and living in poverty, they weave silk cloth, lamenting to the knight, Yvain:

> None of us will ever leave.
> We'll spend our days weaving
> Silk, and wearing rags.
> We'll spend our days poor
> And naked and hungry and thirsty,
> For they'll never pay us what we earn
> . . . .
> We work most nights, and we work
> All day, just to stay alive,
> For they threaten to cut off our arms
> And legs if we rest. No one
> Dares to rest.

A universal lament, we find it also expressed in Chinese with a poem by Tung Hung-to, "Complaint of the Weaving Wife" translated by Elvin; see Penelope Drooker's article, "Silk: the Story of a Culture," in *Handwoven* (January/February 1986), 51:

> Hungry, she still weaves.
> Numbed with cold, she still weaves.
> Shuttle after shuttle after shuttle.
> The days are short,
> The weather chill,
> Each length hard to finish.
> The rich take their rent;
> The clerk the land tax,
> Knocking repeatedly urgent insistence.
> Her husband wants to urge her on,
> But has no heart to do so.
> He says nothing,
> But stands beside the loom.
> The more she tries to get it done
> The more her strength fails her.
> She turns away, choking down her tears,
> And consoles herself that their neighbors

Are poorer and lonelier
For they sold their loom
And next had to sell their son.

2. Adele Coulin Weibel, in *Two Thousand Years of Textiles* (New York: Pantheon, 1952); Dr. P. Quensel, A Vetterli, S. Napier, "Textiles in Biblical Times," in *The Figured Textiles of Europe and the Near East;* Madeleine Ginsburg, *The Illustrated History of Textiles* (New York: Portland House, 1991); Frederick J. Dockstader, *Weaving Arts of the North American Indian* (Thomas Y. Cromwell, 1978); John Becker, *Pattern and Loom* (Copenhagen: Rhodos International Publishers, 1987); Agnes Geijer, *A History of Textile Art* (London: Sotheby Parke Bernet, 1979); Veronika Gevers, *Studies in Textile History* (Toronto, Canada: Royal Ontario Museum, 1977); Francis Paul Thomson, *Tapestry: Mirror of History* (New York: Crown Publishers, Inc., 1980).

3. See Elizabeth Wayland Barber, *Women's Work. The First 20,000 Years: Women, Cloth, and Society in Early Times,* (New York and London: W. W. Norton & Company, 1994), 148.

4. Clothing and cloth have their distinct histories: researchers will examine the relationship between clothing, fashion, and costume in terms of the human body, whereas they will examine cloth, most often, in connection with a society's history and economics of production. Because I am primarily concerned with the text of cloth—whether this text is worn on the body, hung on a wall, or flown like a flag—I will occasionally conflate clothing with cloth, but only in reference to its textual performance and not in terms of that text's relationship to the human body.

5. On this, see Barber, *Women's Work,* 147 n. 1. She claims that writing was invented "not long after the wheel . . . and even then the script was so complicated that only a very few—and highly privileged—individuals could read" (149).

6. Men have occasionally been involved in textile manufacture in the ancient worlds. For example, "[t]he male-operated vertical loom . . . was introduced into Egypt around 1500 B.C.E. By that time, however, Egyptian women and women—only—had already been weaving linen on horizontal looms for fully three thousand years" (Barber 180). By the sixteenth century C.E., weaving had become a male vocation in most parts of Europe, gradually eliminating women's involvement in textile work except in subordinate activities such as carding and spinning. This would continue for another three hundred years. (Three hundred years of weaving dominated by men cannot compare to over seven thousand years of history when weaving was almost exclusively a female practice.)

7. See Rita Felski, *Beyond Feminist Aesthetics: Feminist Literature and Social Change* (Cambridge, Mass.: Harvard University Press, 1989), 19.

8. The Navajo Indian culture furnishes an example of how important textile production is to the sustenance of the tribe, not only economically but spiritually. Whereas women, traditionally, weave the textiles in this society, in the Hopi and Pueblo nations men perform the weaving. Frederick Dockstader suggests that the Hopi male took over the production of cloth because of the intimate relationship between weaving and the sacredness of those symbols woven for the tribe's spiritual rites and rituals. According to anthropologist and writer Mark Bahti (phone interview, Tucson, Arizona; 19 June 1997 at 3:30 P.M.): "Men wove and weave in the Pueblo tribe, and there was or is a house especially for weaving that the women are not allowed in. They kept their weaving practices private and separate. They wove with cotton, because they grew it. Theirs is an embroidery technique, where the woven material functions like a canvas and patterns are embroidered on it. The loom poles are sunk into the ground and the word used for weaving is the same word for growing as in growing agricultural products; a textile grows like a plant out of the ground. This is for the Pueblo/Hopi tribes."

9. A brief history of how England's textile policies influenced large parts of the world demonstrates the importance of textiles and their manufacture throughout human history. Because of England's constant demand for raw fibers—whether flax, wool or cotton—Britain had to seek new land for the production of raw materials to feed its country's looms. The colonizing of India and the American colonies are prime examples. England wanted the American colonies to produce raw materials like hemp and flax. It did not want the colonists to compete with England's textile manufacturing.

So, by forbidding and eventually outlawing the colonists to weave their own textiles, England hoped to ensure the livelihood of English weavers. The Monarchy prevented any looms or loom parts as well as plans for their manufacture to enter the colonies (although some were eventually smuggled in). Instead, the colonists were expected to produce raw materials, spin this fiber and then ship it to England where it was woven into cloth and then sold back to the colonists at inflated prices.

The devastation this policy brought to India is even more telling. India, a country whose textile industry was renowned even before the Roman Empire and certainly long before England existed, became impoverished within a few decades.

For an excellent essay on the English domination of India, see Pico Iyer's essay "The East India Company: Oxbridge-on-the-Hooghly" in *Tropical Classical* (New York: Alfred A. Knopf, 1997), 48–61. According to Iyer's research, the East India Company, originally a group of merchants who received the blessings of Queen Elizabeth I in December of 1599, began a slow and (at its outset) unconscious takeover of India. At first the Company set up trading posts. Eventually, these posts needed defending from local marauders as well as the French who were competing with England for trade, so each post organized its own militia. Because of East India's financial success, England increased its control by the late eighteenth century, as well as becoming a more conspicuous (and threatening) presence in the country. By the time India gained independence in 1947, the social and geographical landscape of the country had changed inexorably. No longer could India depend on the exportation of its textiles that centuries before had guaranteed its economic autonomy. Even the Indian landscape had been altered. The teeming cities of Calcutta, Madras, and Bombay, for instance, had originated from early trading posts of the East India Company, where nothing before had existed.

Both the American colonies and India resisted English domination by undermining the sanctions against weaving textiles as well as through the language of cloth. In her anecdotal collection, *Spin Span Spun: Fact & Folklore for Spinners and Weavers* (Berkley, CA: Wholesale Distributors, 1979), Bette Hochberg writes that the graduating class of Harvard University, 1768, "appeared in handspun and locally woven suits" and in the same year "George Washington commanded his militia to wear homespun uniforms" (36). Similarly, in India, Gandhi sought to restore his country's autonomy by encouraging hand-spinning and weaving among India's poor. In this way, the Indian people would not be reliant on England's textiles. Although this was an ideal that could not be achieved, India nevertheless won its independence, and the spinning wheel abides as a unifying symbol on its flag. Also, see Mahatma Ghandi's book, *Khadi (Hand Spun Cloth) Why and How.*

10. See Barber, *Women's Work,* 163.

11. See John Lechte, *Julia Kristeva* (New York: Routledge, 1990), 123. Emphasis mine.

Chapter 1. Myth, History, and the Material World

1. Sigmund Freud, "Femininity," in *New Introductory Lectures on Psychoanalysis* (New York: W.W. Norton, 1961), 164.

2. I am not concerned, like Sigmund Freud, in whether men or women first invented weaving. Yet I find it interesting that in many different mythologies the invention of weaving was attributed to a female deity (16–19). Freud maintains that if women did invent weaving, then "we should be tempted to guess the unconscious motive for the achievement. Nature herself would seem to have given the model which this achievement imitates by causing the growth at maturity of the pubic hair that conceals the genitals. The step that remained to be taken lay in making the threads adhere to one another, while on the body they stick into the skin and are only matted together. If you reject this idea as fantastic and regard my belief in the influence of lack of a penis on the configuration of femininity as an idee fixe, I am of course defenseless" ("Femininity," 164).

3. Until recently, anthropologists maintained that the date for the "oldest hand-spun weaving fragment" was a little more than 8,000 years old. Bette Hochberg writes, "Any spinner or weaver examining the fragment would recognize the high level of workmanship" (*Spin, Span, Spun,* 13). Also, see Barber's anthropological study, *Women's Work,* for a superb exegesis on weaving in the ancient worlds.

4. See Brenda Fowler, "Find in Europe Suggests that Weaving Preceeded Settled Life," in *The New York Times* (Tuesday, 9 May 1995), C1, C10. She writes, "Pre-historians had underestimated the importance of woven materials in early peoples' lives. Conversely . . . because of their relative abundance, stone tools have been overemphasized in archaeologists' interpretations of prehistoric economies." Also, see Barber's *Women's Work* regarding her thoughts on the invention of writing, pp 147 n. 1 149–50.

5. John Hyslop, *Natural History* (February 1989), reprinted in *Handwoven* (November/December, 1989): 104–5.

6. See Page du Bois, *Sowing the Body,* 3.

7. Nancy Miller, in her work *Subject to Change: Reading Feminist Writing* (New York: Columbia University Press, 1988), writes about this relationship between weaving and female textual practices, saying that she appropriates "as possible tropes of feminist literary agency examples from antiquity of women's weaving" (77). Her interest lies not "so much in weaving, however, as in the representation of writing as instances of a textuality hopelessly entangled with question of its material. Weaving, in that sense, provided me with an irresistible metaphorics: it allowed me to figure a writing identity as grounded and located in a scene of work, thus holding together representation and cultural production" (77). Also, for an excellent book on the study of women's work and women's stories, see Bettina Aptheker, *Tapestries of Life: Women's Work, Women's Consciousness, and the Meaning of Daily Experience* (Amherst, Mass.: The University of Massachusetts Press, 1989).

8. In another version, she is decorating a blanket with porcupine quills, and in even another version she is twining a net.

9. See *The Upanishads: Breath of the Eternal,* translated by Swami Prabhavananda and Frederick Manchester (New York & London: Penguin Books, 1975).

10. Interestingly, Barber posits that "Athena's mythology lies far back in Aegean prehistory, long before the Greeks themselves arrived. The names of Athena and Athens are not Greek or IndoEuropean names but come from an earlier linguistic layer. Furthermore, most of the Greek weaving vocabulary is not IndoEuropean. The proto-Indo-Europeans . . . seem to have had scant knowledge of weaving, their women knowing only how to weave narrow belts and bands. . . . The Greeks clearly

learned how to use the large European warp-weighted loom after they broke off and moved away from the proto-Indo-European community" (243). Barber suggests that the Greeks probably learned weaving from "the indigenous' inhabitants of the Balkans (skilled in weaving since the middle of the Neolithic, perhaps even 5000 B.C.E." (243) and that Athena was originally their deity.

11. Paula Gunn Allen in *The Sacred Hoop: Recovering the Feminine in American Indian Tradition,* (Boston, Mass.: Beacon, 1986) suggests that the contemporary Indian tales about origin, which reflect a patriarchal heritage, are "recent interpolation[s] of the original sacred texts." She proposes that these tales were revised, with "the Christianizing influence" on these "arcane traditions." She maintains that such an influence "would accord with the penchant in the old oral tradition for shaping tales to reflect present social realities" (15). For further information about the possible corruption of the oral tradition, see Allen's book, *Grandmothers of the Light: A Medicine Woman's Sourcebook* (Boston, Mass.: Beacon Press, 1991), 27–32.

12. In Funk & Wagnalls, *Standard Dictionary of Folklore, Mythology, and Legend,* edited by Maria Leach (San Francisco, CA: Harper & Row, Publishers, 1972), 1074.

13. From Paula Gunn Allen, *The Sacred Hoop,* 122. For a classic book on the significance of Spider Woman in Navajo society, see Gladys Reichards's book *Spider Woman—A Story of Navajo Weavers and Chanters* (Glorieta, New Mexico: The Rio Grande Press, 1934). For another book that highlights the importance of Spider Woman in a weaver's life, see Noel Bennet's *Halo of the Sun: Stories Told and Retold* (Flagstaff, Arizona: Northland, 1987).

14. Anthropologist, folklorist, and writer Terry DeWald told this story to me in a phone interview in Tucson, Arizona (19 June 1997; 9:30 A.M.).

15. James Vogh, in *Arachne Rising: the Search for the Thirteenth Sign of the Zodiac* (New York: Dial Press, 1977), 75–95. Also see See J.E. Cirlot, *Dictionary of Symbols* (London: Routledge & Kegan Paul, 1962), 209. Whereas the silkworm, like the spider, spins fibers from its own body, this creature is not a female creative deity in the way that the Spider figure is for the North American Plains Indians and some African tribes. However, the silkworm is said to have been brought forth out of the body of a female deity: "When the Japanese goddess Ukemochi died, her body became the source of all agricultural products. Silkworms emerged from her eyebrows" (Hochberg, 58).

16. See David Jongeward, *Weaver of Worlds: From Navajo Apprenticeship to Sacred Geometry and Dreams. A Woman's Journey in Tapestry* (Rochester, VT: Destiny Books, 1990), 159.

17. See Gemeentemuseum Helmond, in "The Handwoven Communique," edited by Bobbie Irwin, *Handwoven* (November/December 1989), 105.

18. Jane Schneider and Annette B. Weiner, eds., *Cloth and Human Experience* (Washington and London: Smithsonian Institution Press, 1989), 6.

19. Ibid., 6.

20. Frederick J. Dockstader, *Weaving Arts of the North American Indian,* 71.

21. Jiho Sargent, "The Buddha Robe," *Piecework: Needlework & History* 7.6 (November/December 1999): 53–55.

22. Jerome W. Clinton, "Image and Metaphor: Textiles in Persian Poetry" in *Woven from the Soul, Spun from the Heart: Textile Arts of Safavid and Qajar Iron, sixteenth–nineteenth Centuries,* ed. by Carol Bier, 7–11 (Washington, D.C.: The Textile Museum, 1987), 8. A poem written in the eleventh century by a Muslim poet in the court of the Amir of Chaghanian (Khurasan) sports with the metaphorical connection between the making of cloth and the making of poems. Farrukhi of Sistan writes:

> I left Sistan with merchants of fine robes.
> The robe I bore was spun within my heart

And woven in my soul. A silken robe,
Composed of words, that eloquence designed.
I labored hard to draw its warp and woof
From deep within myself. You'll find in it
The rarest figures and the finest metaphors.
This robe is one that water will not stain,
Nor will this robe be burned by any flame.
Its colors won't be touched by earth or dust,
Nor will the ages make its pattern fade.
It was written swiftly, straight from my heart.

For more information on Islamic textiles, see Clive Rogers, *Early Islamic Textiles* (Brighton, England: Rogers & Podmore, 1983).

23. Marcel Griaule, *Conversations with Ogotemmeli: An Introduction to Dogon Religious Ideas* (Ely House, London: Oxford University Press, 1965), 28.

24. Ibid., 74. Griaule writes of this phenomenon that "The sound of the block and the shuttle . . . means creaking of the word' which . . . fills the interstices in the fabric" (73).

25. Ibid., 82.

26. Penelope Drooker, "Silk: the Story of a Culture," 49–51.

27. *Webster's Third New International Dictionary and Seven Language Dictionary* (Chicago, London: G. & C. Merriam Co., 1971), 2365.

28. Roland Barthes, "Work" in *The Pleasure of the Text,* translated by Richard Miller (New York: Farrar, Straus and Giroux, 1975), 76. For Barthes, the text is the mother's body. The appropriate body for the text, however, is the textile. We are here concerned with origins.

29. See Houston Smith's chapter on "Buddhism," in *The World's Religions: Our Great Wisdom Traditions,* (New York: HarperCollins, 1991), 140. Thus, says Smith, "the Tantras are texts that focus on the inter-relatedness of things."

30. From the Associated Press, "Word for Word," reprinted in "The Handwoven Communique," edited by Bobbie Irwin, *Handwoven* (November/December 1989), 104.

31. J. Hillis Miller, "Ariadne's Thread: Repetition and the Narrative Line," *Critical Inquiry 3* (Autumn 1976): 74. Also see Miller's *Ariadne's Thread: Story Lines* (New Haven and London: Yale University Press, 1992).

32. Virginia Woolf, *A Room of One's Own* (New York and London: Harcourt, Brace & World, 1957), 43–44.

33. John Keats, letter to J. H. Reynolds, dated 19 February 1818, in *Letters of John Keats,* selected and edited by Robert Gittings (Oxford, New York: Oxford University Press, 1970), 65–67.

34. Sir Walter Scott, *The Heart of Midlothian,* (London, New York: Oxford University Press, 1982), 158.

35. Roland Barthes, "Work," 76.

36. Susan Gubar "'The Blank Page' and the Issues of Female Creativity," *Critical Inquiry* 8 (Winter 1981): 260.

37. See Geoffrey Hartman, "The Voice of the Shuttle: Literature from the Point of View of Literature," in *Beyond Formalism: Literary Essays 1958–1970* (New Haven and London: Yale University Press, 1970), 342–43.

38. See Susan Gubar, 260.

Chapter 2. The Semiotics of Cloth and Thetic (Re)Production

1. See Kelly Oliver's critique of Julia Kristeva's theories in her book *Reading Kristeva: Unraveling the Double-bind* (Bloomington and Indianapolis: Indiana University Press, 1993), 2. I often refer to this work when trying to explain to my readers Kristeva's complex theories.

2. John Lechte, *Julia Kristeva* (New York: Routledge, 1990), 53. This book has also been a useful source for my own understanding and explication of Kristeva.

3. See Lechte, 99.

4. See Oliver, 3.

5. Ibid., 3.

6. See Julia Kristeva, *Revolution in Poetic Language*, translated by Margaret Waller (New York: Columbia University Press, 1984), 25. Henceforth I will refer to this work with the abbreviation *RPL* to differentiate it from other texts I will be referring to by her.

7. See Kristeva, *RPL*, 27. The signifying process depends on both semiotic and symbolic elements. Oliver writes: "The semiotic moves both inside and beyond the Symbolic. The semiotic, however, does not move within the symbolic. Within signification, the symbolic is heterogeneous to the semiotic. The symbolic is the element within the Symbolic against which the semiotic works to produce the dialectical tension that keeps society going" (10). My readers will note the discrepancy between capitalization and non-capitalization of symbolic in this book. In my own writing, I will refer to the *Symbolic* as that realm wherein we live, speak, and articulate our existence as autonomous beings, whereas the lower-cased term *symbolic* will refer to the activity of articulation within the Symbolic.

8. See Kristeva, *RPL*, 27.

9. From a personal letter written by Dr. Shari Benstock to me, dated 6 June 1994. Dr. Benstock introduced me to and helped shape my understanding of the theories of Sigmund Freud, Jacques Lacan, Julia Kristeva, and Jacques Derrida. This book could not have been written without her guidance and mentorship.

10. Psychosis occurs when the child/adult refuses to identify with the Law of the Father. "The psychotic circulates (linguistically speaking) forever in a closed network of signifiers that cannot open up, or build on themselves. They 'freeze' or become paralytic. There are degrees of psychosis, of course; people can move in and out of psychotic states" (Benstock, from a letter).

11. See "Word, Dialogue and Novel," in *The Kristeva Reader*, edited by Toril Moi (New York: Columbia Press, 1986), 48. Henceforth reference to this work will be done with the abbreviation *KR*.

12. See Oliver, 40.

13. See Nathaniel Hawthorne's novel, *The Blithedale Romance* (New York, New York: Penguin Classics, 1983), 6.

14. Ibid., 113.

15. Ibid., 114.

16. See "Alastor; or, the Spirit of Solitude," in *Shelley's Poetry and Prose*, selected and edited by Donald H. Reiman and Sharon B. Powers (New York and London, W. W. Norton & Company, 1977), pp. 69–87. Although written relatively early in Shelley's career (1815), Alastor's "Veiled Maid" finds representation in many of his other works, particularly "The Witch of Atlas" (dated 1820, 347–67) and "Epipsychidion" (dated 1820, 371–88). The Witch is so beautiful, that she weaves a veil to partially conceal herself (stanzas 12 and 13), and in "Epipsychidion," the persona discusses at length his life-long quest for this "veiled maid," which he now imagines existed all

along in the form of Emilia. The final section of the poem becomes a journey to remove this veil between them—made up of geographical distance, social constraints and the body itself—and merge with his chosen epipsyche, "one Spirit within two frames" (11. 573–74).

17. See Julia Kristeva's essay "Place Names," (271–94) in her collection, *Desire in Language: a Semiotic Approach to Literature and Art,* ed. by Leon S. Roudiez (New York: Columbia University Press, 1980), 283. Henceforth referred to with the abbreviation *DL*.

18. See Oliver, 22.

19. Ibid., 22.

20. Ibid., 4.

21. See Roland Barthes, *The Pleasure of the Text,* 9 (emphasis in the original). Lechte notes that Barthes has "a special place in Kristeva's intellectual and personal trajectory. 'He is the precursor and founder of modern literary studies', wrote Kristeva in 1971" (65).

22. Ibid., 25.

23. See Oliver, 23. Prior to the mirror stage and castration, the mother's body provides the infant all gratification and pleasure. At this stage, both Lacan and Kristeva agree, that for the infant the mother possesses the phallus; she is the phallic mother. At times I will use the terms "phallic mother" and "pre-oedipal mother" interchangeably (as does Lacan). According to Freud, "exposure of the phallic mother's lack is necessary in order to initiate sexual difference" (Oliver, 55); hence, the mother's lack makes her body threatening to the child. On the other hand, Kristeva views the mother's "castration" as only one factor in separation. She posits that the child views the mother's body as menacing not because it represents lack, but "because it is the canal out of which it came. . . . And, insofar as the child was once on the other side of that canal, its autonomy is threatened. . . . It fears being sucked back into the mother through her sex" (Oliver, 55).

24. Freud suggests that the daughter's oedipal situation with the mother initiates guilt feelings. In other words, pre-oedipal feelings of identification and attachment toward the mother are supplanted with a desire "to get rid of her mother and take her place with her father" (166). Coleridge seems to be describing in this scene the actual moment when a female subject (Christabel) passes from the pre-oedipal identification with the mother to an oedipal identification with the father. At first, Christabel behaves in "unconscious sympathy" with Geraldine (signaling her pre-oedipal connection with this mother-of-sorts), so that after she sees the woman's "serpent eyes," Christabel makes a "hissing sound." Immediately following this moment, Christabel regains her ability to speak and, resisting her previous identification with Geraldine, "entreats" her father "this woman [to] send away!" refusing even to address this woman by her proper name.

25. To some extent this idea reverses Barthes's notion that "The text is a fetish object, and *this fetish desires men*" (*Pleasure of the Text,* 27). Instead, the text seeks its own origins (through the agency of its author), desiring only the marks of its own production. For the text, then, the textile comprises a symbol of the text's own materiality, and as a metaphor for the maternal body, constitutes for the text a fetish object.

26. William Blake would link the infant's relationship with the mother's body to the state of Beulah—a perfectly secure condition where all needs are met, but which if remained in for too long endangers the psyche's own growth and individuation. Blake's visionary works deal with this problem of abjection. Blake cannot quite conceive of an adequate "location" for his most autonomous, created beings; his narratives continually return to various projections of Vala, the maternal body, who

inspires desire and disgust. What redeemed humanity would look like, and what their condition would be like, forms a major concern in Blake's ouevre.

27. Kristeva, *Revolution in Poetic Language,* 45.

28. See Shari Benstock, *Textualizing the Feminine: on the Limits of Genre* (Norman, Oklahoma: University of Oklahoma Press, 1991), 29.

29. Consequently, the weaving process emulates the manner in which the Symbolic is constituted, by an "order of borders" (analogous to the textile's salvage and design), "discrimination" (the warp), "and difference" (what I would call the weft) (Oliver, 56).

30. See Kristeva, *RPL,* 26.

31. Ibid., 28

32. Ibid., 26

33. See Kristeva, "From One Identity to an Other," in *Desire in Language,* 136. Kristeva points out an important constituent of poetic language, that though "[l]anguage as symbolic function constitutes itself at the cost of repressing instinctual drive and continuous relation to the mother" [and that] . . . the unsettled and questionable subject of poetic language (for whom the word is never uniquely sign) maintains itself at the cost of reactivating this repressed instinctual, maternal element" (136). As a metaphor for the "maternal element" the textile in these stories compromises the symbolic function of its designs by threatening to unravel them at any moment.

34. See Lechte, 129.

35. See Oliver, 56.

36. See Kristeva, "Stabat Mater" in *KR,* 162.

37. See book 2 of Edmund Spenser's *The Faerie Queene,* "The Legend of Sir Guyon or the Knight of Temperaunce," ed. Thomas P. Roche and C. Patrick O'Donnell, Jr. (New York and London: Viking Penguin Inc., 1987), 203–382.

38. See Kristeva, *Revolution in Poetic Language,* 47.

39. Ibid., 27.

40. Ibid., 27.

41. Ibid., 28.

42. Lord Alfred Tennyson, "The Lady of Shalott" in *Poems of Tennyson,* ed. Jerome H. Buckley (Boston: Houghton Mifflin Company, 1958), 25–29.

43. Carl Plasa maintains that in this kind of reading, the poem recognizes that 'life' is inherently antipathetic to the possibility of an ongoing artist production—an insight taken in turn to be enacted by the death which befalls the Lady" (247). Plasa then goes on to explore the poem in terms of its gendered spaces and "sexual politics": "The Lady of Shalott," he contends, addresses the "Woman Question . . . in a systematically ambivalent manner, at once upholding and dislocating patriarchal assumptions about the issues which the question entails' those of gender, sexuality, the institution of marriage, and the space occupied by women in society" (248).

44. Sandra M. Gilbert and Susan Gubar, *The Madwoman in the Attic: The Woman Writer and the Nineteenth-Century Literary Imagination* (New Haven: Yale University Press, 1979), 617–18.

45. See Julia Kristeva, "Motherhood According to Bellini," in *Desire in Language,* 265. Joseph Chadwick indicates this in his statement that "Traditional portrayals of a woman gazing into a looking-glass or pool (Milton's Even in Book IV of *Paradise Lost,* for example) invoke a feminine autonomy achieved through narcissism. The glass or pool represents the woman as one who is her own object of desire and thus achieves a kind of sexual self-sufficiency" (18).

46. Ibid., 265.

47. See Kristeva, "Giotto's Joy," *DL,* 220.

48. I acquired this information through my own experience as a weaver as well as from my research into the subject. Christopher Ricks has also connected Tennyson's mirror to the actual domain of weaving; see his edition of *The Poems of Tennyson* (London and Harlow, 1969) 357.

49. See Elizabeth Grosz, "The Body of Signification," in *Abjection, Melancholia, and Love: The Works of Julia Kristeva,* ed. John Fletcher and Andrew Benjamin, 80–103 (New York: Routledge, 199), 93.

50. See Michel Foucault, *The Archaeology of Knowledge and the Discourse on Language,* trans. A. M. Sheridan Smith (New York: Pantheon, 1972), 150.

Chapter 3. The Greek Web: Arachne and Philomena, Penelope and Helen of Troy

See Richard Lattimore's translation of *The Iliad of Homer* (Chicago & London: University of Chicago Press, 1951): 23:700–705. I refer to this translation throughout this book.

1. Women were frequently depicted on Attic vases holding spindles, which were often confused or interchangeable in these portraits with hand-held mirrors "as both conveyed the same meaning," as signs "of feminine grace and charm" See Eva C. Keuls, "Attic Vase-Painting and the Home Textile Industry," in *Ancient Greek Art and Iconography,* edited by Warren G. Moon (Madison, Wisconsin: University of Wisconsin Press, 1983), 21.

2. See Eva Keuls, 209.

3. It has been suggested that women were actually locked in these rooms. See Susan Walker's essay, "Women and Housing in Classical Greece: the Archaeological Evidence," in *Images of Women in Antiquity,* ed. Averil Cameron and Amelie Kuhrt (Detroit: Wayne State University Press, 1983).

4. See Eva Keuls, 214.

5. See Ann Bergren's article "Language and the Female in Early Greek Thought," in *Arethusa* 16 (1983): 73. Bergren traces the concept of *mētis* "or transformative intelligence'" (71) to the goddess Mētis, swallowed by Zeus after their marriage. Athena, whom Bergren calls the daughter of Mētis, takes over the characteristics of her mother, not only as the goddess of weaving but as one who wields "the power of transformation, the power to change shape continuously" (73). Bergren continues, "The female as weaver of mētis thus (re-)enters the divine cosmos as a perpetually virgin daughter, loyal solely to her father. And Zeus as sovereign male appropriates a quality that the text has attributed to him from the start" (73). More discussion of this occurs in part 3 of this chapter, "Helen and Penelope."

6. See Marcel Detienne and Jean-Pierre Vernant, in *Cunning Intelligence in Greek Culture and Society,* trans. Janet Lloyd (Atlantic Highlands, New Jersey: Humanities Press, 1978), 237–38. Bergren also states that "mētis is . . . analogous to poetic song at the level of diction, since both are objects of the verb *huphainein* to weave (n. 18 in "Language and the Female").

7. Elizabeth Wayland Barber suggests that there is factual evidence for the existence of poisoned garments that obsessed the ancients and their mythology. She states that "ancient texts now suggest that the soft mineral *realgar,* which is a dark purplish red (a favorite royal color), was one of several stones sometimes crushed and used as pigments—for cloth, among other things. Realgar also upon occasion was known as dragon's blood, as its bright color typically occurred splashed across the surface of harder rocks. But realgar has another property: It is the arsenic ruby,'

sulfide of arsenic—a deadly poison if kept in prolonged contact with the skin. I have collected estimates that a month or so of wearing a garment colored royal purple with arsenic would be sufficient to do one in . . . after (ironically) giving the victim an especially lovely skin complexion for a few days" (234).

8. See Marcel Detienne and Jean-Pierre Vernant, 137–38. The authors state, in lines attributed to Orpheus by Aristotle, "that which is living is produced (ginesthai to zoion) in the same way as a net is woven (homoios . . . tei tou diktuou plokei)" (138).

Clotho spins for each human being their thread of life, Lachesis measures the length of each life span, and Atropos cuts the thread when a life is to end. Though the Morae merely carried out Zeus' orders, propitiatory offerings were also made to the sisters. See *Standard Dictionary of Folklore, Mythology, and Legend,* 741.

9. See Elizabeth Wayland Barber, 155.

10. See Ann Bergren's article, "Language and the Female in Early Greek Thought," 7–72.

11. See Euripides, *Ion,* in *The Bacchae and Other Plays,* trans. by Philip Vellacott (England, Maryland, Victoria: Penguin, 1972), 84.

12. Both linen and wool were spun and woven into garments. "The woolen garments were as a rule coloured, the linen ones white. The decoration for men at least was generally confined to borders, but for women it sometimes formed a frieze or an all-over pattern; figured scenes as well as linear ornaments were used. The designs were either woven into the material, or embroidered on it, or painted" (Richter, 369).

13. See Bergren, "Language and the Female in Early Greek Thought," 72.

14. See T. E. Lawrence's translation, *The Odyssey of Homer* (New York and Oxford: Oxford University Press, 1991), 10:221–24. I refer to this translation throughout this book.

15. *The Odyssey,* 5:61–62.

16. See Walter Pater's Greek Studies: A Series of Essays (London: MacMillan and Company, 1911), 12. The relationship between weaving and the body is examined more thoroughly in the following chapter on Blake's *The Four Zoas.*

17. From Aristotle's *Poetics* (16.2), a phrase taken from Sophocles' lost play, *Tereus.* Also, the subject (a "trope") of a much-debated article by Geoffrey H. Hartman, "The Voice of the Shuttle: Language from the Point of View of Literature" in *Beyond Formalism: Literary Essays 1958–1970* (New Haven and London: Yale University Press, 1970): 337–55.

18. See Bergren, "Language and the Female in Early Greek Thought," 72.

19. See David Jongeward's book, *Weaver of Words: From Navajo Apprenticeship to Sacred Geometry and Dreams,* 65.

20. Once these signs are communicated to Procne, the sister becomes enraged and sets about destroying Tereus and Itys, who, for these weavers, constitute agents of the male prerogative that has oppressed them. Philomela's text, however, can offer no new language or vision to replace the phallogocentric world represented by Tereus and Itys.

21. From Kristeva's essay, "From One Identity to An Other" in *Desire in Language,* 136. She writes that the language of the Symbolic always "constitutes itself at the cost of repressing instinctual drive and continuous relation to the mother" 136.

22. Kristeva, "From One Identity to An Other," 136. Kristeva's conception of poetic language—"for whom the word is never uniquely sign"—relies on her theory of the semiotic.

23. I use *grammata* in the sense that Ann Bergren employs it in her "Language and the Female in Early Greek Thought," as a pictorial and/or linguistic form of writing.

24. See the following works for further discussion: Patricia Klindienst Joplin's "The Voice of the Shuttle is Ours" in *Stanford Literature Review* 1 (Spring 1984): 25–53; Nancy K. Miller, "Arachnologies: The Woman, the Text, and the Critic," in her book, *Subject to Change;* Geoffrey H. Hartman, "The Voice of the Shuttle: Language from the Point of View of Literature," in *Beyond Formalism: Literary Essays 1958–1970,* (New Haven and London: Yale University Press, 1970), 337–55; Jane Marcus, "Still Practice, A/wrested Alphabet: Toward a Feminist Aesthetic" in *Tulsa Studies in Women's Literature* 3 (Spring/Fall 1984): 79–97.

25. See Ovid, *Metamorphoses,* trans. A. D. Melville (Oxford, New York: Oxford University Press, 1986), 317.

26. "[I]t was among the mountains of Thrace that this gloomier element in the being of Dionysus had taken the strongest hold . . . so, in those wilder northern regions, people continued to brood over its darker side, and hence a current of gloomy legend descended into Greece" (Pater, 45–46). Whether or not "the sacred women of Dionysus ate, in mystical ceremony, raw flesh and drank blood" (48) can not be ascertained, but the Greek imagination was haunted by the possibility that Thrace practiced this form of worship.

27. A country is often symbolized as a mother or beloved; thus, Cathleen ni Houlihan represents Ireland. Originally pure and beautiful, Cathleen is also England's whore, wronged by her own countrymen who allow her to exist in servitude. I contend that in Ovid's tale, Procne and Philomela represent Athens, but become unalterably contaminated by their association with Thrace.

28. See Ovid, 323.

29. See Patricia Klindienst Joplin, "The Voice of the Shuttle is Ours" in *Stanford Literature Review* 1 (Spring 1984): 26.

30. See Ovid, 329.

31. See Adele Coulin Weibel, *Two Thousand Years of Textiles: The Figured Textiles of Europe and the Near East* (New York: Pantheon, 1952), 12. Purple was a difficult dye to obtain, unless derived from a mixture of woad "[u]sed as a base with madder" (9). Woad was a principal dye used in Greece and the ancient world.

32. See Joplin, 38.

33. In the more ancient source of Apollodorus, Philomela weaves not a tapestry but a robe, which in this argument could be symbolic of Philomela's own body that she offers to Procne. Her body, no longer pure, is stained with signs of its desecration. See *Apollodorus: The Library,* 98–101.

34. See Geoffrey Hartman, "The Voice of the Shuttle: Literature from the Point of View of Literature," 351.

35. See John Lechte in his book *Julia Kristeva,* 49.

36. See Ovid, 329.

37. Ovid writes that when Procne saw Itys "her wrath fell away, and her eyes, though all unwilling, were wet with tears that flowed in spite of her. But when she perceived that her purpose was wavering through excess of mother-love, she turned again from her son to her sister" (333).

38. See Julia Kristeva, *Revolution in Poetic Language,* trans. Margaret Waller (New York: Columbia University Press, 1984), 26.

39. Ibid., 25.

40. Ibid., 50.

41. Ibid.

42. Ibid., 28.

43. See Shari Benstock, *Textualizing the Feminine: On the Limits of Genre* (Norman, Oklahoma: University of Oklahoma Press, 1991), 31.

44. See Kristeva, *Powers of Horror: An Essay on Abjection,* trans. Leon S. Roudiez (New York: Columbia University Press, 1982), 4.

45. See Walter Pater, *Greek Studies: A Series of Essays* (London: MacMillan and Company, 1911), 48. Euripides' Bacchae illustrates this "ceremony" in the sacrifice of Agaue's son, Pentheus, to the maenads.

46. Sir Phillip Sidney dismisses this kind of female activity when he says of women's tasks: "Truly, a needle [shuttle] cannot do much hurt, and as truly can not do much good. With a sword thou mayest kill thy father, and with a sword thou mayest defend thy prince and country" (*Defense of Poetry,* 139).

47. See Joplin, 45.

48. See Ovid, 321.

49. See Ruth Padel, "Women: Model for Possession by Greek Daemons" in *Images of Women in Antiquity,* ed. Averil Cameron and Amelie Kuhrt (Detroit: Wayne State University Press, 1983), 5.

50. See Padel, 5–6.

51. See Ovid, 179.

52. There is debate as to which sister became the nightingale. Ovid had Philomela changed into the nightingale, but since she was tongueless the more ancient Greek source, Apollodorus, has Philomela changed into a thrush or swallow that can only twitter, and reserves the nightingale's fate for Procne. Ovid states that the breasts of both birds "even now. . . . have not lost the marks of their murderous deed, their feathers are stained with blood" (335).

53. See Ovid, 335. The hoopoe is a small bird of red and black plummage, whose "habits are said to be filthy: it nests in its own droppings and eats insects and worms from dunghills" (*Dictionary of Folklore Mythology and Legend,* 502). Interestingly, the fate of the two sisters parallels the mythological sirens, who were often depicted in Greek art as birds with women's heads, most often appearing as two in number (see J. R. T. Pollard, "Muses and Sirens," in *The Classical Review* V II[2]: June 1952, 60–63). The sirens, too, are connected with Dionysus and with Thrace.

54. Geoffrey Hartman writes of this scene: "Philomela, when her voice is restored through art, participates for a moment in divinity. She triumps over a terrible doom, yet the recognition she brings about continues a tragic chain of events" (in "The Voice of the Shuttle," 351).

55. See Ovid, 293

56. Ibid., 291.

57. See J. Hillis Miller, *Ariadne's Thread: Story Lines* (New Haven and London: Yale University Press, 1992), 82.

58. See Joplin, 49.

59. The myths Arachne illustrates in her tapestry are also myths that Ovid recounts in the *Metamorphoses.* His tales make sport of the lust and fraudulence of the gods.

60. See Ovid, 295.

61. See Lechte, 35.

62. Ibid., 54. Used by Lechte and Kristeva to describe Joyce's *Finnegans Wake.*

63. Ibid., 109.

64. Ibid., 106.

65. See Ovid, 297.

66. Ibid., 295.

67. See *Dictionary of Folklore, Mythology and Legend,* 820.

68. Ibid., 530.

69. See Ann Bergren, "Language and the Female in Early Greek Thought," 72.

70. See Mihoko Suzuki, *Metamorphoses of Helen: Authority, Difference, and the Epic* (Ithaca and London: Cornell University Press, 1989), 249.

71. See Ovid, 297.

72. See Suzuki, 249.

73. Ibid., 249–50.

74. See Ovid, 295.

75. See Shari Benstock, 31.

76. Kristeva defines the death drive in terms of Freud's use of the phrase: "For although drives have been described as disunited or contradictory structures, simultaneously 'positive' and 'negative,' this doubling is said to generate a dominant 'destructive wave' that is [the] drive's most characteristic trait: Freud notes that the most instinctual drive is the death drive" (from *Revolution in Poetic Language,* 28).

77. See Nancy Miller, *Subject to Change: ReadingFeminist Writing* (New York: Columbia University Press, 1988), 83–84.

78. See Lechte, 99–100.

79. See Ovid, 299

80. See Joplin, 50–51.

81. According to Virgil's *Georgics,* 5:236–49.

> For often, unobserved, the spotted newt
> Gnaws at the combs, and swarms of skulking beetles
> Crowd the house, and the empty-handed drone
> Settles down to dine on others' food.
> Fierce hornets bring superior armaments
> Against the bees, or nasty moths get in,
> Or spiders, those insects Minerva hates,
> Suspend their sagging nets across the door.

82. See Henry T. Riley's note in his translation of Ovid, *The Metamorphoses of Ovid* (London: George Bell and Sons, 1884), 195.

83. See Suzuki, 249.

84. See James Vogh, *Arachne Rising: the Search for the Thirteenth Sign of the Zodiac* (New York: Dial Press, 1977), 54. See Mihoko Suzuki's *Metamorphoses of Helen,* 242–57, and J. H. Miller's "Ariachne's Broken Woof" for a discussion on how these two goddesses have been conflated in Classical and Renaissance literature. Robert Graves suggests that the seals found at Cretan Miletus imprinted with spider emblems connects "the spider cult" with "the Cretan trade of spinning and weaving." See *The Greek Myths,* vol. 1 (Edinburgh, Great Britain: Penguin, 1955).

85. See Elizabeth Barber's, *Women's Work The First 20,000 Years: Women, Cloth, and society in Early Times,* better than any other book on this subject, charts the growth and demise of the textile industry from the Paleolithic Age (20,000 B.C.) to Classical Greece (500 B.C.).

86. Robert Graves also suggests this possibility, and says that Athena's "vengeance on Arachne may be more than just a pretty fable, if it records an early commercial rivalry between the Athenians and the Lydio-Carian thalassocrats, or sea-rulers, who were of Cretan origin" (*The Greek Myths* 1:100 n. 6). Graves mentions that the seals with spider emblems were found "at Cretan Miletus—the mother city of Carian Miletus and the largest exporter of dyed woolens in the ancient world—[that] suggest a public textile industry operated there at the beginning of the second millennium B.C." (100 n. 6).

87. See Vogh, 57. These signs were as follows: "1. Jupiter as a bull seduces Europa. (Taurus) 2. Jupiter pursues Asterie. (Arachne) 3. Jupiter seduces Leda, who bears

him twins. (Gemini) 4. Neptune is disguised as a river god. (Cancer) 5. Phoebus is dressed in a lion's skin. (Leo) 6. Erigone, the virgin. (Specifically said to be Virgo) 7. Danae weighs gold in her lap. (Libra) 8. Jupiter as a spotted snake. (Scorpio)" (Vogh, 55), and etc. Vogh situates Arachne as the thirteenth sign of a traditional twelve-sign zodiac; Arachne, the spider, was purportedly the charioteer of the zodiac, the one that propels the zodiac across the sky. Accordingly, her cult, perhaps a variation of the tree-cults popular in Celtic as well as Cretan civilization, was either notoriously secretive or suppressed.

88. See Vogh, 57.

89. Graves writes of these "hanged goddesses": "At Petsofa in Crete a hoard of human heads and limbs, of clay, have been found, each with a hole through which a string could be passed. If once fixed to wooden trunks, they may have formed part of Daedalus' jointed dolls, and represented the Fertility-goddess. Their use was perhaps to hang from a fruit-tree, with their limbs moving about in the wind, to ensure good crops. Such a doll is shown hanging from a fruit-tree in the famous gold ring from the Acropolis Treasure at Mycenae. . . . Ariadne, the Cretan goddess, is said to have hanged herself (*Contest of Homer and Hesiod* 14), as the Attic Erigone did. . . . Artemis the Hanged One, who had a sanctuary at Condyleia in Arcadia (Pausanias: viii. 23.6), and Helen of the Trees, who had a sanctuary at Rhodes and is said to have been hanged by Polyxo (Pausanias: iii. 19.10), may be variants of the same goddess" (Graves 1:298 n. 10).

90. See Elizabeth Wayland Barber, 116.

91. Ibid., 225.

92. In many cultures the spider is a benefactor and guide. I have already mentioned that coins were found in Crete embossed with a spider. And it was Ariadne, one of the "hanged goddesses," who gave Theseus a ball of thread that he might retrace his way through the Minotaur's labyrinth or web. Miller tells us that "[t]he Minotaur, as Ruskin saw, is a spider, Arachne . . . weaver of a Web which is herself" ("Ariadne's Thread: Repetition and the Narrative Line," 72–73).

93. Ann Bergren, "Helen's Good Drug', Odyssey iv, 1–305," in *Contemporary Literary Hermeneutics and Interpretation of Classical Texts* (Ottawa: Ottawa University Press, 1981), 31–32.

94. Athena is the patron goddess of both Penelope and her husband, Odysseus. Wily and cunning, unlike the Athena we encounter in Ovid's tale of Arachne, the Athena of Homer's Odyssey is a master of disguise and transformation. Detienne and Vernant note that Athena is traditionally the goddess of wisdom, skills, and warfare; "weaving and woolwork also involve the *mētis* of Athena" (185 n. 33).

95. Helen's status in the Iliad is different from her status in the *Odyssey*. "In the Iliad, at the beginning of her literary tradition, the figure of Helen is marked by radical undecidability" (Suzuki 18). She is not wholly condemned as the cause of the Trojan War, and so her relationship with Homer constitutes a positive view of her. It is an idea, however, that is constantly questioned in the Iliad. See Mihoko Suzuki's *Metamorphoses of Helen: Authority, Difference, and the Epic.*

96. See *Webster's Third New International Dictionary* (Chicago, London, Sydney, Toronto, Geneva, Tokyo: Encyclopedia Britannica, Inc., 1971).

97. See *The Odyssey,* 2:116–19, 121:

> . . . dowered with the wisdom bestowed by Athene,
> to be expert in beautiful work, to have good character
> and cleverness, such as we are not told of, even of the ancient
> queens, the fair-tressed Achaian women of times before us,
> . . . .
> . . . for none of these knew thoughts so wise as those Penelope knew—

98. From *The Iliad,* 3:125–28.

99. See Bergren, "Language and the Female in Early Greek Thought," 79. Barber writes that "we even possess pieces of two story cloths from Greek tombs in the Black Sea colonies" (154, fig. 9.6). The Bayeux Tapestry is another (and much later) example of a storytelling cloth; Katharine MacCornack suggests that "the technical, semiotic devices used in the Bayeux Tapestry have their roots in the secular oral tradition" (101), just as Helen's tapestry would have been a woven/written text representing the oral poem.

100. Bergren, 79.

101. See Barber, 153–54 and 229.

102. See Barber, 154.

103. Mihoko Suzuki writes of the "elevated" status of Helen in the *Iliad:* "It is only the poet of the *Iliad,* however, who endows Helen with subjectivity and an inwardness that makes her akin to Achilles, the foremost male warrior of the epic. From the *Odyssey* on, Helen is always present in the texts to be studied, but as myth—either an emblem of doubleness or of duplicity on the one hand, or a trivial cardboard figure on the other—to be scapegoated and repudiated" (16–17).

104. See Barber, 211.

105. See Nancy Arthur Hoskins, "The Bayeux Tapestry: an eleventh-century epic embroidery," 79, in *Handwoven* (January/February 2000): 78–80. Hoskins writes, "The tapestry belonged in 1476 to the Cathedral of Bayeux and was hung in the nave during special religious celebration. It has survived being used to cover a wagon, being rolled from one storage drum to another for display, the danger of being sliced up into sections, and numerous wars." Currently, the Bayeux tapestry is on permanent display in a renovated seminary, Centre Guillaume-le-Conquerant in Normandy, France. For an critique on the influence oral tradition had in the composition of this tapestry, see Katharine MacCornack's essay, "The Bayeux Tapestry: Does it follow the French Oral Epic?" in *Constructions* (1985), 95–104.

106. See L. L. Clader, *Helen: The Evolution from Divine to Heroic in Greek Epic Tradition* (Leiden: E. J. Brill, 1976), 7–8, 11.

107. Detienne and Vernant, 239.

108. See Bergren, 79.

109. See Suzuki, 28.

110. Ibid., 75.

111. Ibid., 88.

112. See Suzuki, 75.

113. *The Odyssey,* 24:196–98.

114. See Euripides, *The Bacchae and Other Plays,* trans. Philip Vellacott (England, Maryland, Victoria: Penguin, 1972), 236.

115. *The Odyssey,* 16:31–35.

116. *The Odyssey,* 8:276–81.

117. See Mieke Bal, "Sexuality, Semiosis and Binarism: A Narratological Comment on Bergren and Arthus," in *Arethusa* 16 (1–2) (1983): 122.

118. See Barber, 153–54.

119. See Jane Marcus, "Still Practice, A/wrested Alphabet: Toward a Feminist Aesthetic," in *Tulsa Studies in Women's Literature* 3 (Spring/Fall 1984): 84.

120. See Clader, 7.

121. See Bruno Gentili, "The Interpretation of the Greek Lyric Poets in Our Time: Synchronism and Diachronism in the Study of an Oral Culture," in *Contemporary Literary Hermeneutics and Interpretation of Classical Texts* (Ottawa: Ottawa University Press, 1981), 111.

122. Sea snails, particularly murex, were a major source for the purple dye; how-

ever, each snail when squeezed "produces only a single drop of the splendid dye" (Barber, 113–14).

123. Kristeva discusses the excessive blue in Giotto's paintings as one place where the symbolic is not privileged. (See Kristeva's "Giotto's Joy" DL 210–36.) This idea is also discussed in chapter 4, in relationship to the Lady of Shalott.

124. See Barber, 119. Admittedly, this is a controversial point, but it does answer some important questions about the nature of Helen and Menelaos's relationship. Barber recounts the scene in the *Odyssey* when Odysseus arrives in the land of the Phaiakians. A young princess, Nausikaa, advises Odysseus to go to her parents' home and lay his head first on her mother's feet: "For if she has thoughts in her mind that are friendly to you, then there is hope that you can see your own people, and come back to your strong-founded house, and to the land of your fathers" (6:313–15). Barber comments about this important scene: "No married woman ran the Classical Greek household or made its principal decisions. These peculiarly un-Greek instructions, however, are perfectly in line with what we know of matrilineal societies in which the men spend much of their time away. Since the woman owns and controls the house, she has control of which guests may stay in the house" (119). Furthermore, Barber suggests that although "[w]omen were virtually household prisoners in fifth-century Athenian society in particular. . . . [This] seems to have been the typical state of affairs from shortly before the time of Homer onward. There are many exceptions, however, in the Mycenaean world, most notably with Helen of Troy. Not only does her husband, Menelaos, carry on a ten-year war to retrieve her, but then, far from punishing her (as later Greek husbands of wayward wives were known to do—usually by death), he sits around placidly while she tells stories of her escapades to their guests! The reason that he had to fetch her back can only be a matter of succession" (119).

125. See Barber, 229.

Chapter 4. The Loom of Language and the Garment of Words in William Blake's *The Four Zoas*

1. During the Middle Ages in England, women had been allowed to own and govern textile shops. The Wife of Bath is a literary example of this phenomenon (see Mary Carruthers, "The Wife of Bath and the Painting of Lions" in *PMLA* 94 [1979], 209–22). The Renaissance saw the usurpation of textile production by the exclusively male Guilds. Women were prohibited from owning textile shops, forbidden to weave high grade fibers, and eventually were permitted only to spin. See: Eric Kerridge, *Textile Manufacture in Early Modern England;* Merry E. Wiesner, "Spinsters and Seamstresses: Women in Cloth and Clothing Production" in *Becoming Visible: Women in European History,* 2d ed.; ed. Renate Bridenthal, Claudia Koonz, and Susan Stuart (Boston, Massachusetts: Houghton Mifflin Company, 1987). Judith C. Brown, "A Woman's Place Was in the Home: Women's Work in Renaissance Tuscany" in *Rewriting the Renaissance;* Renate Bridenthal, Claudia Koonz, and Susan Stuard, *Becoming Visible: Women in European History,* 2d ed. (Boston, Massachusetts: Houghton Mifflin Company, 1987).

Weaving became a male enterprise beginning with the European Renaissance and the formation of Guilds. In England by the sixteenth century, weaving had also become a male vocation, gradually eliminating women's involvement in textile work except in subordinate activities such as carding and spinning. Throughout the eighteenth century, the home cottage industry provided England with spun and woven cloth for export. The British, during the early settlement of the American colonies, allowed women to weave coarse material (shoddy) for home-use only. But by the early Industrial Age of the late eighteenth century, weaving and spinning had been almost abolished in the home, as factories began to replace the smaller-scale cottage industries. Wordsworth and Coleridge, alert to this change, each wrote about the devastating effects industrialization had on the economy of the Lakes. See Kurt Heinzelman, "The Cult of Domesticity: Dorothy and William Wordsworth at Grasmere," in *Romanticism and Feminism,* ed. Anne K. Mellor, 52–78 (Bloomington and Indianapolis: Indiana University Press, 1988).

Though new inventions spread throughout many different trades and businesses, the textile industry made such remarkable advancements that it transformed not only the industrial base of England but the economics governing industry and trade all over the world. Textiles fast became the major enterprise for enriching and expanding the British Empire. Beginning with James Hargreaves' invention of the "Spinning Jenny" in 1764, followed by Samuel Crompton's cotton-spinning machine "the Mule" in 1779 (and its automated version in 1790), not only could more than one thread be spun at a time, but a finer, more even thread could be manufactured, finally competitive with that spun by hand in India.

Along with the invention of the power loom in 1787, the rate of cloth production increased so rapidly that England flooded the markets of Europe, America, India and eventually China and Japan, with inexpensive, high-quality woven fabrics. Gradually, England eliminated the textile industries of these countries (particularly that of India), and turned them into producers of the raw fiber England needed. The loom was once again returned to women in the late nineteenth century when weaving was no longer a practical means toward earning a living.

2. Although Urizen also "weaves" intellectual nets and webs, Blake never pictures Urizen working at a loom; the woven material of Urizen's fallen intellect issues from his body like the secretions of a spider:

> . . . & wherever he traveld a dire Web
> Followd behind him as the Web of a Spider dusky & cold
> Shivering across from Vortex to Vortex drawn out from his mantle of years
> A living Mantle adjoind to his life & growing from his Soul.
>
> (6:44–47)

His mind itself is the loom manufacturing the deceitful garments and veils, the books of "the Direful Web of Religion" (8:76). The tropology of the loom, however, is reserved for the female characters (and their male Spectres) alone.

Cirlot notes that the spider is the weaver of the world, sitting at its center (290). Likewise, Blake writes of Urizen's "Direful Web of Religion" that "heavy it fell / From heaven to hevn thro all its meshes altering the Vortexes / Misplacing every Center" (8:176–78). Also, see Leland E. Warren, "Poetic Vision and the Natural World: the Spider and his Web in the Poetry of William Blake" *Enlightenment Essays* VI:1 (Spring, 1975): 50–62.

I suggest that the weaving metaphor, though primarily a female activity, so fascinated Blake that it became a pervasive symbol for creativity, both for his male and female characters.

3. See Irene Tayler, "The Woman Scaly," in *Blake's Poetry and Designs,* 547.

4. Alicia Ostriker remarks that in Blake's poetry the female constitutes nature, "[T]o be born was to be maternally entrapped and even crucified by her" (75). Also along these lines, see Anne Mellor, "Blake's Portrayal of Women," in *Romanticism and Feminism* (Bloomington and Indianapolis: Indiana University Press, 1988), and

Susan Fox, "The Female as Metaphor in William Blake's Poetry," *Critical Inquiry* 3 (Spring, 1977): 507–19.

5. Most likely, Blake would have been aware of the popular ballads of his day, "Paddy the Weaver," "The Weaver and the Chambermaid" and "The Weaver's March / The Gallant Weaver," by Robert Burns, which all have as their theme the love interests of male weavers. Revived by Carla Sciaky in her album, *Spin the Weaver's Song* from Propinquity Records, 1992.

6. See Arthur Symons, *William Blake* (London: Archibald Constable and Company, 1907), 110. *The Four Zoas* "exists in seventy sheets of manuscript, of uncertain order, almost certainly in an unfinished state, perhaps never intended for publication, but rather as a storehouse of ideas." It was never engraved, but a portion of the poem was written on the proof sheets to Blake's illustrations for Young's *Night Thoughts.* Some Blake scholars think that these illustrations complement the text of *The Four Zoas,* and were in part intended for the manuscript.

David Wagenknecht states that "Milton *is* the thematic consummation, or fulfillment, of the concerns evident in *Vala/The Four Zoas*" (216 of *Blake's Night: William Blake and the Idea of Pastoral* [Cambridge, Mass.: Harvard University Press, 1973]). McNeil maintains a similar view, and states that *The Four Zoas* "shares the thematic ambitions of Milton *and Jerusalem* . . . [but] goes beyond the innovations of both its companion epics." See Helen T. McNeil, "The Formal Art of The Four Zoas," 373, in *Blake's Visionary Forms Dramatic,* ed. David V. Erdman and John E. Grant, 373–90 (Princeton: Princeton University Press, 1970). According to Symons, *The Four Zoas* "is both full of incidental beauty and of considerable assistance in unravelling many of the mysteries in *Milton* and *Jerusalem*" (111).

7. See Northrop Frye, *Fearful Symmetry: A Study of William Blake* (Boston: Beacon, 1947), 269.

8. I am indebted to Dr. Kathryn Freeman (Associate Professor of English, University of Miami) who presented *The Four Zoas* from this perspective, in her graduate seminar at the University of Miami, Spring, 1992. See her book *Blake's Nostos: Fragmentation and Nondualism in "The Four Zoas,"* (New York, New York: SUNY, 1997).

9. Any summary of the Zoas risks reduction of this very complex poem. For instance, Blake plays with notions of time and space, so that an action that occurs—at the psychic level—over a hundred thousand years, may only constitute seconds in actual (historical) time. The incongruity of time and space first occur in Night the First:

> Then Eno a daughter of Beulah took a Moment of Time
> And drew it out to Seven thousand years with much care & affliction
> And many tears & in Every year made windows into Eden
> She also took an atom of space & opend its center
> Into Infinitude & ornamented it with wondrous art
>
> (1:222–26)

10. Helen T. McNeil remarks that, "the high rant and bone-crushing agony of most of the poem are not merely the idiosyncrasies of a private horrific vision. They are . . . the actual and inescapable conditions of the riot of mental powers in every fallen man" (390).

11. The scenes of disharmony, in which the Zoas begin to split and divide against themselves, do not happen consecutively but are continuous with one another. The idea that Enion's quarrel with Tharmas begins the Zoas' dysfunctional relationships only arises because it is the "first" scene the reader encounters. Blake's actions do not occur in a linear progression.

12. Hilton also suggests that Blake employs the spider/web/weaving metaphor—Urizen—in an ironic reversal of the eighteenth century's predilection for the spider as symbol of the intellectual man, its woven web a creative product of the intellect. As Urizen, the Zoa of Reasoning, exemplifies, this web serves only to entrap the mind of its maker, and has nothing to offer the redemptive world.

13. This section in Hilton's book develops further those ideas first introduced by David V. Erdman in *Blake: Prophet Against Empire,* (rev. ed. Anchor Books, Garden City, New York: Doubleday, 1969). Erdman writes "In *The Four Zoas* Blake first fully demonstrates his awareness of the implications of history in the industrial epoch" (330).

14. Jane Schneider and Annette Weiner in *Cloth and Human Experience* (Washington and London: Smithsonian Institution, 1989), suggest that the meaning of cloth altered with the advent of capitalism. They remark convincingly that "[c]apitalist production and its associated cultural values reordered the symbolic potential of cloth in two interrelated ways. First, altering the process of manufacture, capitalism eliminated the opportunity for weavers and dyers to infuse their product with spiritual value and to reflect and pronounce on analogies between reproduction and production. Second, by encouraging the growth of fashion—a consumption system of high velocity turnover and endless, every-changing variation—capitalist entrepreneurs vastly inflated dress and adornment as a domain for expression through cloth. Despite these shifts of emphasis and the worldwide expansion of capitalist manufacturing and fashion, ancient cloths and traditions of making them continue to re-emerge with political—indeed often subversive—intent, above all in societies emerging from colonial domination" (4).

15. See Chretien de Troyes, *Yvain: The Knight of the Lion,* 155–56, 158.

16. David V. Erdman, *Blake: Prophet Against Empire,* 229–30.

17. See William Blake, *Jerusalem,* plate 67:26–27. References to *Jerusalem* and *The Four Zoas* are from *The Complete Poetry & Prose of William Blake,* rev. ed., ed. David V. Erdman (New York: Doubleday, 1988).

18. See Morton D. Paley, "The Figure of the Garment in *The Four Zoas, Milton, and Jerusalem,*" in *Blake's Sublime Allegory: Essays on "The Four Zoas," "Milton," "Jerusalem,"* edited by Stuart Curran and Joseph Anthony Wittreich, Jr. (Madison, Wisconsin: University of Wisconsin Press, 1973), 119–39.

19. Ibid., 131. Morton Paley states, "Our concern is particularly with the garment as an ambiguous symbol of the body in the three long poems, but we must begin by considering the weaving theme, as for Blake a garment was first of all a woven object" (120).

20. Walter Pater, *Greek Studies: A Series of Essays,* 12.

21. See *Jerusalem,* plate 59:45–46, 48, 54–55.

22. See *Thomas Taylor the Platonist: Selected Writings,* ed. Kathleen Raine and George Mills Harper, Bollingen Series LXXXVIII (Princeton, New Jersey: Princeton University Press, 1969), 305.

23. Ibid., emphasis mine.

24. See *The Four Zoas,* 8:208–9, emphasis mine. This phallic imagery issues a strong challenge to Freud's notion that weaving conceals the female weaver's lack of a penis. Instead, it suggests that these weavers are in fact possessed of the phallus.

25. Marcel Detienne and Jean-Pierre Vernant, 163 n. 14.

26. See Tayler, 305.

27. See Nelson Hilton, *Literal Imagination: Blake's Vision of Words* (Berkeley, Los Angeles, London: University of California Press, 1983), 145.

28. Mary Oliver calls the abject "something repulsive that both attracts and repels. It holds you there in spite of your disgust" (55). Indeed, when Vala falls into "experi-

ence," she exhibits a rampant and distorted sexuality that both fascinates and disturbs. Blake exhibits his own ambivalence toward Vala by depicting her in the poem as a veiled body. Her veils conceal the maternal body as well as the imaginary phallus of the pre-oedipal mother.

To launch into a discussion worthy of the Vala figure would require a chapter in itself. Therefore, I will limit my observations to the major weavers of this poem.

29. *The Four Zoas,* 1:121–22.

30. Ibid., 1:86–87.

31. Ibid., 1:123–25.

32. Ibid., 8:187.

33. Imbued by Blake with almost godlike powers, these female Emanations and their spectres spin and weave in the tradition of the Greek Moirai or Fates who, too, have power over mortal life and death. Thus Blake writes:

> In Eden Females sleep the winter in soft silken veils
> Woven by their own hands to hide them in the darksom grave
>
> (1:65–66)

And, "in soft / Delight they die & they revive in spring with music & songs" (1:67–68).

Northrop Frye comments on Blake who parallels his weavers alongside the Greek Fates. They are "spinning, weaving and cutting the threads of life according to a monotonous program of tyranny and mystery, [which] comes primarily through a sense of being wrapped up inside nature like a mummy, or a worm in a cocoon" (266–67). In *Blake and Tradition* (volumes 1 and 2, Bollingen Series XXXV–11 [Princeton, New Jersey: Princeton University Press, 1968]), Kathleen Raine records passages from Gray's ode "The Fatal Sisters," a Celtic equivalent to the Greek Fates that Blake had illustrated. In this poem "A man from Caithness saw twelve weird women enter a hollow hill: . . . they were employed about a loom, and as they wove, they sang [a] . . . dreadful song" (1:88–89).

34. See Elizabeth Grosz, *Jacques Lacan: A Feminist Introduction* (New York: Routledge, 1990), 67.

35. See Alicia Ostriker, "The Thieves of Language: Women Poets and Revisionist Mythmaking," in *The New Feminist Criticism: Essays on Women, Literature, and Theory* (New York: Pantheon, 1985), 77.

36. See *Webster's Third New International Dictionary,* 1966 edition.

37. See *The Four Zoas,* 8:183–84.

38. Ibid., 8:113–14.

39. See Thomas Taylor, 298–99.

40. This is one of the main points expressed by Helen T. McNeil. She maintains, "Action . . . is not a consequence of thought in *The Four Zoas,* but rather the way a thought is expressed" (388).

41. See McNeil, 388.

42. See Jacqueline Rose, "Introduction II," in *Feminine Sexuality: Jacques Lacan and "the ecole freudienne,"* ed. Juliet Mitchell and Jacqueline Rose, trans. Jacqueline Rose (New York and London: W. W. Norton & Company, 1985), 31.

43. See Julia Kristeva, *Revolution in Poetic Language,* 24.

44. Ibid., 79–80.

45. Ibid., 79.

46. I will later deal with the issue of "language" in the Zoas; whereas I include these non-linguistic utterances in my definition of speech, I further distinguish them as marking the difference between semiotic and symbolic elements.

47. *The Four Zoas,* 1:69–72, emphasis mine.

48. Jacqueline Rose states: "Lacan's account of childhood then follows his basic premise that identity is constructed in language, but only at a cost. Identity shifts, and language speaks the loss which lay behind that first moment of symbolisation" (31–32). Tharmas's "Identity shifts" when Enion splits from him, indicating a fall for them both into language and gender.

49. See Donald Ault, *Narrative Unbound: Re-Visioning William Blake's "The Four Zoas"* (Barrytown, New York: Station Hill Press, 1987), 53, emphasis mine.

50. See Jean H. Hagstrum, "Babylon Revisited, or the Story of Luvah and Vala," in *Blake's Sublime Allegory,* ed. Stuart Curran, 101–17 (Madison, Wisconsin: University of Wisconsin Press, 1973), 113. Hagstrum maintains that "The tabernacle, the place of the sacred elements, is one of Blake's images for the enclosing of the male organ by the female. Both fallen sexuality and fallen religion hide the bread and wine from the light of common experience" (113).

51. *The Four Zoas,* 1:85–86.

52. Ibid., 1:123–24.

53. Ibid., 1:150–53.

54. See Wagenknecht's account on this.

55. See Donald Ault, 56.

56. Ibid., 57.

57. See John Milton, *Paradise Lost,* 2:650–51.

58. *The Four Zoas,* 1:183, 186.

59. Ibid., 4:287.

60. Ibid., 1:155.

61. Ibid., 1:29.

62. Ibid.

63. Ibid., 1:172.

64. See Blake's poem, "For the Sexes: the Gates of Paradise," ll. 46–50, in *The Complete Poetry and Prose of William Blake,* my emphasis.

65. *The Four Zoas,* 1:102–3.

66. Ibid., 8:212.

67. See Paul de Man, *The Rhetoric of Romanticism* (New York: Columbia University Press, 1984), 2.

68. See Northrop Frye, 267.

69. *The Four Zoas,* 1:72.

70. Ibid., 8:182.

71. Ibid., 8:287.

72. Ibid., 4: 28–29.

73. See Donald Ault, 251.

74. *The Four Zoas,* 4:56–57.

75. Ibid., 4:51.

76. Ibid., 9:511. Although Tharmas commands Enitharmon to weave, Enitharmon accomplishes her work in a spirit of creative joy; under no circumstances does her activity seem obligatory or suggestive of exploitation. Again, I suggest that Blake derives his weaving symbolism, in *The Four Zoas,* not from current sociopolitical themes (linking weaving to the Industrial Revolution) but from more ancient, mythological sources.

77. *The Four Zoas,* 8:50–54.

78. Ibid., 8:73–74.

79. Ibid., 7:84–85.

80. Ibid., 8:40–41.

81. Ibid., 8:97.

82. Ibid., 8:35–36.

83. See S. Foster Damon, *A Blake Dictionary: The Ideas and Symbols of William Blake* (Providence: Brown University Press, 1965), 253. Paley cites Damon's definition, and elaborates further: "Though built in pain, it provides a way for the Spectres to find their way back to paradise through the world of Generation" (125). Stephen Cox also cites Damon in this regard, albeit tentatively (see *Love and Logic: The Evolution of Blake's Thought* [Ann Arbor: University of Michigan Press, 1992], 193).

84. *The Four Zoas,* 8:23–24.

85. Ibid., 8:27–28.

86. Ibid., 8:191.

87. Ibid., 8:191–92.

88. Ibid., 8:218.

89. Ibid., 8:219.

90. Ibid., 8:37, 50, 113, 182, 210–11, my emphasis.

91. See Morton Paley, 131.

92. Ibid., 123.

93. See James Rieger, "'The Hem of Their Garments': The Bard's Song in Milton," in *Blake's Sublime Allegory: Essays on "The Four Zoas," "Milton," "Jerusalem,"* 277. Rieger uses this model to understand Milton through its four levels of discourse, levels that tend to contradict and obscure each other if not seen as mutually exclusive states of experience.

94. *The Four Zoas,* 8:211–15.

95. See Northrop Frye, 267.

96. Ibid.

97. Paley agrees with this analogy: "The 'Created Body' previously referred to by the Spectre is seen as analogous to a work of art, to be given form and substance by the artist, and both are aspects of incarnation" (122).

98. *The Four Zoas,* 7:229–30.

99. Ibid., 1:94–95.

100. See Hagstrum, 105.

101. *The Four Zoas,* 4:92, 911.

102. See Rieger, 273.

103. *The Four Zoas,* IVX:90–91, 92–93.

104. Ibid., 9:344.

105. Ibid., 9:387.

106. Ibid., 7:489.

107. I am indebted to Kathryn Freeman for this idea. Paley remarks that the last plate of *Jerusalem* (38), which shows "Enitharmon with a spindle in her upraised left hand and a distaff in her right, weaving" indicates that "[p]resumably the weaving of garments is not going to stop in Eternity" (138).

108. *The Four Zoas,* 3:196.

109. Ibid., 9:678–84.

110. See Ault, 439.

111. *The Four Zoas,* 9:710–11.

112. See Rieger, 27.

Chapter 5. "A Magic Web with Colors Gay": Representation of the Lady of Shalott in Pre-Raphaelite Art

1. Many of our earliest examples for the representation of women weaving come to us from the painted vases of Attic Greece that depict women at work carding,

spinning and weaving in the *gynaikonitides.* Eva C. Keuls provides important research on the iconography of "women's work"-weaving and water-bearing—illustrated vases intended for use by women but which "reflect a male-centered viewpoint," particularly a tendency toward voyeurism; these scenes, Keuls argues, "are semiotic in nature, and use repetitious pictorial stereotypes laden with conventional associations" (214). Keuls traces in the development and increasing popularity of these vases, with their intimate scenes of female activity, a complexity in the "vocabulary of iconographic codes" (216). See "Attic Vase-Painting and the Home Textile Industry." For an interesting discussion of nineteenth-century art, cloth work, and portrayal of the body, see Rozsika Parker's, *The Subversive Stitch: Embroidery and the making of the feminine,* (New York: Routledge, 1989).

2. A Greek vessel used for oils or ointments.

3. *The Tapestry Weavers,* also known as *The Fable of Arachne,* painted by Velazquez between 1657–59. Madlyn Miller Kahr notes in her book, *Velazquez: The Art of Painting* (New York: Harper & Row, 1976) that one of the women spinning yarn is portrayed with her skirt "pulled up above her left knee, so that an unusual expanse of bare leg is visible" (206).

4. Kristeva mentions this process in which paintings rely on "the framework of [a] narrative" ("Giotto's Joy," *DL,* 211) but at the same time experience "free rein" (211).

5. Ibid., 210.

6. See Margaret Miles, "The Virgin's One Bare Breast: Female Nudity and Religious Meaning in Tuscan Early Renaissance Culture," in *The Female Body in Western Culture: Contemporary Perspectives,* edited by Susan Rubin Suleiman (Cambridge, Mass.: Harvard Books, 1985), 196.

7. See Kristeva, "Giotto's Joy," *DL,* 214.

8. See Jerome H. Buckley, *The Pre-Raphaelites* (Chicago, Illinois: Academy Chicago Publishers, 1986), xvi. Buckley continues, "Pre-Raphaelitism involved a peculiar intimacy, conveyed by a close observation of specifics, especially visual details, or a close analysis of moods—the peculiar heightening of individual impression and emotion. The quality was to be experienced rather than defined" (xvi). Martin Harrison calls the Pre-Raphaelites "narrative artists"; their favorite authors were Malory, Tennyson, Shakespeare, and Keats (*Pre-Raphaelite Paintings and Graphics* [New York and London: St. Martins, 1973]).

9. Needless to say, Siddal became quite ill from this modeling job, and never fully recovered.

10. See George Brandon Saul, *Traditional Irish Literature and Its Backgrounds: A Brief Introduction* (Lewisburg: Bucknell University Press, 1970), 33.

11. See Douglas Hyde, *A Literary History of Ireland: From Earliest Times to the Present Day* (New York: Barnes & Noble, 1967), 344.

12. Ibid., 301. Hyde writes of Cuchulain, "[H]e recognized . . . that his virtue was indeed overcome, and that his geasa (tabus) were broken, and that the end of his career had arrived, and that his valour and prowess were destroyed," 344.

13. Both Joseph Chadwick and Carl Plasa emphasize the inevitability of the Lady's artistic arrest and consequent death. Plasa states that "the death which the text eventually imposes upon the Lady is only the formal or explicit culmination of a process which commences much earlier" (250). Plasa locates her inevitable demise in her failure "to appropriate the gaze" (257), suggesting that Lancelot kills her into art when she, as the artist, must instead "kill" him. Chadwick maintains that the Lady's death signifies the problems inherent in her "position as an artist, a poet of sensation" (24–25), which for him signifies a male position; later on in his essay Chadwick equates the Lady of Shalott wholly with her body as a representation of the

"poem of sensation—the Romantic artwork" (26) and its complex implications for the nineteenth century. See Carl Plasa, "'Cracked from Side to Side': Sexual Politics in The Lady of Shalott'" in *Victorian Poetry* 30:3–4 (Autumn–Winter 1992): 247–63, and Joseph Chadwick, "A Blessing and a Curse: the Poetics of Privacy in Tennyson's The Lady of Shalott'" in *Victorian Poetry* 24:1 (Spring 1986): 13–30.

14. See Isobel Armstrong, 72 in *The Sun is God: Painting, Literature and Mythology in the Nineteenth Century,* ed. J. B. Bullen (Oxford: Clarendon, 1989), 49–108.

15. Ibid., 51.

16. See Chadwick, 14. Joseph Chadwick states that "[t]he poem . . . identifies itself as feminine: Keats's Grecian urn is a 'still unravished bride of quietness'; Coleridge's Eolian harp is 'Like some coy maid half yielding to her lover'; and Shelley's skylark sings not only 'Like a Poet hidden / In the light of thought,' but also 'Like a highborn maiden / In a palace tower.' Even inanimate or animal emblems for the work of art—urn, harp, skylark—must themselves be emblematized by figures of autonomous (unravished, coy, maidenly) femininity" (15).

17. All quotations from "The Lady of Shalott" are taken from *Poems of Tennyson,* ed. Jerome H. Buckley (Boston, Mass.: Houghton Mifflin Company, 1958).

18. As Chadwick suggests, 16.

19. See John Ruskin, *Praeterita: The Autobiography of John Ruskin,* ed. Lord Kenneth Clark (London, England: Oxford University Press, 1978), xi.

20. Chadwick states that all of the critics he has read survey "the Lady's death as a sign of some conflict between art and 'ordinary living,'" and none of these critics link "the Lady's femininity" to "that death." On the other hand, Chadwick insists that "her particular form of femininity is precisely what gives that death its meaning" (15–16). In other words, like those critics he censures, Chadwick also locates that poem's meaning in the Lady's death.

21. See Kristeva, "Art, Love, and Melancholy," 24.

22. See Kristeva, "Giotto's Joy," *DL,* 215.

23. Rossetti's drawing of "The Lady of Shalott" (1858–59), also examined in this essay, was chosen instead for the cover illustration. Hunt engraved another picture of the Lady of Shalott (3 5/8" x 3 1/8"), similar to his painting, which he also intended for the Moxon edition.

24. See Bronkhurst, 249.

25. The painting I've chosen here is housed at Wadsworth Atheneum, Hartford, Connecticut. A smaller version, painted during the same period, hangs in City Art Gallery, Manchester.

26. See Bronkhurst, 249.

27. Kathleen S. Sullivan, a registered art and antique appraiser, provided me with this information. The idea of the turtledoves may have been suggested to Hunt through his familiarity with the marriage and courting mirrors.

28. See Armstrong, 72.

29. See Deborah Cherry, "The Lady of Shalott," in *The Pre-Raphaelites,* the Tate Gallery (Millbank, England: Penguin, 1984), 266.

30. Ibid.

31. With thanks to Dr. Paula Harper (Associate Professor of Art History, University of Miami) for her insights and guidance in examining the Shalott pictures.

32. See Helena Michie, *The Flesh Made Word: Female Figures and Women's Bodies* (New York, Oxford: Oxford University Press, 1987), 123.

33. See Kristeva, "Giotto's Joy," *DL,* 215.

34. This constitutes a different kind of verisimilitude than the one Kristeva promotes as constitutive of the semiotic chora. Kristeva would most likely judge the Pre-Raphaelite style as an enslavement to the Symbolic. For her, verisimilitude and

mimesis are different from "truth": "Although mimesis partakes of the symbolic order, it does so only to re-produce some of its constitutive rules" (*Revolution in Poetic Language,* 57). The Pre-Raphaelites' adherence to detail, however, is often what makes their paintings seem so unreal.

Kristeva's discussions on "mimetic verisimilitude" are limited to language—poetry, in specific. She says, "Mimesis, in our view, is a transgression of the thetic when truth is no longer a reference to an object that is identifiable outside language; it refers instead to an object that can be constructed through the semiotic network but is nevertheless posited in the symbolic and is, from then on, always verisimilar" (*Kristeva Reader,* 110).

35. The exception here is E. E. Siddal.

36. See Kristeva, "Giotto's Joy," *DL,* 216.

37. See Buckley, xvi.

38. See Kristeva, "Giotto's Joy," *DL,* 225.

39. Ibid.

40. See Cirlot, 290.

41. Mythic elements and echoes are discussed in terms of their ironic reversals in Armstrong's article, 57.

"The Lady of Shalott" has long been an enigma to scholars. Isobel Armstrong remarks that the poem "studies to create a form which, as Ruskin was later to say, appears not to know its own meaning. It is curiously unaccountable and sourceless. Its strategy is to be opaque, preferring and evading interpretation simultaneously, so that the strategy itself becomes a form of signification" (50).

42. See Eric Newton, *The Romantic Rebellion* (New York: St. Martin's Press, 1963), 124.

43. Ibid., 57.

44. Ann C. Colley focuses her discussion of "The Lady of Shalott," in part, on this scene: "the citizens of Camelot, [are] looking at the inscribed name and wondering what to do with it: Who is the Lady of Shalott, and what is the meaning of her presence in Camelot?" ("The Quest for the Nameless' in Tennyson's The Lady of Shalott,'" in *Victorian Poetry* 23:4 [Winter 1985]: 369). Colley maintains that "when the Lady of Shalott asserts her name into the consciousness of Camelot"—the name that appears on her boat—"she wounds and ruptures the synecdochic order of the dull-witted society and exposes its emptiness" (375). My analysis differs from Colley's in that I conceive that difference between the Lady of Shalott and Camelot as one which sustains them both; it is analogous to the difference/dependence of the semiotic and symbolic realms.

45. See Lechte, 45.

46. See Kristeva, "The Novel as Polylogue," in *Desire in Language,* 190–91.

47. See Kaja Silverman, *The Acoustic Mirror: The Female Voice in Psychoanalysis and Cinema* (Bloomington and Indianapolis: Indiana University Press, 1988), 73. Silverman studies what she calls "the fantasy of the maternal voice" in terms of the cinema; she defines "fantasy" to mean a "reading of a situation which is fundamentally irrecoverable, rather than to posit it as a simple illusion" (73).

48. Lancelot, then, represents the pre-oedipal mother for the Lady of Shalott, whereas the Lady represents the same for those in Camelot. According to Kristeva, gender has little to do with the pre-oedipal mother, who also possesses the phallus: "In Kristeva's scenario, the husband is the phallic mother for the woman, while the wife is the mother that allows the man to remain a child. . . . [She] argues that the woman finds her mother in her husband" (see Oliver, 80–81).

49. See Jacques Derrida, "Différence," in *Margins of Philosophy,* trans. Alan Bass (Chicago, Illinois: University of Chicago Press, 1982), 17.

50. Ibid.
51. See Oliver, 13.
52. See chapter 1 for discussion of the *thetic.*
53. This mirror is an appropriate tool for the weaver who sees in its reflection the "right side" of her tapestry as it takes shape beneath her hands; perhaps, then, the Lady is inventing the world of Camelot as she weaves, and the shadows revealed in the glass represent, rather, what has already been woven on her loom. Isobel Armstrong also suggests this possibility (63).
54. See Newton, 57.
55. See Kristeva, "The Novel as Polylogue," in *DL,* 175.
56. Ibid., 159.
57. Ibid., 162.
58. See Scarry, xiv.
59. Siddal remains the exception; the artist's refusal to sexualize the Lady indicates Siddall's identification with her. Also, note that although her illustration depicts the curse, she still portrays the Lady in a positive relationship with her work.

Chapter 6. Uniquely Feminine Productions

1. See Julia Kristeva, *Revolution in Poetic Language,* 70–71.
2. See Elizabeth Meese, "Defiance: The Body (of) Writing / The Writing (of) Body," in *Crossing the Double-Cross: The Practice of Feminist Criticism* (Chapel Hill: University of North Carolina Press, 1986), 119.
3. See Jacob Needleman, *Time and the Soul* (New York, London, Toronto, Sydney, Aukland: Currency/Doubleday, 1998), 42.
4. Sir Philip Sidney, *The Defense of Poesy* (1595).
5. See "Ancient Awakening," in *Handwoven* (September /October 1984): 53.
6. Ibid.
7. See Mihoko Suzuki, *Metamorphoses of Helen: Authority, Difference, and the Epic,* 34–36.
8. See Kristeva, *Revolution in Poetic Language,* 70–71.
9. See Margaret Homans, *Bearing the Word: Language and Female Experience in Nineteenth-Century Women's Writing* (Chicago and London: University of Chicago Press, 1986), 2.
10. See Rozsika Parker, *The Subversive Stitch,* 3.
11. Ibid.

Bibliography

Alderman, Sharon. "Simple Gifts." *Handwoven* (November 1982): 40–42.

Allen, Paula Gunn. *Grandmothers of the Light: A Medicine Woman's Sourcebook.* Boston, Mass.: Beacon Press, 1991.

———. *The Sacred Hoop: Recovering the Feminine in American Indian Traditions.* Boston, Mass.: Beacon, 1986.

"Ancient Awakenings." *Handwoven* (September/October 1984): 51–55.

Aptheker, Bettina. *Tapestries of Life: Women's Work, Women's Consciousness, and the Meaning of Daily Experience.* Amherst: University of Massachusetts Press, 1989.

Apter, Emily. *Feminizing the Fetish: Psychoanalysis and NarrativeObsession in Turn-of-the-Century France.* Ithaca, New York: Cornell University Press, 1991.

Armstrong, Isobel. "Tennyson's 'The Lady of Shalott': Victorian Mythography and the Politics of Narcissism." *The Sun is God: Painting, Literature and Mythology in the Nineteenth Century.* Edited by J. B. Bullen. Oxford: Clarendon, 1989. 49–108.

Armstrong, Nancy. *Desire and Domestic Fiction: A Political History of the Novel.* New York, Oxford: Oxford University Press, 1987.

Arthur, Marylin B. "The Dream of a World Without Women: Poetics and the Circles of Order in the *Theogony Proemium.*" *Arethusa* 16 (1983): 97–116.

———. "Cultural Strategies in Hesiod's *Theogony:* Law, Family, Society." *Arethusa* 15 (1982): 63–82.

Atwood, Margaret. *Lady Oracle.* New York: Ballantine Books, 1976.

"Aubusson vs. Gobelins." *Handwoven* (March/April 1988): 88.

Ault, Donald. *Narrative Unbound: Re-Visioning William Blake's "The Four Zoas."* Barrytown, New York: Station Hill Press, 1987.

Badone, Donalda. "Paisley." *Handwoven* (January/February 1987): 39–41, 83.

———. "Peruvian Textiles." *Handwoven* (September/October 1988): 52–54.

Bal, Mieke. "Sexuality, Semiosis and Binarism: A NarratologicalComment on Bergren and Arthur." *Arethusa* 16 (1–2) (1983): 117–35.

Barber, Elizabeth Wayland. *Women's Work: The First 20,000 Years. Women, Cloth, and Society in Early Times.* New York and London: W. W. Norton & Company, 1994.

Barolini, Teodolinda. "Arachne, Argus, and St. John: Transgressive Art in Dante and Ovid." *Mediaevalia* 13 (1982): 207–26.

Barthes, Roland. *The Pleasure of the Text.* Translated by Richard Miller. New York: Farrar, Straus and Giroux, 1975.

———. "From Work to Text." In *Textual Strategies: Perspectives in Post-Structuralist Criticism,* 73–81. Edited by Josue V. Harari. Ithaca, New York: Cornell University Press, 1979.

Barzilai, Shuli. "Borders of Language: Kristeva's Critique of Lacan." *PMLA* 106:2 (March 1991): 294–305.

Becker, John. *Pattern and Loom.* Copenhagen: Rhodos International Publishers, 1987.

Bennett, Noel. *Halo of the Sun: Stories Told and Retold.* Flagstaff, Arizona: Northland, 1987.

Behrendt, Stephen C. *History and Myth: Essays on English Romantic Literature.* Detroit, Michigan: Wayne State University Press, 1990.

Benstock, Shari. *Textualizing the Feminine: On the Limits of Genre.* Norman, Oklaho Mass.: University of Oklahoma Press, 1991.

Berger, John. *Ways of Seeing.* New York, New York: Penguin, 1972.

Bergren, Ann. "Helen's 'Good Drug', *Odyssey* iv, 1–305." *Contemporary Literary Hermeneutics and Interpretation of Classical Texts.* Ottawa: Ottawa University Press, 1981.

———. "Helen's Web: Time and Tableau in the Iliad." *Helios: Journal of the Classical Association of the Southwest* 7 (1980): 19–34.

———. "Language and the Female in Early Greek Thought." *Arethusa* 16 (1983): 6–95.

———. "Sacred Apostrophe: Re-Presentation and Imitation in the Homeric Hymns," *Arethusa* 15 (1932): 83–108.

Blake, *William Blakes's Poetry and Designs.* Selected and edited by Mary Lynn Johnson and John E. Grant. New York and London: W. W. Norton & Company, 1979.

———. *The Complete Poetry and Prose of William Blake.* Newly revised. Edited by David V. Erdman. New York: Doubleday, 1988.

Bier, Carol. "Textiles and Society." In *Woven from the Soul, Spunfrom the Heart: Textile Arts of Safavid and Qajar Iran, 16th–19th Centuries,* 1–6. Edited by Carol Bier. Washington, D.C.: The Textile Museum, 1987.

Bly, Robert. *The Kabir Book: Forty-four of the Ecstatic Poems of Kabir.* Boston: Beacon Press, 1977.

Brandes, Kendra. "The Language of Textiles." *Handwoven* (January/February 1988): 82.

Bridenthal, Renate, Claudia Koonz, Susan Stuard, eds. *Becoming Visible: Women In European History* (Second Edition). Boston, Mass.: Houghton Mifflin Company, 1987.

Bronkhurst, Judith. "The Lady of Shalott." *The Pre-Raphaelites.* The Tate Gallery. Millbank, England: Penguin, 1984. 249.

Brown, Judith C. "A Woman's Place Was in the Home: Women's Work in Renaissance Tuscany." *Rewriting the Renaissance: Discourses of Sexual Difference in Early Modern Europe.* Chicago and London: University of Chicago Press, 1986.

Buckley, Jerome H. *The Pre-Raphaelites.* Chicago, Illinois: Academy Chicago Publishers, 1986.

Burkhauser, Jude. "Ancient Art/Modern Spirit." *Handwoven* (January 1982): 55–56, 65, 90.

———. "The Tweed Weavers of Glenmore." *Handwoven* (May 1982): 56–58.

Caws, Mary Ann. "Ladies Shot and Painted: Female Embodiment in Surrealist Art." In *The Female Body in Western Culture: Contemporary Perspectives.* Edited by Susan Rubin Suleiman. Cambridge, Mass. & London, England: Harvard Books, 1985.

Carruthers, Mary. "The Wife of Bath and the Painting of Lions." *PMLA* 94 (1979): 209–22.

Carter, Anne Babson, "Scenes and Stitches." *Americana* 15 (September/October 1987): 33–36.

Chadwick, Joseph. "A Blessing and a Curse: The Poetics of Privacy in Tennyson's 'The Lady of Shalott.'" *Victorian Poetry* 24:1 (Spring 1986): 13–30.

Cherry, Deborah. "The Lady of Shalott." *The Pre-Raphaelites.* The Tate Gallery. Millbank, England: Penguin, 1984. 266.

Cirlot, J. E. *Dictionary of Symbols.* London: Routledge and Kegan Paul, 1962.

Clader, L.L. *Helen: The Evolution from Divine to Heroic in Greek Epic Tradition.* Leiden: E. J. Brill, 1976.

Claridge, Laura. *Romantic Potency: The Paradox of Desire.* Ithaca: Cornell University Press, 1992.

Clark, Gillian. *Women in the Ancient World.* New Surveys in the Classics, No. 21. Oxford, New York, Toronto: Oxford University Press, 1989.

Clinton, Jerome W. "Image and Metaphor: Textiles in Persian Poetry." In *Woven from the Soul, Spun from the Heart: Textile Arts of Safavid and Qajar Iron, 16th–19th Centuries,* 7–11. Edited by Carol Bier. Washington, D.C.: The Textile Museum, 1987.

Colley, Ann C. "The Quest for the 'Nameless' in Tennyson's 'The Lady of Shalott.'" *Victorian Poetry* 23:4 (Winter 1985): 369–78.

Cox, Stephen. *Love and Logic: The Evolution of Blake's Thought.* Ann Arbor: University of Michigan Press, 1992.

de Lauretis, Teresa. *Technologies of Gender: Essays on Theory, Film, and Fiction.* Bloomington and Indianapolis: Indiana University Press, 1987.

de Man, Paul. *The Rhetoric of Romanticism.* New York: Columbia University Press, 1984.

———. *Romanticism and Contemporary Criticism: The Gauss Seminar and Other Papers.* Baltimore and London: Johns Hopkins University Press, 1993.

Damon, S. Foster. *A Blake Dictionary: The Ideas and Symbols of William Blake.* Providence: Brown University Press, 1965.

Damrosch, Leopold Jr. *Symbol and Truth in Blake's Myth.* Princeton, New Jersey: Princeton University Press, 1980.

Daniloff, Ruth. "Where Tradition Looms." *American Way* (March, 1992).

Derrida, Jacques. "Differance." *Margins of Philosophy.* Trans. Alan Bass. Chicago, Illinois: University of Chicago Press, 1982. 1–27.

Detienne, Marcel and Jean-Pierre Vernant. *Cunning Intelligence in Greek Culture and Society.* Translated by Janet Lloyd. Atlantic Highlands, New Jersey: Humanities Press, 1978.

DeWald, Terry. Folklorist and Anthropologist. Phone Interview. Tucson, Arizona (19 June 1997: 9:30 A.M.).

de Troyes, Chretien. *Yvain: The Knight of the Lion.* Translated by Burton Raffel. New Haven annd London: Yale University Press, 1987. 155–60.

Dietrich, Mary G. "The Fiber Arts of Chile." *Handwoven* (September/October 1988): 57–63.

Dickinson, Emily. *The Complete Poems of Emily Dickinson.* Edited by Thomas H. Johnson. Boston, Toronto, London: Little, Brown and Company, 1960.

Dinesen, Isak. "The Blank Page" *Last Tales.* New York: Doubleday, 1957.

Dingley, R.J. "Misfortunes of Philomel." *Parergon* 4 (1986): 76–86.

Dockstader, Frederick J. *Weaving Arts of the North American Indian.* Thomas Y. Crowell, 1978.

Dorfman, Deborah. *Blake in the Nineteenth Century: His Reputation as a Poet from Gilchrist to Yeats.* New Haven: Yale University Press, 1969.

Drooker, Penelope. "Silk: the Story of a Culture." *Handwoven* (January/February 1986): 49–51.

Dubois, Page. *Sowing the Body: Psychoanalysis and Ancient Representations of Women.* Chicago and London: University of Chicago Press, 1988.

Eliot, George. *Silas Marner.* A Signet Classic. Markham, Ontario: New American Library, 1960.

Erdman, David V. *Blake: Prophet Against Empire.* Anchor Books, revised edition. Garden City, New York: Doubleday, 1969.

Euripides, *The Bacchae and Other Plays.* Translated by Philip Vellacott. England, Maryland, Victoria: Penguin, 1972.

Felski, Rita. *Beyond Feminist Aesthetics: Feminist Literature andSocial Change.* Cambridge, Mass.: Harvard University Press, 1989.

Ferguson, Margaret W., Maureen Quilligan, Nancy Vickers, eds. *Rewriting the Renaissance: Discourses of Sexual Difference in Early Modern Europe.* Chicago and London: University of Chicago Press, 1986.

Flowers, Betty S. and Lynda E. Boose, eds. *Daughters and Fathers.* Baltimore and London: Johns Hopkins University Press, 1989.

Foucault, Michel. *The Archaeology of Knowledge and the Discourse on Language.* Translated by A. M. Sheridan Smith. New York: Pantheon, 1972.

———. "What Is an Author?" In *Textual Strategies: Perspectives in Post-Structuralist Criticism,* 141–60. Edited by Josue V. Harari. Ithaca, New York: Cornell University Press, 1979.

Fowler, Brenda. "Find in Europe Suggests that Weaving Preceeded Settled Life." *The New York Times* (Tuesday, 9 May 1995): C1, C10.

Fox, Susan. "The Female as Metaphor in William Blake's Poetry." *Critical Inquiry* 3 (Spring, 1977): 507–19.

Frater, "In the Language of Folk." *El Palacio* 94 (Spring 1989): 44–53.

Frazer, Sir James George. *The Golden Bough: A Study in Magic and Religion.* New York: The Macmillan Company, 1924.

Freeman, Kathryn. *Blake's Nostos: Fragmentation and Nondualism in "The Four Zoas."* New York, New York: SUNY, 1997.

Freud, Sigmund. *New Introductory Lectures on Psycho-Analysis.* New York: W. W. Norton, 1961.

Frosch, Thomas R. *The Awakening of Albion: The Renovation of the Body in the Poetry of William Blake.* Ithaca and London: Cornell University Press, 1974.

Frye, Northrop. *Fearful Symmetry: A Study of William Blake.* Boston: Beacon, 1947.

Gallagher, Kate. "Action." *Handwoven* (September/October 1985): 11.

———. "Waulking Tweeds at the Marshfield School of Weaving." *Handwoven* (September/October 1985): 10.

Garner, Shirley Nelson, Claire Kahane, Madelon Sprengnether, eds. *The(M)other Tongue: Essays in Feminist Psychoanalytic Interpretation.* Ithaca: Cornell University Press, 1985.

Geijer, Agnes. *A History of Textile Art.* London: Sotheby Parke Bernet, 1979.

Gentili, Bruno. "The Interpretation of the Greek Lyric Poets in Our Time: Synchronism and Diachronism in the Study of an Oral Culture." In *Contemporary Literary*

Hermeneutics and Interpretation of Classical Texts, 109–20. Ottawa: Ottawa University Press, 1981.

Gevers, Veronika. *Studies in Textile History.* Toronto, Canada: Royal Ontario Museum, 1977.

Gilbert, Sandra M. and Susan Gubar. *The Madwoman in the Attic: The Woman Writer and the Nineteenth-Century Literary Imagination.* New Haven: Yale University Press, 1979.

Gilchrist, Alexander. *Life of William Blake: With Selections from his Poems and Other Writings.* Vol. 1. Yorkshire, England: EP Publishing Limited, 1973.

Ginsburg, Madeleine. *The Illustrated History of Textiles.* New York: Portland House, 1991.

Glenn, Edgar M. *The Metamorphoses: Ovid's Roman Games.* Maryland and London: University Press of America, 1986.

Graves, Robert. *The Greek Myths: Volume One.* Edinburgh, Great Britain: Penguin, 1955.

———. *The White Goddess: A historical grammar of poetic myth.* New York: Creative Age Press, 1948.

Griaule, Marcel. *Conversations with Ogotemmeli: An Introduction to Dogon Religious Ideas.* Ely House, London: Oxford University Press, 1965.

Grosz, Elizabeth. *Jacques Lacan: A Feminist Introduction.* New York: Routledge, 1990.

———. "The Body of Signification." In *Abjection, Melancholia, and Love: The Works of Julia Kristeva.* Edited by John Fletcher and Andrew Benjamin. New York: Routledge, 1990. 80–103.

Gubar, Susan. "'The Blank Page' and the Issues of Female Creativity." *Critical Inquiry* 8 (Winter 1981): 243–65.

Hagstrum, Jean H. "Babylon Revisited, or the Story of Luvah and Vala." In *Blake's Sublime Allegory,* 101–17. Edited by Stuart Curran. Madison, Wisconsin: University of Wisconsin Press, 1973.

Haigney, Catherine. "Vala's Garden in Night the Ninth: Paradise Regained or Woman Bound?" *Blake/An Illustrated Quarterly* (Spring 1987): 116–23.

Hakonardottir, Hildur. "Icelandic Weaving: Saga in Wool." *Handwoven* (May/June 1987): 62–63.

"The Handwoven Communique." Edited by Bobbie Irwin. *Handwoven* (November/December 1989): 104–5.

Harari, Josue V. "Critical Factions/ Critical Fictions." In *Textual Strategies: Perspectives in Post-Structuralist Criticism,* 17–72. Edited by Josue V. Harari. Ithaca, New York: Cornell University Press, 1979.

Harrison, Martin. *Pre-Raphaelite Paintings and Graphics.* New York and London: St. Martins, 1973.

Harrison, Martin and Bill Waters. *Burne-Jones.* London: Barrie & Jenkins, 1973.

Hartman, Geoffrey H. "The Voice of the Shuttle: Literature from the Point of View of Literature." In *Beyond Formalism: LiteraryEssays 1958–1970,* 337–55. New Haven and London: Yale University Press, 1970.

Hawthorne, Nathaniel. *The Blithdale Romance.* New York, New York: Penguin Classics, 1983.

Heinrich, Linda. "Weaving with Linen: The Cloth of the Ancients." *Handwoven* (March/April 1989): 39–44.

Heinzelman, Kurt. "The Cult of Domesticity: Dorothy and William Wordsworth at Grasmere," 52–78. In *Romanticism and Feminism.* Edited by Anne K. Mellor. Bloomington and Indianapolis: Indiana University Press, 1988.

Helmond, Gemeentemuseum. "The Handwoven Communique." Edited by Bobbie Irwin. *Handwoven* (November/December 1989): 105.

Hepburn, Ian. "Gandhi and Other Threads." *Handwoven* (September/October 1991): 20, 28.

Herzfeld, Michael. "The Excavation of Concepts: Coommentary on Peradotto and Nagy." *Arethusa* 16 (1983): 57–68.

Hicks, Norman C. "Spindle." *Shuttle, Spindle, and Dyepot* (Summer 1975): 63–64.

Hilton, Nelson. *Literal Imagination: Blake's Vision of Words.* Berkeley, Los Angeles, London: University of California Press, 1983.

Hite, Molly. *The Other Side of the Story: Structures and Strategies of Contemporary Feminist Narrative.* Ithaca: Cornell University Press, 1984.

Hively, Evelyn. "Weaving Myths." *Handwoven* (March 1982): 10–13.

Hochberg, Bette. *Spin, Span, Spun: Fact and Folklore for Spinnners and Weavers.* Berkley, California: Wholesale Distributors, 1979.

Homans, Margaret. *Bearing the Word: Language and Female Experience in Nineteenth-Century Women's Writing.* Chicago and London: University of Chicago Press, 1986.

Homer, *The Iliad of Homer.* Translated by Richard Lattimore. Chicago & London: University of Chicago Press, 1951.

Homer, *The Odyssey of Homer.* Translated by T. E. Lawrence. New York and Oxford: Oxford University Press, 1991.

Hoskins, Nancy Arthur, "The Bayeux Tapestry: an Eleventh-century Epic Embroidery." *Handwoven* (January/February 2000): 78–80.

Hyde, Douglas. *A Literary History of Ireland: From Earliest Times to the Present Day.* New York: Barnes & Noble, 1967.

Hyslop, John. *Handwoven* (November/December 1989): 104–5.

Irigaray, Luce. *This Sex Which Is Not One.* Translated by Porter. Ithaca, New York: Cornell University Press, 1985.

Iyer, Pico. "The East India Company: Oxbridge-on-the-Hooghly." In *Tropical Classical,* 48–61. New York: Alfred A. Knopf, 1997.

Johnson, Beth. "The Tweed of Harris." *Handwoven* (November 1981): 47–48.

Johnson, David M. *Word Weaving: A Creative Approach to Teaching and Writing Poetry.* Urbana, Illinois: National Council of Teachers of English, 1990.

Johnson, Geraldine Niva. "Weaving Rag Rugs: A Women's Craft in Western Maryland." *Handwoven* (May/June 1986): 12.

Johnson, Mary Lynn and Brian Wilkie. "On Reading *The Four Zoas:* Inscape and Analogy." In *Blake's Sublime Allegory: Essays on "The Four Zoas," "Milton," "Jerusalem."* Edited by Stuart Curran and Joseph Anthony Wittreich, Jr., 203–32. Madison, Wisconsin: University of Wisconsin Press, 1973.

Jongeward, David. *Weaver of Worlds: From Navajo Apprenticeship to Sacred Geometry and Dreams. A Woman's Journey in Tapestry.* Rochester, Vermont: Destiny Books, 1990.

Joplin, Patricia Klindienst. "The Voice of the Shuttle is Ours." *Stanford Literature Review* 1 (Spring 1984): 25–53.

Kahr, Madlyn Millner. *Velazquez: The Art of Painting.* New York, Hagerstown, San Francisco, London: Harper & Row, 1976.

Kalniete, Sandra. "Modern Latvian Tapestry." *Soviet Literature* 3 (1987): 178–82.

Kamuf, Peggy. *Signature Pieces: On the Institution of Authorship.* Ithaca and London: Cornell University Press, 1988.

Keats, John. *Letters of John Keats.* Selected and edited by Robert Gittings. Oxford, New York: Oxford University Press, 1970.

Kelly, Joan. *Women, History, & Theory: The Essays of Joan Kelly.* Chicago and London: University of Chicago Press, 1984.

Kerridge, Eric. *Textile Manufacture in Early Modern England.*

Keuls, Eva C. "Attic Vase-Painting and the Home Textile Industry." In *Ancient Greek Art and Iconography.* Edited by Warren G. Moon. Madison, Wisconsin: University of Wisconsin Press, 1983. 209–30.

Klonsky, Milton. *William Blake: The Seer and His Visions.* New York: Harmony Books, 1977.

Knapp, Peggy A. "Alisoun Weaves a Text." *Philological Quarterly* 65 (1986): 387–401.

Kristeva, Julia. *Desire in Language: A Semiotic Approach to Literature and Art.* Edited by Leon S. Roudiez. Translated by Thomas Gora, Alice Jardine, and Leon S. Roudiez. New York: Columbia University Press, 1980.

———. *Powers of Horror: An Essay on Abjection.* Translated by Leon S. Roudiez. New York: Columbia University Press, 1982.

———. *The Kristeva Reader.* Edited by Toril Moi. New York: Columbia University Press, 1986.

———. *Revolution in Poetic Language.* Translated by Margaret Waller. New York: Columbia University Press, 1984.

Krondahl, Hans. "From Hand to Hand: Swedish Weaving Today." *Handwoven* (May/June 1987): 34–35.

Lacan, Jacques. *Feminine Sexuality: Jacques Lacan and "the ecole freudienne."* Edited by Juliet Mitchell and Jacqueline Rose. Translated by Jacqueline Rose. New York: W. W. Norton & Company, 1985.

Lawlor, Robert. *Voices of the First Day: Awakening in the Aboriginal Dreamtime.* Rochester, Vermont: Inner Traditions International, Ltd., 1991.

Larkin, David. *The English Dreamers: A Collection of Pre-Raphaelite Paintings.* Toronto, New York, London: A Peacock Press/Bantam Book, 1975.

Lechte, John. *Julia Kristeva.* New York: Routledge, 1990.

———. "Art, Love, and Melancholy in the Work of Julia Kristeva." In *Abjection,Melancholia, and Love: The Works of Julia Kristeva.* Edited by John Fletcher and Andrew Benjamin. New York: Routledge, 1990. 24–41.

Leviton, Richard. "Voices from the Dreamtime." *Yoga Journal* (September/October 1992): 66–70, 114–15.

Link, Margaret. *The Pollen Path.* Palo Alto, California: Stanford University Press, 1956.

Linton, Joan Pong. "*Jack of Newbery* and Drake in California: Narratives of English Cloth aand Manhood." *ELH* 59(1): 23–51.

Lister, Raymond. *The Paintings of William Blake.* Cambridge, London, New York, New Rochelle, Melbourne, Sydney: Cambridge University Press, 1986.

McCrosky, Judy. "Lentswe La Oodi Weavers." *Handwoven* (March/April 1988): 39–41.

McGann, Jerome J. "Shelley's Veils: A Thousand Images of Loveliness." In *Romantic and Victorian: Studies in Memory ofWilliam H. Marshall.* Edited by W. Paul Elledge and Richard L. Hoffman, 198–218. Rutherford, Madison, Teaneck: Fairleigh Dickinson University Press, 1971.

McNeil, Helen T. "The Formal Art of *The Four Zoas.*" In *Blake's Visionary Forms Dramatic.* Edited by David V. Erdman and John E. grant. Princeton: Princeton University Press, 1970. 373–90.

Macdonald, Don. "Harris TweEdited by" *Handwoven* (September/October 1989): 68–73.

MacCornack, Katharine. "The Bayeux Tapestry: Does it follow the French Oral Epic?" in *Constructions* (1985): 95–104.

Mactoux, Marie-Madeleine. *Penelope: Legende et Mythe.* Centre de Recherches D'histoire Ancienne. Vol. 16. Paris: Annales Litteraires de L'Universite de Besancon, 1975.

Marcus, Jane. "Liberty, Sorority, Misogyny." In *The Representation of Women in Fiction: Selected Papers from the English Institute, 1981.* New Series, no. 7. Edited by Carolyn G. Heilbrun and Margaret R. Higonnet. Baltimore and London: Johns Hopkins University Press, 1983.

———. *Virginia Woolf and the Language of Patriarchy.* Bloomington and Indianapolis: Indiana University Press, 1987.

———. "Still Practice, A/Wrested Alphabet: Toward a Feminist Aesthetic." *Tulsa Studies in Women's Literature* 3 (Spring/Fall 1984): 79–97.

Marsh, Jan & Pamela Gerrish Nunn. *Women Artists and the Pre-Raphaelite Movement.* London, Great Britain: Virago, 1989.

Marshall, Kathryn. "Searching the Sacred Universe." *American Way* (1 March 1992): 56–61, 86–90.

Massey, Michael. *Women in Ancient Greece and Rome.* Cambridge, New York, Melbourne: Cambridge University Press, 1988.

Meaney, Janet. "Three English Textile Museums." *Handwoven* (November/December 1991): 23–24.

Meese, Elizabeth. "Defiance: The Body (of) Writing / The Writing (of) Body." In *Crossing the Double-Cross: The Practice of Feminist Criticsm.* Chapel Hill: University of North Carolina Press, 1986. 117–31.

Mellor, Anne K. *Romanticism and Feminism.* Bloomington and Indianapolis: Indiana University Press, 1988.

Melville, Herman. *Moby Dick.* New York: The Modern Library, 1926.

Michie, Helena. *The Flesh Made Word: Female Figures and Women's Bodies.* New York, Oxford: Oxford University Press, 1987.

Miles, Margaret. "The Virgin's One Bare Breast: Female Nudity and Religious Meaning in Tuscan Early Renaissance Culture." In *The Female Body in Western Culture: Contemporary Perspectives.* Edited by Susan Rubin Suleiman. Cambridge, Mass.: Harvard Books, 1985.

Miller, J. Hillis. "Ariadne's Thread: Repetition and the Narrative Line." *Critical Inquiry* 3 (Autumn 1976): 57–77.

———. "Ariachne's Broken Woof," *The Georgia Review* 31 (1977): 44–60.

———. *Ariadne's Thread: Story Lines.* New Haven and London: Yale University Press, 1992.

Miller, Nancy K. *Subject to Change: Reading Feminist Writing.* New York: Columbia University Press, 1988.

Nagy, Gregory. "Sema and Noesis: Some Illustrations," *Arethusa* 16 (1983): 35–55.

Needleman, Jacob. *Time and the Soul.* New York, London, Toronto, Sydney, Aukland: Currency/Doubleday, 1998.

Nelson, Lila. "Weaving in Rural Norway: A Living Tradition." *Handwoven* (May/June 1987): 52–54.

Newton, Eric. *The Romantic Rebellion.* New York: St. Martin's, 1963.

Oliver, Kelly. *Reading Kristeva: Unraveling the Double-bind.* Bloomington and Indianapolis: Indiana University Press, 1993.

"One Hundred Years Ago in Handweaving." *Handwoven* (May/June 1986): 27.

Ostriker, Alicia. "The Thieves of Language: Women Poets and Revisionist Mythmaking." In *The New Feminist Criticism: Essays on Women, Literature, and Theory.* New York: Pantheon, 1985.

Ovid. *Ovid in Six Volumes: III. Metamorphoses.* Translated by Frank Justus Miller, Ph.D. Cambridge, Mass.: Harvard University Press, 1977.

———. *Metamorphoses.* Translated by A. D. Melville. Oxford, New York: Oxford University Press, 1986.

———. *The Metamorphoses of Ovid.* Translated by Henry T. Riley, B.A. London: George Bell and Sons, 1884.

Padel, Ruth. "Women: Model for Possession by Greek Daemons." In *Images of Women in Antiquity.* Edited by Averil Cameron and Amelie Kuhrt. Detroit: Wayne State University Press, 1983. 94–126.

Paley, Morton D. "The Figure of the Garment in *The Four Zoas, Milton,* and *Jerusalem.*" In *Blake's Sublime Allegory: Essays on "The Four Zoas," "Milton," "Jerusalem."* Edited by Stuart Curran and Joseph Anthony Wittreich, Jr. Madison, Wisconsin: University of Wisconsin Press, 1973. 119–39.

Panofsky, Erwin. *Studies in Iconology: Humanistic Themes In the Art of the Renaissance.* New York: Oxford University Press, 1939.

Parker, Rozsika. *The Subversive Stitch: Embroidery and the Making of the Feminine.* New York: Routledge, 1989.

Parslow, Virginia. "Flax: From Seed to Yarn." *Handweaver and Craftsman* (Spring 1952): 30–31, 45.

Pater, Walter. *Greek Studies: A Series of Essays.* London: MacMillan and Company, 1911.

Peradotto, John. "Texts and Unrefracted Facts: Philology, Hermeneutics and Semiotics," *Arethusa* 16 (1983): 15–33.

Plasa, Carl. "'Cracked from Side to Side': Sexual Politics in 'The Lady of Shalott.'" *Victorian Poetry* 30: 3–4 (Autumn-Winter 1992): 247–63.

Pollard, J. R. T. "Muses and Sirens," *The Classical Review* V II(2): June 1952, 60–63.

Pope, Alexander. *The Odyssey of Homer.* New York: The Heritage Press, 1942.

The Pre-Raphaelites. London: Tate Gallery Publications Department and Penguin, 1984.

Raine, Kathleen. *Blake and Tradition.* Volumes 1 and 2. Bollingen Series XXXV–11. Princeton, New Jersey: Princeton University Press, 1968.

——— and George Mills Harper, eds. *Thomas Taylor the Platonist: Selected Writings.* Bollingen Series LXXXVIII. Princeton, New Jersey: Princeton University Press, 1969.

Rantanen, Kirsti. "Finnish Textile Art: From Byzantine to Bauhaus." *Handwoven* (May/June 1987): 68–69.

Rawlings, Marjorie Kinnan, "The Magnolia Tree," *Sisters of the Earth: Women's Prose and Poetry About Nature.* New York: Vintage, 1991.

Reed, Myrtle. *Love Letters of a Musician.* New York and London: G. P. Putnam's Sons (The Knickerbocker Press), 1901.

Reichard, Gladys. *Spider Woman—A Story of Navajo Weavers and Chanters.* Glorieta, New Mexico: The Rio Grande Press, 1934.

Rieger, James. "'The Hem of Their Garments': The Bard's Song in *Milton.*" In *Blake's Sublime Allegory: Essays on "The Four Zoas," "Milton," "Jerusalem."* Edited by Stuart Curran and Joseph Anthony Wittreich, Jr. Madison, Wisconsin: University of Wisconsin Press, 1973.259–80.

Rose, Jacqueline. "Introduction II." In *Feminine Sexuality: Jacques Lacan and "the ecole freudienne".* Edited by Juliet Mitchell and Jacqueline Rose. Translated by Jacqueline Rose. New York and London: W. W. Norton & Company, 1985.

Rubin, Nancy Felson. "Introduction: Why Classics and Semiotics?" *Arethusa* 16 (1983): 5–14.

Ruskin, John. *Praeterita: The Autobiography of John Ruskin.* Edited by Lord Kenneth Clark. London, England: Oxford University Press, 1978.

Sargent, Jiho. "The Buddha Robe." *Piecework: Needlework & History.* VII.6 (November/December 1999): 53–55.

Saul, George Brandon. *Traditional Irish Literature and Its Backgrounds: A Brief Introduction.* Lewisburg: Bucknell University Press, 1970.

Schneider, Jane and Annette B. Weiner, eds. *Cloth and Human Experience.* Washington and London: Smithsonian Institution Press, 1989.

Sciaky, Carla. "Paddy the Weaver," "The Weaver and the Chambermaid," "The Weaver's March / The Gallant Weaver." *Spin the Weaver's Song.* Prompinquity Records, 1992.

Scarry, Elaine. "Introduction." In *Literature and the Body: Essays on Populations and Persons.* Edited by Elaine Scarry. Selected Papers from the English Institute, 1986. New Series, no. 12. Baltimore: Johns Hopkins University Press, 1988. vii–xxvi.

———. "Work and the Body in Hardy and Other Nineteenth-Century Novelists." *Representations* 3 (Summer 1983), 90–123.

Schliske, Doreen. "Weaving with the Past." *Handwoven* (November1982): 15.

Schmeckebier, Laurence E. *Modern Mexican Art.* Minneapolis: University of Minnesota Press, 1939.

Scott, Sir Walter. *The Heart of Midlothian.* London, New York: Oxford University Press, 1982.

Shelley, Mary. *Mary Shelley: Collected Tales and Stories.* Edited by Charles E. Robinson. Baltimore and London: Johns Hopkins University Press, 1976.

Shelley, Percy Bysshe. *Shelley's Poetry and Prose.* Edited by Donald H. Reiman and Sharon B. Powers. A Norton Critical Edition. New York, London: W. W. Norton & Company, 1977.

Silverman, Kaja. *The Acoustic Mirror: The Female Voice in Psychoanalysis and Cinema.* Bloomington and Indianapolis: Indiana University Press, 1988.

Showalter, Elaine. "Feminist Criticism in the Wilderness." In *The New Feminist Criticism: Essays on Women, Literature and Theory.* Edited by Elaine Showalter. New York: Pantheon, 1985. 243–70.

Smith, Houston. *The World's Religions: Our Great Wisdom Traditions.* New York: HarperCollins, 1991.

Sollors, Werner. *The Return of Thematic Criticism.* Harvard English Studies 18. Cambridge, Mass. and London, England: Harvard University Press, 1993.

Spenser, Edmund. *The Faerie Queene.* Edited by Thomas P. Roche and C. Patrick O'Donnell, Jr. New York and London: Viking Penguin Inc., 1987.

Standard Dictionary of Folklore, Mythology and Legend. Edited by Maria Leach. San Francisco, CA: Harper & Row, Publishers, 1972).

Strickler, Carol. "Dearest Daughter." *Handwoven* (November 1982): 37–38.

———. "Inspiring Words" *Handwoven* (November/December 1984): 44–46.

Suleiman, Susan Rubin. *The Female Body in Western Culture: Contemporary Perspectives.* Cambridge, Mass.: Harvard University Press, 1985.

Suzuki, Mihoko. *Metamorphoses of Helen: Authority, Difference, and the Epic.* Ithaca and London: Cornell University Press, 1989.

Symons, Arthur. *William Blake.* London: Archibald Constable and Company, 1907.

Talley, Charles. "Danish Textiles." *Handwoven* (May/June 1987): 44–45.

———. "Reflections on the Weaver's Art." *Handwoven* (May/June 1987): 32–33.

Tayler, Irene. "The Woman Scaly. In *Blake's Poetry and Designs.* Edited by by Mary Lynn Johnson and John E. Grant. New York and London: W. W. Norton, 1979. 538–52.

Taylor, Thomas. *Thomas Taylor the Platonist: Selected Writings.* Edited by Kathleen Raine and George Mills Harper, Bollingen Series LXXXVIII, Princeton, New Jersey: Princeton University Press, 1969.

Tennyson, Lord Alfred. Edited by *Poems of Tennyson.* Edited by Jerome H. Buckley. Boston, Mass.: Houghton Mifflin Company, 1958.

Thomson, Francis Paul. *Tapestry: Mirror of History.* New York: Crown Publishers, Inc., 1980.

Vogh, James. *Arachne Rising: the Search for the Thirteenth Sign of the Zodiac.* New York: Dial Press, 1977.

Wagenknecht, David. *Blake's Night: William Blake and the Idea of Pastoral.* Cambridge, Massachusetts Harvard University Press, 1973.

Walker, Rossiter. *William Blake in the Art of His Time.* A Faculty-Graduate Student Project. University of California, Santa Barbara. The Regents of University of California, 1976.

Walker, Susan. "Women and Housing in Classical Greece: the Archaeological Evidence." *Images of Women in Antiquity,* Edited by Averil Cameron and Amelie Kuhrt. Detroit: Wayne State University Press, 1983.

Warren, Leland E. "Poetic Vision and the Natural World: the Spider and his Web in the Poetry of William Blake." *Englishtenment Essays* VI:1 (Spring, 1975): 50–62.

Watkinson, Raymond. *Pre-Raphaelite Art and Design.* Greenwich, Connecticut: New York Graphic Society, 1970.

Webster's Third New International Dictionary and Seven Language Dictionary. Chicago, London: G. & C. Merriam Co., 1971.

Wehrhahn-Stauch, Dr. L. "Introduction." *CIBA Review* 1 (1967): 2–7.

———. "Near Eastern Animal Motifs." *CIBA Review* 1 (1967): 8–17.

———. "Chinese Animal Motifs." *CIBA Review* 1 (1967): 18–28.

———. "Symbolic Animals of Christendom." *CIBA Review* 1 (1967): 29–45.

Wehrlin, Max. "Raw Silk for the Handweaver." *Handweaver and Craftsman* (Spring 1955): 22–23, 59.

Weibel, Adele Coulin. *Two Thousand Years of Textiles: The Figured Textiles of Europe and the Near East.* New York: Pantheon, 1952.

Weiner, Annette B. and Jane Schneider, eds. *Cloth and Human Experience.* Washington and London: Smithsonian Institution, 1989.

Weiskel, Thomas. *The Romantic Sublime: Studies in the Structureand Psychology of Transcendence.* Baltimore and London: Johns Hopkins University Press, 1976.

Welles, Marcia L. *Arachne's Tapestry.* San Antonio, Texas: Trinity University Press, 1986.

Wescher, H. "Great Masters of Dyeing in 18th Century France." *CIBAReview* (February 1939): 626–41.

West, Virginia. "From the Far West: Carpets and Textiles of Morocco." *Handwoven* (May 1981): 14, 16–17.

Wilkie, Brian and Mary Lynn Johnson. *Blake's "Four Zoas": The Design of a Dream.* Cambridge, Massachusetts and London, England: Harvard University Press, 1978.

Wilson, Kax. "America's Linen." *Handwoven* (March/April 1989): 49–53.

Witherspoon, Gary. *Language and Art in the Navajo Universe.* Ann Arbor, Michigan: University of Michigan Press, 1977.

Woolf, Virginia. *A Room of One's Own.* New York and London: Harcourt, Brace & World, 1957.

"Word for Word." Reprinted in "The Handwoven Communique." Edited by Bobbie Irwin. *Handwoven* (November / December 1989): 104.

Wyatt, David M. "The Woman Jerusalem: *Pictura* versus *Poesis.*" *Blake Studies* 7 (1975): 105–24.

Index

Numbers in boldface indicate illustrations